Caught
by the
COLLAR

EUGENE G. AKINS III

ISBN 978-1-64079-982-0 (paperback)
ISBN 978-1-64079-983-7 (digital)

Christian Faith Publishing, Inc.
832 Park Avenue
Meadville, PA 16335
www.christianfaithpublishing.com

Printed in the United States of America

This book is dedicated to all the men, women and
children who have been disrespected, devalued,
exploited and abused by clergy and
religious organizations of all denominations.

Introduction

GROWING UP IN A Pentecostal church, my life spanned an era where we were still called "holy rollers" to a time when it was fashionable to "feel the Spirit." I had Baptist friends who talked about people catching the Holy Ghost in their services, but it was not really allowed. The person feeling it would be corralled, sat down, and calmed down with fans and wiping with hankies and towels. I lived through a time when I was embarrassed to bring a friend to church because of the ribbing I would get afterward to now seeing the Holy Ghost as a more mainstream character on the religious front, being portrayed on television and in movies. Early in my spiritual journey, I was given the impression that only the people who were in my church (organization) would get to heaven. As I grew, matured, and attended school I began to feel that many of the things I was taught didn't make sense, some things just weren't logical. I was made to feel "God is not logical, He is miraculous." Statements like, "You're not going to understand everything," "You are not supposed to understand everything," "You don't have enough faith," "Just believe" were the usual responses to my queries. For a time I thought there was something wrong with me. Maybe they were right, maybe I didn't have enough faith, maybe I didn't really believe, maybe this just wasn't meant for me. In my early adult life there were several cases of clergymen falling into sin in my own community as well as nationally. Preachers were drunk drivers, gamblers, murderers, and adulterers. All over the country they were telling us to do one thing while it seemed they were doing something else. We were supposed to live by one code while they lived by another. Needless to say, I became very disillusioned and confused and for a while even stopped going to church all together. But I guess "train up a child" really worked in my case because I could never shake church try as I may. Even when I consciously and deliberately decided, it was all a fake and I wasn't going back, I found myself missing what I had grown up in. I was a musician (or was trying to be) and my ten brothers and sisters were all at one time or another, a large part of the church choir. We were at church all day Sunday from Sunday school through morning worship which usually went until about 3:00 p.m., back for evening Bible study at 6:00 p.m. and stayed for evening worship getting back home around 10:30 p.m., plus minus. Tuesday night was Bible study, Thursday night was midweek service, Friday or Saturday (sometimes both for different choirs) was choir practice and back again on Sunday. Church was my life, it was in my blood, it defined me.

When I realized I would not be happy trying to live my life without the church I returned, but I was different. I didn't really believe the whole thing was phony, but I knew something was just not right. There were questions being asked that no one seemed to have answers for. Now as an adult I wanted and needed to find my way in the church to find my identity, my purpose. I loved music and at times thought that was my niche, but I just wasn't a good enough musician. As I became more involved in the functioning of the church it seemed to have morphed into something less like a church and more like a business. In many ways this was a good thing the church had grown, a new building and an addition were in place. I began to wonder if my place was somewhere in ministry but my feeling at the time was that the pastor should see that and guide me that way if it was God's desire for me to join those ranks. With my father as my leader by this time, I was sure that he would have encouraged me in this direction if it was to be and since there was nothing from him I looked to other areas.

By this time I had finished college and podiatry school, and with so much time invested in education, I became focused on this area in church. I knew there were many needs that required attention and with the many years I had spent getting a formal education perhaps I could put them to practical use. But the more I tried to apply the principles, I had learned in my schooling to what was being taught at church, I continually and consistently ran into confusion. One of the arguments that I have heard over the years from people who don't believe in God is that the Bible contradicts itself. I began to understand why they said this but that did not keep me from looking for other answers. One of the answers seemed to be in language and the more I leaned on language the more clear things became. The Bible is not contradictory but being written originally in other languages, poor interpretations, and translations might make it appear so. When detractors and pundits study the Bible they are not trying to understand it they are trying to undermine it. So it fits their agenda to take two lines of scripture from the King James Bible, place them next to each other and say, "See, contradiction," and certainly contradiction undermines authenticity and validity. But if you take the time to really "study" the Bible these presumed contradictions disappear.

Another problem that is a product of changing attitudes and philosophies in recent years is a lack of strict adherence to the principles and doctrine that the "Bible" presents. But again if we are not paying close attention to the real meaning of scripture and avoiding the "I believe" approach to what the Bible is saying we will fall into the error of misinterpretation quite easily. For example, Ephesians 5:1 says, "Be Ye followers of God," and the Greek word for followers there is (mimetes) and is translated imitators. I grew up watching several comedians on TV who were impressionists. Their stock in trade was to sound and act like famous people. Men like Rich Little, Frank Gorshin, and Jonathan Winters were some of the best at this art. They studied the mannerisms and the voices of famous people and were able to recreate them such that with your eyes closed and listening you would think you were in the presence of the celebrity being mimicked. If imitating God, we should look like him, act like him, sound like him. Our practices in worship, personal, private, and emotional lives should strive to mimic that of God. Our doctrines should be derived strictly from the scriptures and when it becomes apparent that something does not line up with scripture it needs to be rectified immediately. But this is an area of gross shortcoming not only in the Pentecostal church but others as well, which is probably why we have so many different denominations in Christianity.

There are many issues faced by members of the charismatic/ Pentecostal church members. This book is my attempt to share some examples and hopefully some solutions to this problem. I am not an expert in biblical studies and have no formal training in theology so I am not writing from that perspective. My lifetime experience in the Pentecostal church is the background from which this book will be forged. My sixty-two years of experience in that environment will serve as the backdrop for what will be shared in these few pages. I am a living witness to these issues and the causes and effects related to them. My learning experience is also a testimony to the fact that the personal efforts in studying the Bible can result in understanding things that are not always clear initially. While it is primarily for the benefit of the general church population, I am sure that clergy can greatly benefit from it as well. My intent primarily is to encourage the general church population to become more dedicated to personal bible study which is something that the Pentecostal church is sorely lacking. But while the laity is my target I am sure that the clergy can greatly benefit from it as well, though I fear there will be only a few that are open minded enough to read it. I would like to make it clear that I am not trying to disparage or disrespect any church organization or any of the God fearing patriarchs that have gone before us. But since church leaders have failed to provide adequate instruction in biblical study, many people fail to mature and indeed many leaders fall to sin because they themselves have not grown and matured spiritually even though they are pastors and bishops, etc.

In the Beginning

MY FIRST REALIZATION THAT something was wrong with what I was being taught, or at least the way it was being taught, came while still in high school. It was in the late '70s and I was about sixteen years old. It was in a Sunday night Bible study, YPWW (Young People Willing Workers). The discussion was on Cain and Abel. Genesis 4:10, "And He said (God speaking) what hast thou done? The voice of thy brother's blood crieth unto me from the ground." This was my first red flag.

While growing up, I was considered an intelligent child. I was mature for my age and doing well in school. I was quiet and obedient (for the most part). I was very seldom in any trouble at school and was always very respectful to all adults. I was planning to attend college and for the most part appeared to have a very bright future. Until then, there had only been two college graduates from all the church families combined and both of those had left town to pursue their careers. The congregation was a pretty good size, about a hundred on Sunday mornings. There were several members of the clergy: my grandfather, who was pastor; several elders; and a few ministers, also none of whom had any college education not to mention degrees. In fact, of all the members of the clergy, I think there were only three or four who had graduated from high school. The attendance was quite a bit smaller for the night services, but it did tend to draw what I thought were the younger, more intelligent adults to return. While they were not college graduates, many of them had very good jobs working for major industries in town. In fact, many of them had joined the exodus from urban life to the suburbs. They spoke correct

English as did their children in contrast to us ghetto kids who used *ain't, dis,* and *dat* a lot. I always looked up to "The Camillus Crew," as they were called. I respected their opinions and thought that because of their positions in the community and at work, these were people who knew what they were talking about. Since my father was a manual laborer and there were eleven children in our family, we were not really seen as a part of the important people. Nevertheless, I had always seen my parents as a part of the more intelligent and insightful group, especially my mother. My parents, along with the Camillus group and a few others, comprised the core of my spiritual mentors. These were people I looked to and looked up to especially when it came to God and the church. The day that I was born, I was a member of this church. As I grew, I was indoctrinated with the beliefs of this church. My life's reality was built on what I'd been taught by this church. As far as I was concerned, as were many others, if you were not in my church, you were going to hell! Being an obedient child, I listened, trusted, and believed all the things I was told. There was no reason for me to question anything I'd been taught.

Of course, there had been other things that raised an eyebrow, but I always figured I just didn't understand yet. For example, the preachers always ate first. No matter where we were or what the function if there was food, the preachers would eat first. It didn't matter how many kids were there or how much crying was going on because they were hungry. If the preachers had not been served, those kids would just have to keep crying. And this did not happen only at our church but also when we would visit other churches for special occasions (which usually meant raising money). At the church picnic, the preachers ate first! At your home! The preachers ate first and best. No matter where we were or what the function if food was served the preachers would eat first. It didn't matter how many kids were there or how much crying was going on because they were hungry. If the preachers had not been served those kids would just have to keep on crying. This did not happen only at my church but also when we visited other churches for special services which usually meant raising money. At the church picnic the preachers ate first, in your home preachers ate first and best. To this day I don't think I've ever seen a pastor or bishop allow the children to be served before them. When I was a kid, I thought that maybe this was one of the ways the preachers were paid back for all the things they did for everybody. After all, they were like Jesus, and he was always doing something for somebody. And I never saw in the Bible where Jesus had been paid except for meals.

I never understood "the role call" at the offering table. Many times in our churches if there were funds needed for anything, we would invite another church to ours (or vice versa) supposedly to praise the Lord but really to raise money for that need. Usually there was a particular amount of money desired by the coordinators of the service. Those who were designated to function at the offering table would proceed much like an auction but in reverse. Instead of starting low and going higher, those at the table would start high and end low. Depending on the amount desired those at the table might start by asking, "How many of you are going to sacrifice and give us $500?" If there were any takers (or givers as it were), they would be asked to parade down the aisle and individually bring their gift to the table for all to see. Once the money was on the table, the giver's name would be announced publicly for all to hear. This procedure would be followed for $400, $300, $200, $100, and $50 dollar donations. After that amount, everyone else would be herded to the table like cattle as one group and no names called. During this process if the table workers were not getting the response they desired, they might prod the audience with comments like, "Y'all oughta be shame holdin' onto dat money so tight, das why da lawd can't bless ya" or "Soma y'all spent a hundred dollars to git ya hair done and can't stand to give da lawd more den dat."

I never understood why I could never "catch the Holy Ghost." When we got saved (commit your life to Christ), it was quite a great production. This usually occurred at a revival where an evangelist would preach at church for a week or more hoping to bring someone to the Lord. Each night at the end of the sermon, there would of course be an invitation to the altar for those who wanted to be saved. The children always dreaded revivals because for us there was no "invitation." We were herded to the altar whether we wanted to

11

go or not. There were admonitions like, "You're old enough to know right from wrong"; If you get saved, you won't cause your parents so much trouble; "You been round here long enough now, you ought to be saved by now." We were then marched to the altar where we would "tarry." The act of tarrying is based on the second chapter of Acts where the disciples waited or "tarried" in the Upper Room for the comforter (the Holy Spirit) to make his appearance as Jesus said. The process of tarrying was as follows: each candidate adult or child would stand or kneel facing the altar. They would be coached by an "altar worker" to close their eyes, clap their hands, and say, "Save me, Jesus," over and over and over repeatedly, nonstop. The faster you spoke, the better. The faster you clapped, the better. You were encouraged to speak with speeds that you had never approached in normal conversation and would never have any need to reach unless you worked as the announcer who does the disclaimer at the end of commercials. This rapid speech would impair your breathing pattern. You were unable to swallow normally so saliva would build up in your mouth and sometimes lead to a frothing foam that would then run out of the mouths of the subjects. Noses would begin to run as well as the inevitable production of tears. All these different fluids flowing at the same time did not make a pretty picture. And if you bothered to wipe or clear any of the now clogged passages, you were losing focus. You had to "give it all to Jesus," "Let go and let God." At some point during this process (if they were lucky), some people "got it." The evidence of being saved was the holy dance. The spirit would take control of the person and cause them to "shout," which is dancing, anything from just jumping up and down to different patterns of dance moves limited only by the individual and their "spirit's" creativity. I remember one brother that would point his fingers on both hands as if simulating guns, hold them at his waist, and spin around in circles. People would bound and writhe all over the room usually with their eyes closed, sometimes falling to the floor and rolling around uncontrollably hence the old name for Pentecostals, "Holy Rollers." The sign of the Holy Ghost was "speaking in tongues."

This involved speaking in a language that was prompted by the Holy Ghost. I asked about the language once. From the account of tongues in the book of Acts, it seemed that we should be speaking in French or German or Japanese. I even found myself speaking some words once with an accent that I thought was Oriental while feeling the spirit, but I was told that these were "Holy, unknown languages." When we speak in these tongues, we were supposed to be speaking directly to God. He would know what we were saying. It was always very curious to me that some people spoke in tongues a lot and others not at all. Those that spoke often spoke the same "phrases" or sounds. Sometimes they did have the sound of another language. But at other times it just sounded like gibberish, "Bay, bay, bay bosa, hebalafa, oh sumba day sedie dioria; hes comma nina chevolay." So the answers to my questions seemed very mystical! Answers that may have to wait until God could clear them up for me. These things seemed to be part of the mysteries of the universe and of course I accepted that. But the statement in Bible study was just too much. Logic, reason, and my educational experience to that point would not allow me to digest this one.

As I stated, we were discussing the Cain and Abel story. I don't recall if the focus was on the Bible's first murder looking out for your neighbor or some other aspect of the passage. At some point in the conversation, my grandfather started saying things that sounded as if Abel's blood was speaking. Literally! As if there was a voice coming out of the blood that had been spilled. I was sure that I had misunderstood. I listened a while longer, and there it was again! I couldn't believe it. Now you have to understand this was my grandfather! Grandpop! I loved this man and still do! I miss him a lot even though he's been dead almost forty years. He was stern and honest as a pastor, and as a grandfather, he was like a cross between Rodney Dangerfield and Sinbad. He taught me to fish! He gave me my first paying job! He was always there when we needed him! But the blood, talking? And what made things worse, no one else was going to say anything. They were all just going to sit there and go along with this. Whatever this was. Was everyone else oblivious to the problem? Had I given them too much credit? Was I really that much more educated or intelligent than these people I looked up to? So after sitting and waiting and seeing that no adult would step up to the plate, I did! For a while, I was sorry I did! After that, I began to question more and more. Not verbally, that would only get me more of the same ridicule and a reputation of being a rebel, disrespectful, arrogant, none of which were true. In fact, I think many of those there that night were in total agreement with me and wanted to ask the same question. But one of the things that kept those voices silent is also a reason for the writing of this book. Respect!

Respect is such a powerful word. Men have lived their whole life trying to earn it, and men have died because they weren't deemed worthy of it. It's the one thing we never seem to get enough of, yet too much of it can destroy us and those around us. Ego was not a problem for my grandfather. He was so humble and soft spoken, always looking out for others. He could be just as strong as he needed to be but never excessive. No, in his case, it wasn't the need for respect that was the problem. It was the congregations' need to give it. This I'm sure was partly due to the residual effect of a slave mentality on black America. Be respectful and you won't get whipped. Be more respectful (butt kiss) and you'll get favor. Respect for your elders! Respect was something you owed, a commodity that was bestowed upon everyone over a certain age whether it was deserved or not. This was also a very self-fulfilling practice. You see the more respectful you were, or at least appeared to be, the greater the level of esteem one could garner for themselves. This made it very easy system for "butt kissers" to take advantage of. It may seem very naive to think that an entire congregation would go along with such an error. Perhaps *ignorant* is a better word. But I am convinced that out of respect they remained silent and deemed it better to do so than to question the leader, the man who God had placed in the position of pastor, leader of the flock, the voice of God. So, when I asked, "You're not saying that the blood was talking, are you?" the eyes began to peer at me. They made comments that suggested I was the one who didn't understand. What a nerve I had to question the pastor. Who did I think I was anyway? Later, some of the kids younger than me would tell me things that were said by their parents about me. To this day, I don't know if anyone understood my point of view that night, but I believe that even if they did, they would have remained silent out of respect. Unfortunately, this is not an attitude that existed only in my church at that time but one that was prevalent throughout the culture then and persists even today. So began my journey through a maze of puzzles that I am just now beginning to get solutions for.

One of the subjects that had always puzzled me was what I had been taught about alcohol and what the scriptures say or don't say about it. In our society now, there are more and more Christians who don't think there is anything wrong with drinking wine or other spirits. But I was taught that drinking was a sin! God's people did not drink at all. With this in mind, when we remembered the Lord's Supper we used grape juice. I know that some of the people I've discussed this with think that I'm trying to justify my own drinking. Not at all. I don't drink. I don't even like the taste of alcohol, and I think one of the dumbest things people do is to go out for a good time but can't remember the good time they had because of drunkenness. But it never made sense to me that the all-knowing Christ would not realize the confusion it would cause when he failed to denounce drinking. When he drank wine himself even during the Last Supper, why not just say it? Thou shalt not kill, thou shalt not steal, thou shalt not commit adultery. Why not thou shalt not drink? And if that wasn't bad enough, the very first miracle he performed was to turn water into wine. Some argue that the wine wasn't fermented, that is was only grape juice, or that the Jews would not have used fermented wine because it was unclean. These are interesting points of view but the most important point is what the scriptures say. Part of the problem with this is a simple failure to understand the connection between drinking and drunkenness. The Bible clearly denounces drunkenness. Throughout both the Old and New Testaments, there are multiple examples of the horrors of drunkenness. Yet not once at the end of any of these terrible examples does the scripture say, "See, for this reason, you do not drink alcohol." There is of course the scripture that says don't get drunk (Eph. 5:18). But there is an assumption of drinking when you are told not to get drunk. Think for a minute, you can't get drunk if you are not drinking. No one would be admonished not to get drunk if it was not assumed they were drinking. You would not be told not to speed if you were not driving. You would not be told not to drown if you were not swimming (or in the water). Drunkenness is then the result of an extreme behavior. There are a couple of other words that are treated similarly in the scriptures.

Fornication is one that might help here just from a literary perspective. Fornication basically means inappropriate sexual activity. Sex outside of a heterosexual marital relationship. Sex when the two people involved are not married to each other (adultery, when at least one person is married to someone else). Fornication is a sin. That does not mean that sex is a sin. It means that a very particular type of sex is a sin and not sex in general. One could very easily say, "Be not drunk with sex," and convey the essence of what the word *fornication* means. To be drunk with or in sex is to be out of control (extreme relative to godly standards) in your sexual activity. As crystal clear as the scriptures are about fornication, I have never heard anyone say that sex is a sin. Again with this word there is the assumption that there is the capability of sexual activity. You would not tell someone who was impotent or without sexual organs not to commit fornication/adultery.

Gluttony is another word that sheds light here. Proverbs 23:2 says, "Put a knife to your throat if you are given to gluttony." Gluttony is of course excessive eating, pigging out, getting your eat on. There are many Christians who have no idea what alcohol tastes like, who have never tried a cigarette and turn their noses up at anyone who plays the lottery, but they would have no problem gorging themselves at a meal until it was difficult for them to breathe. Many people have the attitude that since they don't engage in any of the other vices, it's okay for them to overindulge in this one. As a physician, I have firsthand knowledge of and experience with patients who are literally eating themselves to death. One of the most popular and yet most dangerous places for many of God's people is the buffet restaurant. As with fornication, the Bible takes a very clear stand on gluttony but have you ever heard anyone say that eating was a sin? Again, the issue is excess or extreme. No one would suggest that we starve ourselves, that we never eat anything to avoid being guilty of gluttony. But that is exactly what has been done with alcohol. Again with gluttony there is the assumption of eating. You would not caution someone against gluttony if they were not eating. Let me reiterate, I am not advocating drinking. I think drinking alcohol is a very bad choice for all the obvious reasons. Many people speak to the fact that we are not to defile the temple (our bodies 1 Cor. 3:17) by drinking alcohol or smoking, but they are not convicted in the least by diabetes, obesity, hypertension, or cardiovascular issues all of which lead to the destruction and therefore the defiling of the temple. So it's okay to defile the temple with food but not with alcohol? Of course not.

So perhaps part of the reason alcohol has been taught to be sinful is related to a poor understanding of words. But I also think there is an aspect of shepherding involved. By this I mean that those in leadership (shepherds of the flocks) likely looked at the issue of alcoholic beverages and recognizing all the negatives, surmised that the sheep were not capable of making the best choice concerning alcohol. Therefore, as the watchmen over the souls, they instituted teachings that were meant for the good of the people. If you teach that drinking is a sin, you avoid the problems of drunkenness. This sounds good in theory except for the fact that "you can't legislate good behavior." Also, it is not right for the leadership to trick people into obedience. St. John 4:24 says, "We worship Him in spirit and in truth." God wants our obedience to be a matter of choice, not coercion or manipulation. After all, he could have made us obey him whether we wanted to or not. It is not the place of those in leadership to purposely interpret God's word in the way they feel best serves the community or the church. After all, that is what the Pharisees did in developing the Talmud (a codification of Mosaic law). But it is their responsibility to do as 2 Tim. 2:15, "Rightly divide the word of truth," only then can you worship in truth.

I think it is more likely that a failure to understand the context of the scripture in Ephesians is the most important part of this errant idea. When we read in Eph. 5:18, "Be not drunk with wine," logically we think of the social woes of our society that are related to alcohol. Alcoholism, liver disease, and other health issues, driving while intoxicated, and the related-property damage, lost wages and careers, loss of limbs and the loss of lives, family dysfunction, divorce. It is very likely there was some of this in Paul's mind but that was not the primary focus of his writing. In his sermon, "Be not drunk with wine," Pastor John Macarthur outlines the context of Paul's reason for the command. The Ephesian Christians were coming out of a background of pagan religious practices. In their transition to Christ, of course, many old things must pass away. One of the key components of some pagan worship was drunkenness. Their idea was that being intoxicated brought them into a higher state of consciousness and which put them into closer contact with the god they served and thus a greater religious experience. When they became partakers of the Lord's Supper and the Cup of Christ, they equated this wine with their previous practice of getting drunk as a part of worship. That is why in 1 Cor. 10:20 Paul says, "We cannot drink the cup of the Lord and the cup of devils." Paul is speaking primarily of religious practices in worship services and not about the social ills of drinking. But without reading the entire book of Ephesians or at least the entire fifth chapter, it is almost impossible to get any idea that Paul is talking about something far more important than getting "wasted."

Another puzzle had to do with something that is a defining characteristic of Pentecostal religious groups and that is speaking in tongues. Speaking in tongues is a phenomenon whereby persons presumed to be experiencing the presence of the Holy Ghost begin to speak in another language. Of course, the source of this comes from Acts 2. Christ told the disciples to tarry (wait) in the city of Jerusalem, and he would send the promise of the Father (Luke 24:44–49). That promise was the Holy Spirit, which would be the source of power for the disciples to do the work that God had for them. This would include the many miracles performed by the disciples. While waiting in the Upper Room, Acts 2 says, "They were all filled with the Holy Ghost and began to speak with other tongues as the spirit gave them utterance." This occurred on the Day of Pentecost hence the name Pentecostals. So following the example of the Upper Room miracle, Pentecostals believe that the evidence of the presence of the Holy Ghost dwelling with a person is speaking in tongues. I have been a witness to this all my life. People spoke in tongues at almost every church service but not everyone and not me. For a long time,

I desired to speak and actually tried on my own on a couple of occasions. Again, my understanding of the scriptures got in the way.

If you read Acts 2:9–11, you will find several languages listed as those spoken (or heard) in the Upper Room. Parthian, Mede, Elamite, Phrygian, Pamphylian to name just a few. These were all actual languages of the time and geographic area. They were languages that were recognized by people from the respective places, languages that could be learned and interpreted. This was my understanding of tongues so I tried speaking what I thought sounded Oriental. It sounded pretty good to me, and I'll bet I could have fooled someone with the sound, but of course, it was just gibberish. Unfortunately, gibberish is what's spoken by Pentecostals. Not everyone speaks. It seems that speaking is done by those who are most holy or "closest" to God. Or by those who want to appear to be holy or closer to God. It is interesting that those who speak frequently seem to say the same "phrase" regularly. Phrases I can recall include, "Oh sumbudy sedadeee auria," "Bebebebosa," "Acomma nay chevolly," "Ebala Fa."

The biggest problem with glossalalia is that it is not biblical. The disciples were not speaking gibberish. They were speaking recognizable languages that could be understood by anyone versed in that tongue. I am not saying that the Holy Spirit never bestows the true gift of tongues today, but he would certainly also bestow the gift of interpretation as well (1 Cor. 14:27). If this practice is not the same as the tongues caused by the Holy Ghost in Acts, it is likely not prompted or caused by the Holy Ghost. Those who engage in it are then "lying" on the Holy Ghost. That sounds like blasphemy!

Another problem involves the nonspeakers. When you are taught that you should speak in tongues and you don't speak in tongues, you begin to feel there is a problem. Is the problem with you? Maybe you are not saved? Maybe there is some sin that is preventing from "getting it." Maybe you just have not "let go and let God"? A person in this situation can become very frustrated and even depressed if they are doing all they know and all they've been told but not getting the result they expect. This could even lead to them throwing in the towel and giving up on their new life. They are caught in a trap. They are trying to be what they've been told they should be. But since what they've been told is based on half-truths, if not lies, they are unable to reach the expected goal. They are caught on a rollercoaster they chose to ride but there is no exit. The men (and women) in the black and white collars, intentionally or not have them caught in a web that can get more tangled the more they struggle.

So these are a few examples of the holes I've found in my religious upbringing. As I said before, I love my church, and I think the intentions of our founders were sincere and righteous. But with all due respect, there are many things being taught by many groups that need to be clarified and understood for what the scriptures are really trying to say. The Bible is like a cookbook. It has recipes for different things, but if that recipe is not followed what you end up with will not look the way you expected it to. If you leave out two or three ingredients, you can't expect your product to look like the picture. Unfortunately, there are many in leadership roles, ministers, pastors, and bishops who just don't belong there. Many souls as well as personal lives sit in the balance because of inept, self-serving people who call themselves men and women of God. These people will have to answer for the effect they have on the lives of others, but we do not have to sit still and swallow everything that comes at us. Timothy encourages us to study (2 Tim. 2:15). Many years ago lack of education may have been an excuse, but we can no longer hide behind that shortcoming. We must begin to ask questions until we get the answers. That is why so many sincere Christians walk in defeat. The recipe is fouled up!

So what do we do? You can't unbake a cake! The deed is done. Unfortunately, many lives have been irreparably damaged. Damaged when they sought advice from someone who was totally unqualified or only interested in making a decision that would most benefit the advisor. Decisions that were based on the advisor's poor understanding of scripture or their own personal life experiences that in many cases needed serious professional counseling. Telling someone that this man or this woman is not right for you to marry or that this profession is not right for you to pursue. God doesn't want you to do this, or God does want you to do that. We have seen in recent years many cases of those in leadership roles that have serious sexual issues they are struggling with. It is one thing to get advice from a person who has dealt with and overcome these issues, it is quite another to be advised by a person not only still in a struggle but in many cases has not even admitted there is a problem. Sexual infidelity, domestic violence, pornography, and child molestation are all issues that many times confront those in church leadership and we trust these people so much. But the truth of the matter is in many instances church leaders are the worst choices we could make to seek help for such a need.

W. Sybel Lester wrote a book titled *The Black Church Gang* in which he portrays the Black Church as just that, a gang. His premise is based on what he calls "lies, hypocrisy, and neurotic concepts," on which the church is organized. He reports having no respect for this group (leaders or followers). He paints a picture of "power-maddened maniacs who act in the shadow of the Cross trying to hide their true identity." This book was shared with me by a friend in college after conversations about church and my attempts to present Christ. Initially, I was quite offended first by the author and by my friend. Was this how I was perceived? This wasn't how I saw myself, my pastor, or my church. I only read a few pages before putting the book down with no intention of ever picking it up again. The author was obviously someone from the outside looking in and my friend obviously had a made up mind about church and religion. It was not until my decision to write myself that I finally read that book. While I don't agree with Mr. Lester as to the causes, we seem to be in agreement about some of the effects on the lives of church members. The effect can be seen when we try to "unbake" the cake.

There are several ways people seem to react when confronted with the idea that something they believe in is flawed. One is denial. They may be totally capable of understanding there is an issue, but their loyalty and devotion to the organization is more important than quibbling over a couple of minor details. Remaining "steadfast, unmovable, always abounding in the work of the Lord." I'm sure rings in the hearts of these souls. To them remaining loyal to the organization is the same as being loyal to God. Because their faith is based more on emotions and feelings than facts it's difficult for them to grasp the thought that something they've been taught is flawed or just plain wrong. I think these people would likely have the most difficult time changing because they are thinking more with their hearts than their minds. However, if they can see that the organization has actually displeased God with the errant teaching, then change is more likely to occur.

Another reaction is rejection. This is brought on by feelings of betrayal. I confess that this is some of what I felt when first learning of shortcomings in what I'd been taught. I also felt like a sucker or a sap. I felt like I had been taken advantage of. Admittedly, a lot of those feelings were also related to incidents where more than one church leader had been found to be less than stellar and falling short of what I had been taught was godly behavior. There was the aura of "do as I say not as I do." These "guys" are saying this and doing that. Teaching X but doing Y. If God is as real as they say and as powerful as they say, how could they dare stand in his pulpit on Sunday doing the things they do the rest of the week? They can't possibly believe what they are teaching and live the lives they are living. It must be a fake! It must all be a fake, a con, a scam, a game. Just another way for a no good "pimp" to take advantage of unwitting victims. That's like the attitude of "The Black Church Gang." Some people when confronted with this effect will just rebel. They do a complete 180 and go in the opposite direction from the church. They are now driven by anger, disillusion, and confusion. Angry because you can't believe you fell for it all or that you trusted these people, had faith in them, and they were only using you. Disillusion because what you once based your whole life on now seems to be just a fairy tale. Confusion because now you have to figure out which way is up! What is real and what is fake! What was the truth and what was false! Some people don't bother with figuring it out. After all, who can they turn to but another preacher! How could they ever trust anything any of them say now? So in frustration with the whole matter, they just give up. They stop going to church all together. They may continue to believe in God but not in organized religion. Some start looking into other forms of religion, such as the new age movement. Some just give up on God all together.

If they are lucky—no, blessed—they will hang in there. For me, the question always remained but faith continued to burn. I believed what I was taught, the essence of what I was taught. I believed the backbone, the locus crucsis, "Latin for focal point or central point" of what I was taught, was real! I knew there was more to it than a bunch of charlatans, swindlers, and whoremongers. I knew that some of these people were totally sincere and deeply believed and were committed to their belief system. They could not all be wrong! I decided that I had to find out for myself. No matter what the cost and no matter where it led, I had to begin searching and separating the wheat from the chaff. Many times I was very surprised with what I found sometimes even shocked. But ultimately, I was very pleased to learn that I was right! God is real! He wants to have a relationship with us, and he wants us to seek that relationship on a regular basis. But he wants us to seek and worship him in spirit and in truth! He wants our quest for him to be about righteousness and not riches! Second Corinthians 4:18 says, "While we look not at the things which are seen but the things which are not seen." While God does want us to be happy and live prosperous lives that is for him to take care of. Our focus should be on "the things not seen," the eternal. It seems that people have almost forgotten that the focus of holy living is for our benefit primarily in the next life! For us to be pleased in the next life means pleasing God in this life. That requires knowing his truth.

In the next few chapters, I will share some areas where I have gained clarity on God's truth. My hope is that some of these will serve as starting points for many that find themselves searching for answers to questions that seem so hard for some people to respond to. I hope this will bless you as it has blessed me and maybe begin to guide some lost sheep back to the fold.

Obedience
(Weapon of Mass Destruction)

IN 1 SAMUEL 15, there is a story of God giving direction to Saul for the destruction of the Amalekites. He was directed to destroy all the people (men, women, children) as well as all the livestock. When Samuel inquired about the bleating of sheep and lowing of oxen, Saul explained that "the people" had spared the best of the sheep and oxen to sacrifice to the Lord. Samuel's reply, "Behold to obey is better than a sacrifice and to hearken than the fat of rams." Throughout my life as well as today, the obedience of church members has been an important area of focus for church leaders. I'm not speaking just of my church or other Pentecostal organizations but the Catholic Church, which has been one of if not the most controlling organization of all. Growing up, I always looked forward to having fish in the school cafeteria for lunch every Friday. It was a long time before I knew that it was because Catholics could not eat meat on Friday at least back then. So control or obedience has always been a very important issue in the church setting.

As a very young child in the sixties, before my grandfather was pastor, there was Dad Payton. I never heard anyone call him reverend, and it wasn't until after his death I can recall someone using "Elder Payton" to refer to him. But this man was revered. He was quiet and unassuming, and there must have been some health issue because I don't remember him ever standing in the pulpit to preach. He was always sitting. But he was in charge! Not because he demanded it but because people genuinely respected him. There were a few times

24

when I was close enough to touch him that I almost felt like I was near Jesus. On one occasion, he gave me a coin directly in my hand. I really thought he was special then he even had special money, a coin like none I had ever seen before. I held on to that coin for a very long time. Turns out, I had never seen a Canadian dime before. But that's how special he was to everyone. There was an incident in church one Sunday when Dad Payton was publicly reprimanding someone. After a while, the man stood up to walk out while he was being talked to. Dad Payton blasted over the microphone, "Sit down." This grown man stopped in his tracks and took his seat! There were other men like him back then but the difference between now and then, those men weren't looking for reverence.

In today's churches, many of those in leadership desire the reverence described above. The problem is they don't live the lives that garner such treatment. Therefore, they try to cultivate it through other methods. One of the most popular methods is through scripture. The above passage from 1 Samuel is one that is commonly used. Another that is probably the most common is 1 Chronicles 16:22, "Touch not my anointed and do my prophets no harm." For many clergymen, this is the one scripture that is regularly used as the Sword of the Spirit. The problem is that this passage is taken out of context when used to encourage followers toward respecting their leader.

As with Dad Payton, if today's clergy would live lives that truly reflected the image of Christ, they would not have to encourage obedience and respect. It would come automatically. But why is obedience so important to so many? I think one very broad reason lies in the fact that many at least in Pentecostal circles are not in ministry for the right reason. If the reason was for the glory and honor of God, they would be satisfied with knowing they were doing God's will. Their reward would be with God leading and guiding them in all they do and knowing that it all works for the good. There would not be such an obsession with control and having the last say about the smallest little details. The very structure of the Pentecostal church lends itself to exploitation by those with tainted motives. To become a preacher in most of these organizations, the primary requirement is "the call of the Lord." The problem is only the one who is called knows if he really felt a divine urge or if he called himself. His pastor then decides if he is worthy or not. If the pastor is not completely genuine or (up to snuff), then this step in the process is also tainted. I am convinced that this is why we have so many people in ministry who obviously don't belong and thus why there are so many pastors that should not be in these positions. Another part of this reason has to do with ego! Many of these preachers would have no other notoriety, no claim to fame, no title in front of their names, and no letters behind their names if not for "Rev." I know there are some of these men who are totally sincere in their love for the Lord and would never do anything intentionally to discredit God's word. But sincerity does not by itself qualify anyone to lead or teach God's people. On the other hand, I am convinced that there are those who call themselves men (and women) of God who have simply brought their "hustle" from the streets to the pulpit. Of course, they will have to answer to the Almighty!

A "weapon of mass destruction" is defined as a nuclear, radiological, chemical, biological, or other weapon that can kill and bring significant harm to large numbers of humans or cause great damage to human-made, natural structures, or the biosphere. It was first used in reference to aerial bombing with chemical explosives by the Archbishop of Canterbury in 1937. During and after the Iran-Iraq war, Saddam Hussein was condemned by the international community for his use of chemical weapons on Iranian and Kurdish civilians. Saddam continued to pursue an extensive biological and nuclear weapons program in the 1980s. This continued pursuit led to "Operation Desert Fox" in 1998 and ultimately to the second Gulf War. More recently in August 2013, during the height of civil unrest in Syria that government launched a rocket attack against rebels using warheads that were filled with deadly chemicals. US intelligence records and intercepts of this event became the core of the Obama administration's case that linked the Syrian government to the use of outlawed chemical toxins in the death of nearly 1,500 civilians including at least 426 children. These weapons of mass destruction (WMDs) are especially disconcerting in the climate of terrorism the world now finds itself. As was seen in the 9/11 attack on the US, the terrorists' target is more likely civilian than military. However, as dangerous as ISIS and radical Islam and Jihad are, we can fight them because we are aware of them and of their agenda. If understanding and reasoning fail at least, we can protect ourselves by being aware of their methods and strategies. It is this lack of awareness concerning unbridled obedience that I fear puts it on the list of WMDs. Of course, I am not speaking of actual physical body counts (in most cases) but to the devastation in the emotional, spiritual, and financial lives of the countless thousands (perhaps millions) that fall prey to the power mongers who stand behind some of the pulpits in our churches.

I am in no way suggesting disrespect here. Neither is this intended as an act of sedition (Gal. 5:20). This is an attempt to show that what God is calling for is not blind, no questions asked, you say jump I say how high, sheep dumb obedience to our leaders (bishops, pastors, supt., etc.) but to him. Many "men" of God have convinced many of us that obeying them is equal to obeying God and nothing could be further from the truth.

In 1 Samuel 15, Saul's mistake was that he as king made a pastoral decision instead of just doing what God said. There was no excuse! Having no doubt about God's instructions would be a valid point today. He had Samuel, and he knew Samuel had God. But looking at it from a human perspective, it made sense to keep the livestock. After all, they were still in the practice of sacrificing animals as offerings to God, and it made perfect sense to do so with these that were taken as spoils. The key to his decision should have been what God said and not what he thought. Now, our problem today is no Samuel's! That is to say our leaders today do not, in most cases, have the first-hand access to God that Saul did. Oh yeah, they say they have it! They act and sound like they have it! They convince many of us with phrases like, "God said...or God told me to tell you...or I have a word for you...," and they should have access to God. But the sad truth is that many if not most of them are just not as connected to God as they should be.

So, you go to this guy for advice, let's say about your marriage. He may be married b-u-u-t not the best husband you've ever seen.

He may have been married a couple of times with all his ex's still alive. He may treat his wife like an old shoe in public! He may have absolutely no formal education or experience in counseling yet you go to him and trust his advice. Why? Because he is "The Man of God." In Pentecostal circles, we are taught to honor, respect, and obey our leaders not so much for what they have done or the person they have shown themselves to be but for who they are in the church. That is, what title they hold! It does not matter what his or her character is. It does not matter what unsavory or distasteful activity or situations he or she has been involved with in his recent past. The thing that matters most is the title and one of the anchors for this mentality is the verse in 1 Samuel 15 as well as 1 Chronicles 16:22, "Touch not mine anointed and do my prophet no harm." Since these two scriptures are the source of much of the reverence given to clergy rather than the actual evidence of God's influence in their lives and ministries, it is little wonder that so many of our churches are near empty.

On January 1, 1863, President Abraham Lincoln signed the Emancipation Proclamation declaring all persons held as slaves to be freed. This was primarily aimed at African slaves of course. That seems like quite a long time ago, and certainly we have made great progress in race relations since then. But when you think about it, that's only 154 years ago, maybe five generations. My father is eighty-four and remembers when blacks could not drink from the same water fountains as whites. So today in 2017, much of the generation before mine is still tainted with almost direct residual effects of slavery. One of those effects was the importance and influence of obedience. In the days of slavery, disobedience could literally mean your life. If you were so brash as to run away from your master, you could legally be killed. Learning to read could cost you life or limb. Obedience was foundational to having a "good" life. For another one hundred years after Lincoln's proclamation, full grown, adult black men were required to use phrases like "Yes, sir boss," when addressing white men. It took 101 years after being declared free for the Congress of the United States of America to enact the Civil Rights law of 1964. So in 2017, it has only been fifty-three years that the government of the United States has recognized (at least on paper) that black people are to be respected as human beings! To put it mildly, respect has been and continues to be a difficult commodity for the black community to be confident with and I believe this is one of the reasons obedience has held such a high place in the black church culture. It has been the one place that a black man could rise easily with little or no qualifications to a place of prominence and notoriety in his community.

The potential devastation from WMDs cannot be exaggerated. I believe the same can be said about an inappropriate or blind obedience. I call it a weapon because used intentionally or ignorantly, the consequence is the same, Satan is victorious. Yes, I believe there is Satanic influence possible whenever people are convinced to believe weird things. I know some people think it's weird to believe in God. But what I mean by weird is taking a mainstream, traditional belief system and tweaking it to fit your own feelings, desires, needs, etc. For example, there have been a number of people who have claimed to be Jesus Christ over the years;

Ann Lee (1736–17840), "Shakers"—Her followers believed she was the female incarnation of Christ.

Arnold Potter (1804–1872)—Latter Day Saints schismatic group. He claimed the spirit of Christ entered his body and he became "Potter Christ," son of the living God. In an attempt to ascend to heaven, he jumped off a cliff and died.

William W. Davies (1833–1906)—Latter Day Saints schismatic group, "Kingdom of Heaven." He claimed to be the Archangel Michael. When his son was born, Feb. 11, 1868, he said the infant was the reincarnated Jesus Christ. When a second son was born, he was declared to be God the Father.

Haile Selassie I (1892–1975)—He did not claim to be Christ but his followers believed him to be. When he became emperor of Ethiopia in 1930, this was taken as confirmation of the Revelation 5:5, return of the Messiah.

Sun Myung Moon (1920–2012) was believed by members of the "Unification Church" to be the Messiah. He and his wife were believed to be the restored Adam and Eve and therefore the parents of humankind.

Jose Luis de Jesus Miranda (1946–2013)—"Growing in Grace," based in Florida. He claimed to be the resurrected Christ and later the Antichrist as well, stating that "Antichrist means no longer following Jesus of Nazareth as he lived in the days of His flesh."

There is David Koresh of "The Branch Davidians," Marshall Applewhite of "Heaven's Gate," Joseph Di Mambro of "The Order of The Solar Temple." Probably the most well known of these figures though is Jim Jones and his "People's Temple."

In 1978 in Jonestown, Guyana, 911 followers of Jones participated in a murder/suicide under the direction and insistence of Jones himself who later died from a self-inflicted gunshot wound to the head. Over the years, Jones has been characterized as a paranoid drug addict with power infatuation who claimed to be the reincarnation of Jesus, Buddha, and Gandhi. He was an untrained preacher who really began preaching as a young child. He had a very strong religious zeal as a child after exposure to many churches in the town of Lynn, Indiana, where he grew up. He was often left to himself as his mother worked a lot and his father seemed to have no interest in him. So this man was troubled from the very beginning of his life. His troubles led him to church as it does with many people. His church background was Pentecostal. As tragic as this incident was, the real tragedy is that it did not have to happen. This man obviously had psychological issues that led to his mental deterioration. I have so much empathy for those who died at his hand. I know what it is to trust and have faith in a system and a group of people that you rely on. Thinking that whatever they tell you is true and good and good for you. Even in cases where you don't understand, you believe that this group or these people have your best interest in mind. You are willing to go wherever they say, do whatever they say, and be whatever they say you should be because they are like Christ in your life. They are your shepherds, and we, like sheep, are to follow and obey. *But we are not sheep!* I believe that if you carefully study the sheep/shepherd examples used in the Bible you will see they speak more to the responsibility of the shepherd for the sheep than they do to our character becoming like sheep. Many in leadership want us to be like the sheep in the Bible, but they don't want to be like the shepherd. The bottom line is that a large portion of those deaths were related to blind obedience. These were people blindly following a leader who was no longer following his leader (God).

So how could the Jonestown tragedy have been prevented or at least diminished? At first glance, it seems like a no-brainer! Why would anybody kill themselves willingly at the direction of someone else? What, are they nuts? But in several of the examples mentioned above, that's exactly what happened. I think the answer lies in the title of a radio ministry "Back to the Bible." In 2 Timothy 2:15, we are told to "study to shew thyself approved unto God, a workman that needeth not to be ashamed, rightly dividing the word of truth." That is the way the verse appears in the King James translation, which occurred in 1611. At that time, the word *study* meant strive or to be diligent. With that in mind, we see the American Standard Bible giving, "Be diligent to present yourself approved to God as a workman who does not need to be ashamed, handling accurately the word of truth." Apparently in Jonestown, 2 Timothy 2:15 was not regularly ascribed to. I am convinced that if some of the victims had been "studying" scripture on their own, there would have been fewer casualties. We need to get back the Bible literally. This is one of if not the biggest problem in Pentecostal churches today. Too much focus on the emotional (feelings or physical experience) the visual, the financial, the political, and not enough on the Word! Looking at Jonestown as well as the other cult tragedies, lives would have been saved if they were really into their Bibles. Now of course I wasn't there but allow me to deduce to my conclusion.

In the beginning of his ministry, it may have seemed that Jim Jones was preaching the gospel message. This may have seemed evident from the impact he was having on the community in Indianapolis as well as after the move to San Francisco. He was fulfilling the great commandment to love thy neighbor as thyself. Or was he? When you look closer at the influences on his life, Marxism and Communism were more likely his motivators than was the Gospel. In fact, a very close look at what Jones had been involved in before Jonestown sounds much more like a politician than a preacher. But if they had gone "Back to the Bible," they would have been able to see that Jones was not so much about the Gospel as he was about the government. If they had not only listened to what he was saying but correlated it with the Bible, it would have been apparent that the two did not mesh. This of course pertains to the members who were there for spiritual reasons probably those who had been there the longest. But if you have never been exposed to a biblical environment and your leader is not telling you that you should study for yourself, then how would you know this. Then these people who have been inspired by this man and have witnessed the great things he has done and experienced perhaps being one of the many he has helped, these people become focused on the things they see. Improvements in the neighborhood, food coops, integration activism, all very good things. And all things that God would smile about. But the longer you stay on a road when you're lost, usually the harder it is to find your way back. Many of these people lost their way. I'm sure there were those who just wanted to be a part of something better and something new and something different. There are always those who just want to be a part of the latest "trend." But for those looking for truth, looking for righteousness, looking for God, "trending" can be very dangerous. So they would have had to step outside the box, recognize there was something wrong and ask, "Why does God need a spaceship?" This is where obedience becomes a problem. When obedience to a leader prevents my questioning his directives, that's a problem. When the fear of being disrespectful outweighs the need to get clarity, that's a problem. When sheep have wolves for shepherds, that's a problem!

So people are taught to obey the leader. They are made to feel sinful if they don't. Because he is believed to have this close relationship with God; if you disobey him, it's as if you are disobeying God.

So why do people stay in these situations? Well, we are talking for the most part about people who are totally committed to their faith. They sincerely love God and desire to please him at all cost. So there is no way they would want to appear disobedient to a leader. But I think that a couple of other words come into play as well. Faithful is one of those words. Faithfulness is a very important aspect of the believer's walk. It is defined as "the concept of unfailingly remaining loyal to someone or something and putting that loyalty into consistent practice, regardless of extenuating circumstances." The "consistent" practice aspect would be called into question if a person were perceived as disobedient. You are not seen as being faithful if you don't jump when the pastor says jump. You are not a faithful servant if you question what the pastor says or teaches. You are not bearing you burdens, or exhibiting long-suffering if you are always giving the pastor the third degree. It is always the desire of the committed soul to hear the pastor (and therefore God) say, "Well done, thy good and faithful servant."

Another word to consider is promotion. As Matthew 25:23 continues, "Thou hast been faithful over a few things, I will make you ruler over many." It is quite a shameful state of affairs but politics has entered the church. This is of course nothing new and will be touched on later, but it is unfortunately a harsh reality. That being the case, a person who is viewed as combative, insubordinate, or noncompliant could hardly expect to get opportunities for ministerial promotions no matter how qualified they might be. So anyone who desires to work in a certain capacity or just to retain a position they love and are very competent in should not be perceived as "rocking the boat." For these and other reasons, many people "bite their tongues." They hold back opinions, questions, and comments that are contrary and in many cases correct to keep from rocking the boat. So in many ways, people in this situation are brainwashed. "To make someone adopt radically different beliefs by using systematic and often forcible pressure," that is the definition of brainwashing. They have been made to adopt or at least adhere to beliefs that they may not totally agree with. The method is very systematic in the use of scripture (though errantly) and doctrine. Though the pressure is rarely physical, the force exerted on the emotions the psyche and the spirit are all too real. It is in this climate that some well-meaning though unqualified men and women are allowed to serve as ministers and pastors. It is the very nature of the Pentecostal church that allows it to be a breeding ground for incompetence and conmen.

In my humble opinion, the nature of the Pentecostal church is to overemphasize the importance of the mystical and unseen intangible aspects of the religion. In so doing the qualifications for service are heavily weighted on those intangibles. So in most cases, the most important question is "your calling." Did God call you to the ministry? Was the call in a dream or a vision! Did you hear a voice? Were Mom and Dad always saying, "You look like a preacher, or you are going to be a preacher?" Or was it just something you always wanted to do. Unfortunately because of the intangible nature of the credential, it is not possible to verify them. So in a best-case scenario you have a preacher who is at least sincere in his heart. There is a hope that at some point he will realize or be inspired to follow 2 Timothy and study God's word with the attention it deserves. To follow the Bereans from Acts 17 who searched the scriptures daily. With a pure heart as a starting point, it is hopeful that he will seek the fullness of God in his life and ministry. If he will humble himself and pray and seek God's face and guidance and most of all search the scriptures to understand what is the full and perfect will of God then he will hear from heaven. He will be filled with the Holy Spirit by being filled with the word. He will look to increase his knowledge of the word through diligent study of all possible sources. He can grow in grace and knowledge and wisdom and develop into the man that God is calling for in this day. Or he can join the club. He can punch his card and pay his dues to be a member of the "Collar Club." This is not an exclusive group. Almost anyone can join. In most cases, it seems the most important thing is having the price of admission. This varies from organization to organization I'm sure, but in some way shape or form, it boils down to cash. And even in the case of young pure heart if he is not careful or falls under the wing of the wrong mentor, he may soon find himself more concerned with anniversaries than Antichrists.

Of course, there is always the worst-case scenario. This would be the entrepreneur. This is the person that recognizes "there's gold in them thar hills." This person sees the church as an ATM (all their money) and his or her main purpose is their own prosperity. Their teaching is focused on giving more than salvation and righteousness. To them, the church is primarily a financial business that happens to deal with souls. Actually, the primary business of the church is souls. It just happens to deal with a little finance. I believe that is why the names of churches have changed in recent years. It's no longer Southside Baptist Church or Living Word Pentecostal Church. Now it's Southside Baptist Ministries or Living Word Pentecostal Ministries. When you see ministries as part of the name, you think of an organization that is doing things in the neighborhood other than having church services and in many cases this is true. There are many great churches that deserve to use that as a part of their name. Many great things are done in and through some of these organizations. But for others, it just gives a reason to raise more funds. Funds that are mainly used to provide a good life for the pastor. Gone are the days of the humble preacher whose car barely starts and who lives in the neighborhood with his members and relied on the offering he would get to live on. Now salaries are negotiated, homes are paid for, and at least once a year a bonus in the form of an anniversary celebration is required of the congregation. If these things are not being done, the flock is not taking good care of their shepherd. The proponents of this kind of activity will of course point out the "muzzle not" scripture. I say "Rolls" not! As in Rolls Royce. Why would anyone who is full of the love of God disgrace the gospel message by owning such an expensive vehicle? Yet this sort of behavior is commonplace now. For example, Benny Hinn's ministry collects more than two hundred million dollars per year and his salary is as he stated more than 500,000 per year. He owns a private jet (guess Creflo is jealous) and lives in a ten million dollar home. Joyce Meyer's ministry is reported to have spent around four million on five homes for her and her children. She is said to live in a 10,000 sq. ft. home with an eight-car garage. Her salary was reported at 900,000 in 2003. Kenneth Copeland flat out refused to submit financial information about his ministry while being under investigation. He owns a twenty million dollar jet. Creflo Dollar's church made sixty-nine million in 2006. The Senate wants to talk to him but he also refused. He was recently in the news in reference to a sixty-five million dollar jet. Eddie Long drives around in a $350,000 Bentley (a car in the Rolls family) and has also refused the Senate information.

With reality television being all the rage, it is not surprising to see that the church has become involved with a few aberrations in this area. There are a few shows that follow people whose lives supposedly center on God. After watching some of these shows, you have to ask yourself what God? I realize we are all human and none of us is perfect. I realize we all have opinions about certain things that may not mesh with others. I also realize that when a network comes calling with big bucks in a TV contract, it must be very hard for people to see that Satan is the one behind it all. I'm glad it was not offered to me because maybe I would have been sucked in as well. But I am so very glad it is not me in the office of a preacher standing before millions as a supposed representative of God. If Christ hadn't died on the cross, some of these shows would have killed him. How any of those preachers could convince themselves that what they were portraying was glorifying God in any way simply speaks to how important the almighty is. Dollar that is. In fact, the only positive thing I saw in most of them was an example of patterns, habits, and attitudes to avoid. But this is what ministry means to some people. And that is why obedience is so important. Without it, the games could not be played and the scams could not be run. They are in many ways nothing more than pyramid plans or Ponzi schemes, but they rely on obedience for success. Over the years, I have heard preachers speak against what is called "The Pew Pastor." These are people who sit in the pews while the leader is in the pulpit and whispers comments about him or what he's saying to others on that pew. Of course, this is a very discourteous practice and should be discouraged. It is sometimes the voice of sedition and should be dealt with as such. But sometimes it is the voice of frustration from a person who has questions but no answers. Perhaps they have asked but not received. Maybe they just don't feel that asking is an option so they are left in limbo. When people are unable to ask or they ask but don't get or understand the answer, it stunts their growth. There is a failure to thrive. As Paul said in 1 Corinthians. 3:2, "I gave you milk and not solid food because you were not yet able to bear it."

As a child in the sixties, we used a word that is today considered degrading and really is not tolerated. In fact, anyone who uses it today would probably be considered ignorant! But in the sixties, everyone used it. The word was *retard* and of course it referred to the mentally handicapped. I will use this term only because it helps to paint a more vivid picture in this example. There was a man in my neighborhood who fell into this category. One of the first things you noticed about him was his bicycle, which had three wheels. This was the way he got around because when he walked, it was very slow and nonfluid. Each step was taken as if he had to think specifically and focus individually on every distinct phase of the gait cycle. He almost appeared to be intoxicated but his arms would flail awkwardly above his head similar to the characteristic motions of a chimpanzee. When he spoke, it was no more than a garble of nonsensical utterances as he tried to mimic speech. He drooled constantly, unable to control even this basic function. This is what a Christian looks like when he/she has not been nurtured in the gospel. Their walk is labored and inconsistent. They may know where they want to go but have no idea how to get there. They often need to be supported to get from one place to another when they should be totally capable of getting there on their own. They tend to fall down over and over and over. It is often difficult to understand them because what they say is a combination of things they are not sure of and things they've heard others say. They are simply unable to function at a level expected of a normal fully mature adult and therefore spiritually retarded. So, blind obedience leads to spiritual retardation and a failure to develop a discerning spirit. Getting answers to questions leads to increased knowledge, which leads to increased understanding and leads to discernment, which we should all be developing. So what is discernment?

Let's start with what discernment is not! 1 Cor. 12:10 lists discernment as a spiritual gift, but it is not only a spiritual gift. In fact, it is not primarily a spiritual gift. The charismatic/Pentecostal movement tends to put great emphasis on the spiritual aspects of our relationship with God. With the discovery of the Holy Spirit, the tangible seems to take a backseat almost to a fault. Many will say, "Well, God is a spirit, and we worship him in spirit." But we also worship him in truth! You can't have one without the other! So when 1 Corinthian lists it as a spiritual gift and Hebrew 4:12 talks about "discerning thoughts," many jump to the conclusion that this is all about an ability to see something that most other people can't. Discernment is defined as "the ability to separate a thing mentally (not spiritually) from another or other things, to recognize something as separate or different, to make out clearly, to recognize the difference." There are many other scriptures that talk about this process outside of the spiritual realm (Phil. 1:9–10). "Abound more and more with knowledge and discernment" (Heb. 5:14), "but solid food is for the mature, for those who have their powers of discernment trained" (Heb. 4:12). "For the word of God is living and active, sharper than any two-edged sword, piercing to the division of soul and spirit, of joints and of marrow and discerning the thoughts and intentions of the heart." There are scriptures that talk about this process using other words (1 Thes. 5:21–22), prove all things (1 John 4:1), test the spirits (Ro. 12:9), abhor evil, cleave to good. In 1 Kings 3:9–12, Solomon asked God for discernment and God called it wisdom. So in this multitude of scriptures, God is calling all of us to get wisdom, knowledge, understanding to be discerning. This is why Timothy said we must study so that we can "rightly divide the word of truth." Rightly divide it from mistake, from misconception, from deception and from error.

So it is our responsibility to study. As the Bereans in Acts 17 study/searched the scriptures to make sure Paul's teaching was in agreement with it, so it is our responsibility to make sure what we are being taught also agrees with the scriptures. If we are not getting the answers we need from our leaders, we are responsible for the effect that lack of information has on our lives. I'm not suggesting a mass exodus from churches (that's already happening), but we have to persevere in our efforts for the truth and the clarity of God's word. It is unfortunate that this situation exists. It is a shame that there are so many pastors and preachers in general who are just plain ill-equipped to function in that capacity. There are so many in leadership who are there for all the wrong reasons. This aberrant brand of preacher has cast a shadow over all the well-meaning shepherds and have become wolves tending unsuspecting flocks, fleecing them not only of their financial means but their spiritual growth. Be not deceived, there will come a time of payment for the damage these leaders have caused in the lives of the people they are charged with. James 3:1 discourages men from being masters (teachers, preachers) because there is greater responsibility placed on these offices. I don't know if some preachers have never read this scripture or they just don't believe it. In many ways, this kind of preacher (pastor, elder, bishop, etc.) is much like Israel and Judah in the time of the prophet Amos. They were so prosperous at this time their focus was misdirected and walked farther and farther away from God's law. Eventually, God sent fire down upon Judah by way of the Babylonians and their destruction of the Temple. Amos 2:6, "Thus saith the Lord; for three transgressions of Israel, and for four, I will not turn away the punishment thereof; because they sold the righteous for silver, and the poor for a pair of shoes."

To Serve Man

ONE OF MY FAVORITE episodes of the classic TV series *The Twilight Zone* involved aliens coming to earth. The plot was that a race of beings presents themselves as good neighbors that just want to help the earth with some problems they have noticed from afar. They don't seem to want anything but to be helpful and supply our planet with some technology that we just can't say no to. The ambassador from afar happens to leave a book laying around that is written in this alien language. The US military employs a linguist/code specialist to decipher the language. After several weeks Mr. Chambers makes out the title of the book but that's all. The title is *To Serve Man*, which seems to go along with all the beneficence the "Kanamits" have shown since arriving. After several months of "serving man," stopping war, famine, and disease the earth's governments decide the new friends are genuine and authorize trips to the alien planet for anyone who is interested. After giving up on decoding the book and not having anything to do since there is no more war, Mr. Chambers decides to visit the alien planet himself. Just as he is about to board the spaceship, his assistant runs into the launch site imploring Mr. Chambers not to get onto the craft. She has continued to work on the deciphering and has found that the book *To Serve Man* is a cookbook! If they had been able to unlock the language, they would have known what the book was all about. They would have been able to save the lives of thousands if they had only known not to get on the ships! Of course, *The Twilight Zone* is not real but this illustrates a similar issue that exist when reading the Bible. I believe there are several mistakes made when reading the Bible that lead to much of the confusion in understanding scripture and therefore errant principles and doctrines. The primary purpose of the Bible is "to serve man." That is to serve, help, support, guide man in his efforts to serve God. If we don't read the service manual or we don't read it correctly or we don't understand what we read, it's like trying to put something together without reading the directions. It takes a lot more time and somehow it doesn't feel sturdy. Then you notice there are things left over that you have no idea what to do with or where they were supposed to go. So let's talk about the Bible.

Most people know that the Bible is a book of books. That is it is made up of several individual writings by many different authors. But many people don't realize there were many other writings that were considered for inclusion into the sacred book. For example, the Gospel of Mary; Jesus's Infancy Gospel 1, 2; the Gospel of Nicodemus; the Epistle of Christ, Laodecians; the Apocalypse of Peter; the Epistle of Barnabas; Shepherd of Hermas; 1 Clement; the Gospel of Thomas; the Lost Epistle to the Corinthians. These are just a few of the many writings that were not included in the final grouping. The sixty-six works that make up the Holy Bible are known as "the canon of scripture." That phrase refers to the list of books recognized as worthy to be included in the sacred writings of a worshipping community. For Christians, it is the group of writings recognized as being of divine inspiration. The word *canon* is from a Greek word (kanon) that means rod as in a special ruler used for measuring. This led to the use of the word as a standard. So in the early church, the canon was the group of writings that were to be used as the basis of any doctrinal philosophy under a Christian heading. Thomas Aquinas said, "Canonical scripture alone is the rule of faith." In 1647, after listing the sixty-six books of the Bible.

The Westminster Confession of Faith added, "All which are given by the inspiration of God to be the rule of faith and life." So while the canon of scripture means the list of books accepted as holy scripture, it also has a sense of "the rule and standard by which belief and Christian life are gauged." So the Bible is a book. It is a sacred and holy book to be revered and esteemed above all others. But it is in fact a book! I think when this fact is overlooked, there are many pitfalls waiting for the reader, so let's look at the book.

So what do I mean it's a book? Well, it has a front and a back, a beginning and an end. It has chapters, paragraphs, sentences, commas, and periods. No, I'm not trying to be funny. The point is these are very important parts of the construct of a book. Without all of these elements, all you have is a bunch of words strung together. In fact, without the spaces, they are just a bunch of letters one next to the other. "Ohwhatagooseiam" has no meaning until the spaces are added to reveal "Oh what a goose I am." If the recipes in a cookbook are not followed accurately, you don't know how your product will turn out. It may look like the picture displayed and taste terrible. It may taste wonderful but does not stand up as firmly as it should. If you don't understand the recipe or measuring or any of the chemistry of cooking, you may do well with some things but with others not so much. Failing to understand the Bible can come from a lack of understanding or failure to recognize the constructs of its creation. So we have all the literary tools that have been employed along with all the different authors and all the different styles. To top it all, none of the contributors were actual writers. So just from a literary standpoint there are many ways that our quest to "rightly divide the word" can be derailed. From this perspective, it is not surprising that there are so many misunderstood concepts in the charismatic/Pentecostal churches, which have always focused on the spiritual/mystic rather than the scriptural aspect of the relationship with God. Because of this spiritual focus, charismatics put more emphasis on what is seen and felt versus what the written word is really trying to say. Because of the focus on the intangible, critical logical thinking often takes a backseat. The idea that Abel's blood was actually speaking could be avoided simply by asking the logical question, does blood speak? Since it does not, this scripture must mean something else. Instead with a mystic focus we allow ourselves to take the leap that something spiritual happens to the blood that allowed it to have the power to do something that no other blood can do simply because God is involved. There is no one who is more logical than God and he would not want his words read without logic. God inspired the authors of the Bible and "God is not the author of confusion" (1 Cor. 14:33). It simply does not make sense that we cast logical analysis aside when trying to understand the Bible. I sometimes joke that when we finally see God, he will probably be shaking his head from side to side in disbelief at the things that some of us have gotten wrong. Logic has to be a part of "rightly dividing the word of truth."

Not understanding what kind of book you are reading can diminish your ability to understand the meaning of the book. For example, there are three kinds of books in the Old Testament: historical, poetic, and prophetic. The history books are Genesis, Exodus, Leviticus, Numbers, Deuteronomy, Joshua, Judges, Ruth, 1 and 2 Samuel, 1 and 2 Kings, 1 and 2 Chronicles, Ezra, Nehemiah, and Esther. The poetry is Job, Psalms, Proverbs, Ecclesiastes, and Songs of Solomon. The prophetic are Isaiah, Jeremiah, Lamentations, Ezekiel, Daniel, Hosea, Joel, Amos, Obadiah, Jonah, Micah, Nahum, Habakkuk, Zephaniah, Haggai, Zechariah, and Malachi. To understand the Bible, there must be clarity between these books.

The history is that of the nation of Israel and her relationship to God. It is the history and foundation of the Jewish religion. It is a history of the law and the evidence of man's inability to keep the law. It records the rituals of the worship and the remedies for the sin. These rituals and remedies do not, however, apply to us as Christians today. Quite frankly, there is not a lot of trouble in this area. We don't have a lot of Christian churches advocating burnt offerings and animal sacrifice or observing the many festivals of the OT. That is very good because they don't apply to Christians they apply to Jews. When we read the OT, it is important to understand we are not reading a book on how to be a Christian, we're reading how to be a Jew. Of course there are exceptions. The Ten Commandments carry over into the NT because they are a part of the foundation of righteous living and a life that pleases God. They are fundamental to our understanding of God and what he expects from us. Since God does not change what he expects from us does not change whether Jew or Christian. Therefore all of the ideas in the commandments can be found in some form throughout the NT.

I. Thou shalt have no other God before me. (Matt. 4:10, Lk. 4:8)

II. Thou shalt not make any graven image. (Acts 15:20, 1 Cor. 10:7, 14)

III. Thou shalt not take name of the Lord in vain. (Mk. 6:9, Lk. 11:12, Matt. 15:8, 9, 12:36)

IV. Remember the Sabbath day. (Matt. 12:8, 12; Mark 2:27, 27, 28; Lk. 6:5)

V. Honor thy parents. (Matt. 19:19, Mk. 10:19, Eph. 6:1–3)

VI. Thou shalt not commit murder. (Matt. 5:21; Mk. 10:19; Ro. 13:9)

VII. Thou shalt not commit adultery. Matt. 5:27, 28, 32; Matt. 19)

VIII. Thou shalt not steal. (Matt. 19:18, Ro. 13:9, Eph. 4:28)

IX. Thou shalt not bear false witness. (Matt. 15:19, 20, 19:18; Ro. 13:9)

X. Thou shalt not covet. (Lk. 12:15, Ro. 7:7, Ro. 13:9)

These NT verses that parallel the commandments are just a few of the multitude of verses that can be found to do so. These foundational ideas occurring in both the old and new testaments illustrate a principle that should be recognized when studying the Bible and that is "recurring themes."

The idea of recurrence is that anything of theological importance that should be observed by NT Christians will be found in the NT more than once or it will be stated as a command if found only once. If something from the OT should be observed by us, it will be found in the NT such as the scriptures above relating the ideas of the Ten Commandments. God's grace, his love, mercy, and longsuffering are all prominent themes in the OT and all are very obvious in the NT. It is impossible to read the Bible with any intelligence and not recognize that God desires our growth toward him in righteousness. Both testaments make this clear over and over with many different writers and situations. We can get it wrong when we fail to realize that God will, more times than not, repeat the important stuff as exemplified in "verily, verily I say unto you." I think he repeats it because he wants to be sure we get it, and he knows how prone we are to lean toward our own understanding. Some things are a little harder to identify as belonging to the old or new testaments or both.

The Sabbath is one of those things. Some denominations believe because the Sabbath was originally observed on the last day of the week that it should continue being observed on Saturday as do the Jews. Most Christian denominations observe Sunday as the day of rest based on Christ rising on that day. The Sabbath is first mentioned in Genesis 2:2–3 when God rested from his creation work on that day and blessed and sanctified that day. In Exodus 31:13–17 the Sabbath is noted as a sign between God and Israel. Exodus 20:8–11 explains that no work should be done on that day, but it says nothing about worship. In the NT, Christ observed the Sabbath in the synagogue (Lk. 4:16, 13:10; Mk. 6:2) but then defied the Pharisees gauge of Sabbath observance with an exorcism (Lk. 4:31–32, 33–36). In Mark 2:27, Jesus states, "The Sabbath is for man and not man for the Sabbath." Nowhere in the Bible are the Gentiles taught to observe the Sabbath nor are they condemned for failing to do so. The disciples gathered in Acts 20:7 for what sounds like the first description of a "church service" because Paul was preaching and this was on the first day of the week. In 1 Corinthian 16:2, a collection was taken also on the first day. In Romans 14:5, Paul forbids observers of the Sabbath condemning nonobservers and he directs us not to be judged by keeping Sabbaths in Colossians 2:16. Jesus, being a Jew, would of course observe the Jewish tradition of worship on the Hebrew Sabbath. His visits to the synagogue were in keeping with what he had grown up with all his life. None of these visits record any of the disciples joining him. One would think that if this were of great importance, we would see at least a couple of instances when they were together at the synagogue. Knowing that his mission was to the whole world and not just the Jews, it seems he didn't focus on something that was after all Jewish. In Matthew 12:8, Jesus declares himself Lord of the Sabbath.

He seems to be saying that he and what he is teaching supersede the Sabbath. He doesn't condemn the Sabbath as evidenced by his own observance, but he refuses to make it a task master as the Pharisees have. He seems to take this thought a step further when he says, "The Sabbath is for man." I believe that means for man's good, for man's benefit, to help man, "to serve man." I believe the Sabbath is a tool that assists man in his endeavor to serve God. Sabbath day observance maintains a regular pattern of communication and interaction with God. Perhaps Christ is saying it's more important that we choose a day than which day we choose. But being omniscient, Christ knew there would come a time and a culture where some men would not have the luxury of not working on Saturday or Sunday as is the case today. Some people pine for the day when they can come to worship services with the others in their church family but the constraints of their employ do not allow that pleasure at this time. What about professional athletes? Should they be deprived the blessings of a God-given physical talent because the games are on a traditional Sabbath? Or should we teach that you can't be a professional athlete and be saved? If a person works on Saturday and Sunday and the Sabbath was made for man, it seems that man should be able to observe another day of the week. The point of the Sabbath is after all to honor and glorify God. If God knows my situation and I set aside Wednesday to keep it holy, wouldn't God be as pleased with me as those who kept traditional worship days? When I was growing up, the answer would be no! And there are those I'm sure now who would agree, no! Quit that job and let God provide you with another. It's more important to come to church on a specific day than to hold onto a good job. So where do you place being a good steward in this scenario? Then there are those pastors who would take the opposite stance and encourage that person to remain employed as long as they are sending their tithes and offering! Both cannot be correct! Christ came to us as a Jew demonstrating how to be a Jew and then taught us that just being a Jew wasn't enough. So it amazes me that it is sometimes difficult to separate things Jewish from things Christian. Perhaps I shouldn't be amazed. Perhaps it is not so much a matter of difficult but a matter of choice. Take tithes for example.

The modern dictionary defines tithing as paying or giving one-tenth of annual production or earnings as a tax for the support of the church and clergy. I grew up with this tradition as did many of today's Christians. My mother often shared her first experiences paying tithes with great pride and joy. When she was a very small child, as young as under ten, whenever she received a gift of money for a birthday or made money doing a chore, she couldn't wait to put her nickel or ten cents in an envelope on Sunday and place it in the tithing vessel. Over the years, I've come to the conclusion that there are basically three categories of tithe payers: The 100%ers, the Spocks, and the tippers.

My parents were 100%ers. This group believes in paying that 10 percent out of every check no matter what happens. They take the tithe off the top and figure out what else will get paid after that. No matter what the need or the emergency, the tithe was to be paid first. Now I have ten siblings, and my father struggled working three jobs most of my life so I know there must have been times when they missed payments. In those cases, there would be an additional amount owed much like a late payment on a loan! The extent to which you adhered to or deviated from timely payment was a reflection of your dedication to God. It was actually considered sinful if tithes weren't paid. If a person aspired to a particular office or position and did not pay tithes, they could forget any such appointments. They could be qualified on a professional and academic level, but if they were not tithing, they were out. I once heard a discussion about tithing and heaven. There was a woman who was tragically killed by an automobile one Monday morning on the way to work. She had missed church the day before (Sunday) and so did not pay her tithes. She had the tithes at home, and they were set aside, but since she did not get them to the church, there was some question as to whether this kept her out of heaven. The woman was loving, kind, faithful, and honest. She was always sacrificing for others and trying to help any and everyone she found in need. I personally knew her and to this day have never heard anyone say anything negative about her but some thought missing one tithe payment might keep her from seeing God!

The next group I call the Spocks (Star Trek). These are the more logical tithers. They believe in paying the 10 percent but not at the expense of letting bills lapse or taking care of real necessities for home and family. These people would say they love God just as much as the first group but do not think it is sensible to pay tithes when there is a financial issue that needs attention. They would be more likely to pay a portion of what they owe in these cases. They would likely recognize that scripture admonishes us toward good stewardship (1 Tim. 5:8) and the wise use of the finances God has provides for us. When speaking to those in this group, you can sense the recognition that failure to pay is not sinful, but they are not able to give chapter and verse as to why they feel this way.

The last group is the tippers. This group basically pays whatever they want to and it usually is nowhere near 10 percent. With these people, it's hard to tell if they are very insightful or just very cheap. It's very interesting that in my experience these are usually the people who have the most financially. Perhaps it's harder to give that larger amount even though all are asked for 10 percent.

Paying tithes has always been a very honored practice in my church but is sometimes taught with a fervor that borders on coercion. Tithing is one of the giving ministries in the church and as such it should be a joyous and happy part of worship. This attitude is encouraged in many services today with clapping and cheering at the prospect of giving to God. This is totally appropriate and in line with 2 Corinthians 9:6, 7, "God loves a cheerful giver," but it's very hard to be cheerful when you are trying to be obedient on one hand and know you really can't afford it on the other. Knowing that the kids need shoes or the car needs a repair but you are taught by someone you trust that you need to learn to sacrifice and lean on God. The pastor tells you that God will bless your giving and how he has been blessed for his giving, but it just never seems to work out for you. So you keep struggling to pay tithes and you keep on struggling while the pastor picks out his next new car. Yes we should be happy about the prospect of giving to God the problem is that now days we're not really giving to God but to the pastor (bishop, etc.) and it's funny that they stop quoting 2 Corinthians 9:7 at v. If they would read through to verse 15, they would see that the funds collected from those cheerful givers should be used at least in part for the benefit of others. Funny how that happens. They can see the part that applies to the sheep but very seldom the part that applies to the shepherd!

So we, like sheep, every Sunday are marched down the aisles of churches all over the country in a parade of all those who are paying tithes. Of course, those who do not walk are just not quite as righteous as those who do. Or like an affirmation of faith recited by the congregation, we are to verbally pledge that we are tithers in front of all and for all to hear. Of course, no one would lie in church! There are even those churches that require a W2 tax form so that they know how much a person should be paying lest you try to "rob God." These are all methods to assure that every man, woman, boy, and girl pay that 10 percent. If that money, even a substantial portion of it was used to benefit those in need, it would not be so bad. And I know that churches have operational costs. But most of the time one of, if not the largest, cost is the pastor's salary. The point is that people should not be bullied or manipulated into paying tithes. If it is to be done, it should be a joyous and happy part of the service and not a moment when you have to stop and wonder if you did the right thing. Will the car note or the mortgage payment is short? But when the scripture is read, "Will a man rob God?" Logic goes out the window because no one who believes in God would want to be guilty of robbing him. Malachi 3:8–10 is probably read in more tithing churches on Sunday than any other scripture. Unfortunately to fully understand this passage, you have to go back to chapter 2. When read before the tithing portion of services, it sounds like a question to each individual hearing the speaker. Will you rob God? The answer is of course, no! Why? Because no one wants to be cursed with a curse from God (verse 9). But if you finish reading verse 9 (ye have robbed me, even this whole nation) a question should come to mind. How can my failure to pay rob the whole nation? The only way that could occur is if I have a responsibility to the whole nation as did the priests and that's exactly who Malachi is talking to. Not the general public but to corrupt priests who have been misappropriating temple funds. Ironically, in using this scripture inappropriately to scare or brainwash God's people into giving, church leaders are guilty of the very thing that Malachi is warning against. The saddest thought in this whole discussion is that tithing is not something that is even taught to Christians of the NT. That's right, tithing is not to Christians.

That may come as a surprise to some but, no, tithing is not taught in the NT. Tithing is not a part of our Christian duties as most tithing churches would have us believe. None of the Apostles address tithing in any of the NT writings. Jesus actually spoke about it once, but he was reprimanding a Pharisee because he tithed even of his herbs but ignored the more important things like justice, mercy, and faithfulness (Matt. 23:23, Luke 11:42, and 18:12). In other words, Jesus was concerned about the attitude in his giving, not what he was giving. This Pharisee was giving out of ritual and to be seen giving almost in a boastful manner. He was very concerned about the trappings of religion, the things that made him appear righteous to men. The truly important things that paint a picture of his soul did not reflect righteousness at all. In the entire twenty-third chapter, Christ is blasting hypocrisy and false teachers who "have a form of godliness." So Jesus was not encouraging tithing, he was encouraging a right heart, purity, and righteousness. More importantly to this subject he was talking to a Jew and not a Gentile and nowhere in scripture does he address Gentiles on this matter. Why is that significant? Because tithing was to the Jews, not the Gentiles. The Gentile Christians were converts from different pagan religions, mostly idolatry. While they brought many practices with them, tithing was not one of them. So if this were an important issue, it surely would have to be taught to them, yet no one teaches or encourages the Gentile to pay tithes in the entire NT. Jesus himself has always acted as a model for things that we are expected to follow in our worship and our living practices (baptism water and spirit, Matt. 3:14–16; communion, Matt. 26:26–29, Luke 22:14–20; servant, St. John 13:1–5; taxes, Matt. 17:24–27) but no record of his paying or suggesting that anyone else pay tithes. So if Jesus were to address this issue for us today, it would likely be with the same reprimanding tone he used with the Pharisee because technically this is a "false teaching."

Technically in the OT, paying tithes was specifically to support the functioning of the temple. Supporters of tithing would argue that this is what tithes do today, support the church but that is not correct. For that to be true, you would have to equate the OT temple (that is the temple built by Solomon) with our present-day churches.

That is an error! The OT temple was the place where the Ark of the Covenant was kept. It was built in the Holy City of Jerusalem (there is only one Holy City). The Ark was representative of the presence of God. The temple was a sacred edifice built specifically to house this one sacred item. The temple was a hallowed, sanctified place where the sacrifices for sins were performed. It was comprised of several courtyards designated for use by specific persons. There was an area to keep the animals before sacrifice, a slaughtering and skinning area, and the altar for burning the sacrifice. There was a special chamber for lepers, a chamber for storage of vestments and a chamber for the bread maker (Shewbread). The most important area was the Holy of Holies, which was the thirty-foot room that the Ark was kept in. This room was separated from the outer Holy Place by a curtain. This was the veil that was torn when Christ died on the cross. Only the High Priest had access to the Holy of Holies, and this was allowed only once a year. On that one day when he entered, he wore a bell that could be heard by the priests on the outside as long as the high priest was moving. If the bell stopped sounding, it was because the high priest had stopped moving. This indicated that he had gone into the Holy of Holies with some uncleansed sin, which made him unworthy to be there and was now dead for his transgression. He was then dragged out by a rope that was tied to him and ran out to the other priests who were standing by in case this occurred. To compare the temple with any church on earth even from a natural standpoint is ridiculous. From a spiritual view, the closest thing to compare in the NT with the temple would be those of us who are redeemed and have God's presence (the Holy Spirit) within us. So to equate the Jerusalem Temple with NT churches is really grabbing at straws. Probably the best comparison is the church with the synagogue, which was the local meeting place for worship and instruction that became prevalent after the destruction of Solomon's Temple. So since there was only one temple that housed the Ark and tithes were collected to support that temple, which was destroyed in AD 70; technically today, tithes are not used for the purpose they were designated in the Bible. I spoke to a rabbi on this matter and his response was that "Jews today do not pay tithes because there is no temple to pay them to." Another problem technically, tithes should be given to a Levite. As priests, it was the job of the Levites to care for the treasury of the temple and thus collect and distribute the tithes (1 Chron. 9:22–28). The rabbi said, "It would be a sin to give the tithes to a non-Levite and a sin for anyone but a Levite to accept them." That means that even if the temple was still standing today unless your pastor, superintendent, overseer, bishop, etc., is a descendant of the tribe of Levi it is a sin to receive tithes. Of course no one (but God) can know if they are in that line because the records of lineage were lost when the temple was destroyed.

So where does tithing come from? To strengthen the idea that tithing is for Christians today and not strictly for O.T. Jews many supporters will point to the first mention of tithe in the Bible. In Genesis 14:17-20 we see Abraham giving tithe to Melchizedek who was the priest of the, most high God and King of Salem (possibly early Jerusalem). Melchizedek was a Canaanite, a non-Jew who served the living God, Abraham's God. There is no further explanation for Melchizedek but there were other non-Jews who served God, Noah, Job, Adam. However, tithe is not mentioned with anyone until Abraham and Melchizedek. Nevertheless, they will say here we have father Abraham initiating the tithing system. But if we read the whole story here we learn that what Abraham gave a tenth of was "the spoils of war" and not a tenth of his earnings or his annual income which is what tithes are based on (Lev. 27:30; Deut. 14:22-23,28; 2Chron. 31: 5-6.) What happened was with three hundred eighteen men, Abraham defeated an alliance of four kings to rescue his nephew Lot. He realized this was done by the power of God and gave a free-will offering to the priest as a show of recognition and gratitude to God for the miraculous victory. There is no record of Abraham paying tithes before this incident even though he was at the time already a very wealthy man. There is no record of Abraham paying tithes ever again after this incident. Abraham even gave the remaining 90% of the spoils back to the owners (Gen. 14: 21-23). So, this does not appear to be the institution of the tithing system we see in Judaism. In fact, the "tenth" is only a portion of the total tithe the Jews were responsible for.

1-Because of their function in caring for the Temple the Levites were not given a portion of the promised land as were all other tribes. Therefore, everyone was required to pay a tenth of their worth to the Levites. (Numbers 18:21)

2-The Levites would then pay 10% of that to the priests. (Numbers 18:25-31) Not all of the Levites were priests.

3-The people were to keep a tithe for themselves to be used for annual pilgrimage and feasting in the name of the Lord. (Deut. 14:22-26)

4-Every three years 10% of that year was to be given for the poor, widows, orphans and the Levites. (Deut. 14:28-29)

So, this is what tithing should look like. This is true tithing. This was part of the Law of the O.T. Christians are under the law of grace. The two concepts are like oil and water, darkness and light, east and west, they don't mix! Speaking of the old covenant Hebrews 8:13 says "In that he hath, a new covenant, he hath made the first old. Now that which decayeth and waxeth old is ready to vanish away." The old covenant is gone. It has served its purpose but it is no longer useful now that we have the blood of Jesus and the grace of God. To hold onto a portion of something that is dead is not sensible. Preachers often use the phrase "anything that is dead should be buried", but because the concept of tithing is beneficial especially to them it is kept on life support by whatever means necessary. James 2:10 says "For whosoever shall keep the whole law, and yet offend in one point, he is guilty of all." So, while the term tithe did appear in scripture before the Jewish nation, the institution of, the practice and command to observe tithing was not given by God until it was given to Moses and the Children of Israel. I am not saying that the O.T. is of no value. I am not saying that we don't need to be bothered with the O.T. as is the teaching of some denominations. There is great wisdom and knowledge there, we get to know and understand God, his nature and personality there. But we are not under the law and we should not be in observance of any of the rituals or ordinances associated with the law no matter how lucrative it is and that's what tithing is, a part of the law. This is why it is so important for us to study the Bible earnestly and thoroughly.

Galatians 3:6–14 contrasts the futility of trying to keep the law with justification by faith. Verse 10 says, "Cursed is everyone that continueth not in all things which are written in the book of the law." Basically, the only way the law could have worked for salvation is if you kept every aspect of it. It was a curse or a condemnation to spiritual death if you didn't keep every part of it. So here we are hanging on to one part of the law tithes, and we are not even observing that fully. We are not told to observe the family tithe (Deut. 14:22–27) or the poor tithe (Deut. 14:28–29) only the sacred tithe, the tithe to the pastor uh bishop, uh, oh the church. But if we hang on to this part of the law, why not other parts like animal sacrifice, kosher foods, observance of feasts and festivals, Rosh Hashanah, Yom Kippur, Passover? Because that would mean we are trying to be Jewish. This is one of the problems Paul had to deal with in both the Corinthian (1 Cor. 7:19) and Galatian (Gal. 6:15) churches. The Jewish converts were trying to impose their traditions on their Gentile counterparts, requiring circumcision and other Jewish practices for them to be saved. Paul explains that it is not circumcision (or other ritual acts) that matter but becoming a new creature within. Perhaps that is why some cannot recognize that the place for tithes is in the OT. Perhaps the new creature still has some growing to do. Growing from the materialistic mentality that makes them drag something from the OT into the church age that even modern-day Jews are not holding on to. Growing to a faith and reliance on God that if he has truly ordained a particular church, he will be faithful to sustain that church and a church that is not sustained by God should close its doors.

Is tithing a sin? Well, if not, it is certainly not directed at NT Christians. And don't make the mistake of using 1 Cor. 16:1–2 where Paul was directing the collection of a special offering that he would pick up and deliver during his travels. In 2 Corinthians 9:7, we are told to give as we purpose in our hearts. God loves a cheerful giver. I grew up paying tithes even as a young teen. I have received many strange looks from tax preparers concerning my tithes for the year. Even as I share this knowledge, it is difficult for me not to pay. I don't believe there is anything wrong with paying tithes. I know of some people who pay 20 and 30 percent, and I do believe God blesses these wonderful souls for what they do. But the NT is our Christian guide, our spiritual handbook, and if Jesus himself and none of the Apostles told us, taught us, or suggested to us that we should pay tithes, then no modern-day preacher should have the audacity to teach it either. The sin of modern tithing is not that some people don't pay but that some people don't pay enough attention to God's word to recognize where tithes belong. To borrow from Paul, to pay tithes is nothing; and to not pay tithes is nothing. But to teach that tithes is what it is not, that is something.

Tithe is an example of a concept that is misunderstood when it is taken out of the time or era to which it belongs. Christians are a part of what is called the "church age," which is defined as the time from Pentecost (Acts 2 to the Rapture foretold in 1 Thes. 4:13–18). Let's look at something that applies directly to the church age, speaking in tongues. Growing up in a Pentecostal church tongues was something I grew up hearing. It was and is one of the defining characteristics of the charismatic churches. As I mentioned earlier, speaking in tongues is thought to be a language prompted by the Holy Spirit and spoken directly to God. The speaker does not know what he/she is saying unless an interpreter is present at the same time. Like tithers, the person who spoke in tongues was looked upon as more spiritual or closer to God. Personally, my only experience speaking came at a revival when I wanted so badly to speak because it was a sign that God was truly in your life. This was a time when I thought I was saved! I was living my life the best I knew and wanted so much to have this deeper relationship with God. It meant that you were really saved that this thing was real. All I had been taught my whole life was real. So I began to speak. I don't remember what I said, but I know I was not out of myself or controlled by the Holy Spirit. But we had been told to "let go and let God," and that's what I was doing. During a revival, we would be taken to the altar and "encouraged" to call Jesus. Each candidate would be verbally coached toward repentance by someone who had already received the Spirit. "Jesus, Jesus, Jesus, Jesus, Jesus, Jesus." We were told to speak faster and faster and faster until to only sound you could hear was "Je, je, Je, Je, Je, Je, Je, Je, Je, Je." After thirty to forty minutes of this, most of us would invariably start to cry, so now there was crying and snif-fling to contend with as well. I think the shear speed we were being pushed to attain was enough to lead to sounds like words but having no meaning. Some were crying because the things being said to you while you called Jesus would cause you to feel guilty about your life or maybe something done recently. They might even use your parents or a dead loved one to spark genuine remorse. After working the altar for an unspecified amount of time, it would be proclaimed by some, "You got it," and others, "You need to come back tomorrow." Those who had it would have "spoken in tongues" and probably "shouted" the holy dance of the Pentecostal church. So what does it mean to speak in tongues? In Acts 2, the miracle of tongues first appeared. The Apostles were among a group of about 120 people gathered to celebrate Passover. The others in the Upper Room were from a vari-ety of nations or regions and therefore languages. By the power of the HS, Peter and the other Apostles present began preaching but in the languages of the foreigners present. These were real languages that could be written down, translated, and learned. They were reg-ular human languages. The scripture in Acts also says that "cloven tongues" appeared and rested upon each of them. So not only was there an audible but a visual miracle. It seems the HS was really try-ing to make a point here. The importance of the events at Pentecost cannot be overstated. This was the day foretold by the prophet Joel, "It shall come to pass that I will pour out my spirit upon all flesh" (Joel 2:28). Before this day, the HS did not reside in a person per-manently. When it was in operation, it would come upon a person to get the work done, and when it was finished, the HS would leave. But now the HS was going to take up permanent residence in indi-viduals that accept Christ. This miracle of tongues and fire made sure that this day stood out from age to age. So because tongues was an indicator of the presence of the HS at Pentecost, most charismatic churches today believe in the appearance of tongues whenever the HS comes into a person's life. Unfortunately, there are several prob-lems with this line of thinking. First, the failure to recognize this was not just a miracle but a necessity. The use of tongues was not just to show that God was at work here and that these guys were his guys. Remember, there was no Internet, social media was centuries away. There was no television, no telephone, and no telegraph. Not even the printing press was available yet so there was no Bible, newspapers, or magazines that could be used to spread this new gospel message. The gospel had to be carried by word of mouth. If this task were left up to the Apostles without the event at Pentecost, it would have required they learn these languages or teach people who spoke these other languages to speak the language of the Apostles. This would have been very time consuming and the gospel would not have been able to spread as quickly as it did. Because there were twelve languages spoken, those who heard this message in their own native tongue were able to take that message back to their region, thereby spreading the gospel like wildfire. Among other things, the appearance of cloven tongues at the Pentecost event may have indicated this wildfire spread of the word of the HS. Another problem with taking tongues as a sign for us today is what happens with the cloven tongues of fire? Since they appeared with the spoken tongues, why aren't they used as a sign as well? How do you take one part of the miracle as a sign and not the other? There is also the problem of glossolalia, which is defined as fluid vocalizing of speech-like syllables that lack any readily comprehended meaning. As I stated earlier, what was spoken at Pentecost were actual languages. What we hear spoken in churches today is glossolalia. Why are we not hearing actual languages today? Some will answer that what we hear today is called unknown tongues (1 Cor. 14:2–4) but in all the Bibles I have seen and all those reported by classmates in Sunday school and Bible studies the word unknown is in italics. Unknown is always written differently than the other words on a slant or with different lettering. The reason for this is that it does not occur in the original scriptures that the Bible was translated from. For some unknown reason, it was placed there by translators. It may have been for the sake of the flow of words in the passages where it is used but in the original scriptures unknown does not appear.

So technically, the modern-day concept of speaking in tongues is based on something that does not exist. Look at Christ as our example. We saw earlier that he was our example in keeping the Ten

Commandments as well as the Sabbath. He meant for us to be baptized in water and with the spirit, so he experienced both of these. In praying, fasting, loving, and giving. In all these integral aspects of our Christian walk, he was our example. Why is it that he never spoke in tongues? He did speak about tongues once in Mark 16:14–20 when telling of the signs that would follow believers. But if you read the entire chapter, several points emerge: (1) He was talking only to the (disciples); there was no one else in that gathering. (2) He was reprimanding them for their failure to believe Mary when she said she had seen him. (3) He was sending them out into the world to preach the gospel. (4) One of the signs that would follow (them) that believe was new tongues. Most Pentecostals take these signs as applying to all who believe, but it is more likely that the "them" Christ was referring to was the disciples there with him and those associated with that core group. Otherwise, it seems he would have taught that speaking in tongues was for all believers as he taught the other things that all believers should be doing. Why are tongues not taught by any disciples but Paul in any book other than Corinthians? In 1 Corinthians, Paul is dealing with a multitude of problems that were facing that congregation. Sexual problems of incest and fornication, marriage and divorce, food offered to idols, pagan feasts, and the Lord's Table. It is in this climate of bringing clarity out of confusion that he discusses speaking in tongues. He never seems to encourage the practice; in fact, he discourages and downplays it. In chapter 13:1–8, he explains that love is more important than tongues. In chapter 14:9, he says, "Yet in church I would rather speak five words with my understanding, that by my voice I might teach others also, than ten thousand words in an unknown tongue." In 1 Cor. 12:30 after asking several rhetorical questions, which were answered no, Paul asks, "Do all speak in tongues?" to which the answer in context of the passage is no! If speaking in tongues is a sign of the Holy Spirit's baptism, why are there so many of these baptisms in the Bible with no mention of tongues? (Acts 2:47; 4:31–33; 9:17–18, 35; 11:21; 14:1, 23; 17:4, 12, 34; 18:8; 19:18). If tongues is a sign of the presence of the HS, why are there so many spirit-related events with no presentation of tongues? (Acts 4:8, 31; 9:17; 13:9, 50). In 1 Cor. 14:26–28, by the inspiration of the HS, Paul lists four rules that should be followed in the functioning of tongues in the church: (1) No more than three should speak at any service. (2) They should speak in order (not at random or haphazardly). (3) There should be an interpreter present. (4) If there is no interpreter, there should not be any tongues spoken in church. Later in that passage (1 Cor. 14:33), in his efforts to bring clarity to the discord, Paul explains, "God is not the author of confusion." He is insinuating that failure to follow these rules will lead to confusion. There may be times that these rules are followed. Maybe even in the presence of a legitimate language. But we all know that for the most part, these rules are never adhered to. If modern tongues is from the HS who issued these rules, why does the HS almost always break its own rules for speaking? The answer of course is it wouldn't, couldn't, and doesn't. There is no way that God who is not the author of confusion would bring about the confusion that exists in our churches relative to the subject of tongues.

Looking at the above information, something very peculiar comes to light. Speaking in tongues ends in the book of Acts! Now I may have missed one or two instances, but it is virtually nonexistent outside of the book of Acts. It is also very interesting that miracles seem to end in Acts as well. In 1 Timothy 5:23, Paul instructed Timothy to use a little wine for his stomach's sake and for his ailing. Why didn't he heal him? In 2 Timothy 4:20, Paul left Trophimus at Miletum sick. In Philippians 2:25–30, he left Epaphroditus sick. Why didn't he heal them? We know that the miracles were done through the power of the HS, so did the HS suddenly lose its power? Of course not, so there must be some other reason that these wonders suddenly came to a halt. Perhaps the events in the book of Acts were meant to authenticate the Apostles as God's chosen messengers and not things that would be done by all believers for all time. Maybe we should not be focusing on the mysterious and the miraculous, after all that is what the Antichrist will use to deceive when he comes on the scene, signs, and wonders. Remember in St. John 20:29 after Thomas needed to see the scars of Jesus's crucifixion to believe he had risen, Jesus said, "Blessed are those who believe and have not seen." What if that phrase "have not seen" was not just referring to have not seen Christ but have not seen miracles, signs, and wonders? After all, our salvation is based on faith and what else is faith but belief! Whosoever shall believe on him shall not perish but have everlasting life. On the other hand, in Matt. 16:4, Jesus said, "A wicked and adulterous generation seeketh after a sign: and there shall be no sign given unto it!"

We also have to ask if glossolalia (modern tongues) is not from the HS, where does it come from? There are several possibilities. Learned behavior is the nice way to say it and brainwashing is probably extreme, but mixed up somewhere between those two words is one source. When you are raised from childhood with this concept, it is the norm. It's like learning the alphabet or to count or talking, that's what you are taught so that's what is normal to you. It's a part of you, it's who you are it defines you. It also takes us back to the concepts of obedience and trust. You trust what you are being told is the truth because you trust the ones telling you. Obedience is a logical next step and comes very easily and is directly proportional to the level of trust. Once you have learned something, it is very hard to "unlearn it" so those who have grown up with the idea of speaking in tongues will likely have a more difficult time even considering the possibility that it is not a biblical concept. I have seen this myself in discussions of this nature where people have almost become angry because of the very suggestion that what they believe, what they have been living and experiencing all their lives might not be what they thought it was. In my experience those who come into the Pentecostal arena from another faith or no church upbringing at all have a much harder time grasping the concept and practice of tongues. There are also those who teach the ability to speak in tongues. However, this is simply a blatant misrepresentation of the word because the Bible clearly calls tongues a gift or a miracle and neither of these can be taught. But because we fail to pay attention to what the word is saying, we often foolishly fall victim to such folly. Another likely source is mental illness. Unfortunately, this can be a factor in the presence of this phenomenon. Schizophrenia is an illness that would easily lend itself to hearing voices and being told to say things. This may seem insulting to suggest, and it is really not my intent but when you eliminate some things as a possible source the things that are left have to be considered. That is why it is so important to know what the Bible says and what the Bible means by what it says. If you believe something with all your heart that turns out to be a lie, it doesn't matter how strong your belief was, it was all for nothing, and it may end up causing problems for you. I think the most dangerous source is Satan! We have to remember that Satan is always trying to copy God. He wants to take God's place. He tries to mimic God at every opportunity. There is a Holy trinity—Father, Son, Holy Ghost—and an unholy trinity—the dragon, the beast, and the false prophet. We know that Christ died and rose from the dead but in Rev. 13:3, the beast (Antichrist) dies from a wound to the head but comes back to life. Christ worked many miracles during his ministry and in Revelation as told in 2 Thessalonians 2:9, Satan will perform signs and wonders. In 2 Corinthians 12:1–4, Paul gives an account of his being caught up into the third heaven and hearing "unspeakable words," presumably angelic language. It would make sense that Satan would try to counterfeit this as well and could be another source for glossolalia. Keep in mind that glossolalia was also used in ancient pagan idol worship. By the way, in that last passage Paul says that it was "unlawful" for man to speak the words he heard so this could not be the tongues that the Apostles spoke neither should we expect to speak them.

Lastly, consider the events in Matthew 12:31–32. Here the Pharisees accuse Christ of healing by the power of Satan. They are rebuked by the Savior but not for disrespect to him, he says they have blasphemed the HS. So what's going on here? Jesus performs a miracle by the power of the HS and the Pharisees say it was done by Satan. This amounts to a lie on or about the HS. Jesus calls this blasphemy! A lie would also fit one of the descriptions that the dictionary uses; the act of insulting or showing contempt or lack of reverence for God or something sacred (the HS). If it is a lie and therefore blasphemy to say that the HS did not do something that it did do, is it not equally a lie and blasphemy to say that the HS is responsible for something that it is not responsible for? If modern-day speaking in tongues is not from the HS, and we say that it is, are we committing blasphemy? One thing's is for sure, if tongues are not from the HS, we are certainly lying on the HS.

Tongues and tithes are examples of what I will call "positive affirmation." This is a concept or doctrine that seems to be supported by scripture as something that should be observed, but the scriptures used for support are misunderstood. The opposite of that would be "negative affirmation." A concept or doctrine that seems to be supported by scriptures as something we should not observe, but again, scriptures used for support are misunderstood. An example of the negative would be the idea that drinking alcohol is a sin. Let me reiterate, I am not condoning the use of alcoholic beverages. I am not a drinker, and I am not writing from this perspective to justify a secret activity of mine. The point is that the topic of alcohol lends itself very nicely to this discussion in many ways. As a negative affirmation scriptures that warn against drunkenness are used to say something the Bible itself does not say (drinking alcohol is a sin). The topic of alcohol demonstrates something else that keeps us from understanding the Bible correctly and that is "societal tunnel vision." This occurs when we try to understand something from an ancient society or culture using our modern standards or ideas. It would be like transporting Paul through time to our present day and trying to explain the Internet to him. He would never understand without looking at many other aspects of our society and specifically communication. In our case, the tunnel vision occurs because we look at alcohol from our societal perspective and not from that of the ancient Christian or Jew. When we do this, we are unable to understand factors that were very important in the writing the scripture as well as the reason for writing it.

If we look at the use of alcoholic beverages from the "it is a sin" point of view, we see all the ills connected to this activity. Our society struggles with the problems related to alcohol so much that alcoholism is now considered a disease in the realm of mental health. There are organizations like MAAD (Mothers Against Drunk Driving) and AA (Alcoholics Anonymous) that battle these problems on a daily basis year in and year out. We see all over the country during summer holidays, high school graduation season, New Year and Christmas celebrations, even around the Super Bowl, TV announcements encouraging those who drink not to drive. From this perspective we see the drunk driving stats, dead adults/teens/children, property damage and loss, jobs, homes and families lost, medical issues of disease, chronic and terminal illness, mental illness and prenatal concerns. While these are all very important issues to us and reasons to avoid alcohol now, many if not most of these issues do not apply to biblical drinking. There were no cars, so no drunk driving therefore probably few teens and children dying as a direct result of drunkenness. Wine was a staple of their diet. It wasn't for recreation or for watching the game, it was an everyday thing. There were few choices for beverages then and with wine being such a staple in their lives, it would have been ridiculous for Paul to say, "Do not drink wine." It would have been like saying to my and many other poor families don't drink Kool-Aid. We didn't have soda, we didn't have juice, and we rarely had milk. It is impossible that Paul would be classifying wine drinking as a sin. So the issue for Paul is not drinking, it is drunkenness as it is with every other scripture that deals with this subject. So if drunkenness is the issue, we have to be honest in our assessment. Not every person who drinks alcohol on a regular basis gets drunk. I would venture a guess that there are those who are regular drinkers who have never been drunk a day in their lives. If this is the case, then drinking is a matter of two things, choice and control. If the Bible has not said that it is a sin, then it falls under liberty and you have a choice. But it is a grave choice! It is a choice of monumental proportion! If you choose to drink, can you control the amount?

Dr. John Macarthur has a wonderful CD on this subject, *Be Not Drunk with Wine*. In it he explains many of the cultural issues related to wine in the NT. Not the issue of drinking because there was no issue. He explains some of the things we need to know to truly understand that Paul was not speaking to drinking but to drunkenness. A couple of points from the CD, the many names used for wine in the Bible and the different product that each name represents.

NT—*Oinos* simply refers to the juice of grapes. The normal NT word for wine (mixed with water).

OT—*Yayin* refers to wine that is mixed, not with other wine, usually with water, sometimes with honey, sometimes with herbs, and sometimes with myrrh. Even when mixed with any of the above, it could also be mixed with water (from a 1901 Jewish encyclopedia).

NT—*Gleukos*, new wine, fresh wine but could also be fermented because it would not take very long, days sometimes. Therefore still potentially intoxicating (Acts 2:13). Also mixed with water.

OT—Tirosh, new wine (Hos. 4:11) mixed with water.

NT—Sikera, strong drink (unmixed)

OT—Shekar, strong drink (unmixed)

So it is very unlikely that the wine most commonly used today is even similar to the wine most commonly used in the Bible. The one closest to ours is probably the unmixed variety (strong drink), which would be the one most likely to cause intoxication. Today's wine is not mixed with water. That is not true of biblical wine. Some of the wine of Bible times was absolutely nonintoxicating.

Prof. Samuel Lee of Cambridge Univ, "Yayin (or Oinos) does not refer only to intoxicating liquor made by fermentation but more often refers to a thick unintoxicating syrup or jam produced by boiling to make it storable."

After this process, the juice that remained was stored in new wine skins. There were times and places where they definitely wanted to eliminate any alcoholic or fermentation capability of what they were using. So it cannot even be said that they always drank alcoholic beverages because there was no refrigeration. So this syrup that was similar to grape jelly could be spread on bread also but when they wanted to drink it they would mix it with water up to 20/1. In this form, it would be unfermented and totally unintoxicating. So this was a very easy way of storing it and as such was the most common form.

Classical historians:

- Horace (35 BC)—"You can quaffe under a shade cups of unintoxicating wine."
- Plutark (AD 69)—"Filtered wine neither inflames the brain nor infects the mind or the and is much more pleasant to drink."
- Aristotle—"The wine of Arcadia was so thick it had to be scraped from the skin bottle which it was stored and dissolve the scrapings in water."
- Virgil (30 BC) talked about the kind of wine that was boiled down to the luscious juice and then preserved.
- Homer (Ninth book of Odyssey)—"Ulysses took in his boat a goat skin of sweet black wine and when it was drunk it was diluted with 20 parts water."
- Dr. Newman, prof. of chem. (Berlin, eighteenth cent.)—"It is observable that when sweet juices are boiled to a thick consistency, they not only do not ferment in that state but are not easily brought into fermentation even when diluted with water.

So! The wine consumed in the Bible is not necessarily the same as what we have today. It was at times a concentrated grape juice with its fermentation and intoxicating properties removed. Another point, at times it was stored as a liquid and liquid would ferment. According to Robert Stein (1975, Christianity Today), "Liquid form was kept in a large jug called an amphore for daily use. From the amphore they would place this unmixed wine into a krater and water would be mixed there and from there to the killix. Mixes would be as high as 20/1 or as low as 3/1. Drinking unmixed wine was considered even by unsaved people as barbaric!"

"The gods have revealed wine to mortals to be the greatest blessing to those who use it aright but to those who use it without measure the reverse. For it gives food to them who take it in strength in mind and body, in medicine it is most beneficial. It can be mixed with liquid and drugs and it brings aid to the wounded. In daily course to those who mix and drink it moderately it gives good cheer. If you overstep the bounds it brings violence. Mix it half and half and you get madness, unmixed bodily collapse." So they mixed it and even to mix it one to one was considered barbarian. Wine was seen in ancient times as a medicine and of course as a beverage. And as a beverage it was always mixed. It was mixed from a paste base or from an amphore to a krater and then it was served not unmixed. The ratio of water might vary but only barbarians drank it unmixed, and unmixed wine was considered strong drink. So wine, oinos, or yayin was always used in referring to wine mixed with water. Below are listed the percent alcohol in today's beverages:

Beer—4% (% alcohol)   9–11/3–1=2.25–2.75% (sub-alcoholic bev.)
Wine—9–11%
Fortified wine (brandy)—15–20%, today 3.2% defines an alcoholic bev.
Liquor—40–50%

If you take today's wine percent alcohol (9–11%) and dilute it to the usual biblical 3 to 1 ratio (3 parts wine + 1 part water = 4 parts), 9–11%/4 = 2.25–2.75% alcohol content if today's wine were diluted as biblical wine was. Today a product has to contain 3.2% alcohol to be considered an alcoholic beverage. Since today's refining process is more geared toward high percent alcohol than was biblical wine making it is probably safe to say that the wine of the Bible was nowhere near 9% alcohol. If diluting modern wine would produce a beverage that would be considered sub or nonalcoholic today, to get drunk from the wine of the Bible you would have to drink a lot more than a couple of glasses. So biblical wine was a wine with a nonexistent or negligible alcohol content and drunkenness was something you set out to do. So Paul was not concerned with people drinking. The average person who drank a normal amount would not get drunk. Paul's concern was with drunkenness with people who got drunk intentionally. He was concerned with Ephesian converts who were holding onto pagan worship practices and getting drunk as a part of church services.

Again I must say, this is not a call for Christians to raise a glass at the neighborhood bar. This is not meant to encourage anyone toward alcohol. With a higher percent alcohol in these beverages today, it's even more important to understand and avoid the dangers they pose. It is as I've said before an attempt to show how we can and do misunderstand God's word when we fail to recognize some simple principles when studying.

Another source of misunderstanding is "contextual clouding." There are some scriptures that are very common place among Christians, laymen as well as clergy. Some of them voice a general theological principle. In the beginning, God created the heavens and the earth. Others, a spiritual truth: "For God so loved the world that He gave His only begotten Son." Still others a simple human emotion; Jesus wept. In all these examples, full grasp of the intended meaning is in hand from the verse alone. Unfortunately, most scriptures do not lend themselves to such simplicity. To get a clear understanding of most of the Bible, it is important to know the "context" of the passage. Context is defined as the whole situation, background, or environment relevant to a particular event, personality, or creation and determining its exact meaning. You might look at context as the plot behind the scripture, who wrote it and why? Who is the writer talking to or about? Where and/or when are they? Clouding occurs when a scripture is used to convey one thought or concept but the context of that scripture conveys another. We had an example of this with Ephesians 5:18 and talking about drunkenness. Many have taken this as speaking to the ills of drinking when actually it speaks to improper religious practices. This happens because many times when we hear a scripture used, i.e., in a sermon, we take for granted the use is correct. We then turn around and use the scripture in the same incorrect way, thus perpetuating the error. The context of a scripture comes from reading some of the passage before and perhaps after the particular verse in question. It may at times require reading a whole or several chapters to fully understand a particular line. To read one verse in the middle of a passage of scripture and expect to get the true meaning in most cases is like starting to read a novel in the middle and expecting to know what is going, most of the time you will end up in the dark.

For the first example of this type error, let's look at the first book, Genesis. "Be fruitful and multiply and replenish the earth," occurs in Genesis twice, 1:28 and 9:1. This verse is integral in support of teaching against the use of birth control. It is also used to support "The Gap Theory," an idea that something happened after Gen. 1:1 to make the world "without form and void" in Gen. 1:2. The means of support in both cases is the word "replenish" but a quick look at that word should suggest a question to the birth controllers. If these were the first people on earth, why is God using a word that means "refill or fill again"? The Hebrew word for *replenish* in this scripture is "male" (pronounced *mawlaw*). It means to fill, to fulfill, to overflow, to full capacity, to fill up to the full extent. So as a verb it does not have quite the same meaning as *replenish* and therefore not meaning to do over or replace. So that doesn't seem to help the gap theory, but it does nothing to discount birth control. But something else was common to both those scriptures, dominion. Dominion is actually stated in the 1:28 scripture and suggested throughout the rest of chapter 9. Dominion suggests supremacy, but it also suggests authority and control. Authority and control both suggest responsibility and stewardship. I don't think God would give us very a high grade for our stewardship of the earth right now. The use of oil and other fossil fuels are on the rise and these are the main problems with the earth's atmosphere and what's called "the greenhouse effect." Coal and oil release sulfur dioxide when burned causing heat to be trapped in the atmosphere, which leads to global warming and other atmospheric changes. These gases cause breathing problems and have been linked to 7 million deaths in 2012. Hunger is a major issue not only in third world countries but in the US. With stewardship being a high biblical priority, I wonder with whom God would be most displeased, a man who fathered twenty children knowing he could barely provide for one, or a man who used contraception (not abortion) to keep the size of his family within the range of his income?

Because God told Adam and Eve to be fruitful and multiply, it is taken as an act of disobedience (by those who oppose birth control) when a married couple chooses not to have children. It is also seen by some as playing God when we take control of this function. It is felt that just as God is in control of when we die and we should have no say in our death, birth is also the domain of God, and if he wants you to have twenty children, it is his will. I have even heard some clergy say that "if a couple is not planning to have children they should not get married." The problem with this line of thinking relative to this scripture is the failure to consider context. The context of both the scriptures is the dawn of humanity, the birth of mankind. From the perspective of the chapters involved (creation and the flood), there are no people! Since God created man to serve him, it is logical that he would encourage procreation. But should this be taken as support against birth control? Let's look at some of the family sizes of that day. That should give us some insight into the patterns and trends of the time.

Most of us know the story of Cain and Abel, the sons of Adam and Eve. But Seth was also a child of the first couple (Gen. 4:25), so we know that they had at least three children. In fact, Gen. 5:4 tells us that more were born after Seth (and he begat sons and daughters). Sons means more than one and daughters means more than one. It is safe to assume then that Adam and Eve had at least four children other than the three that are well known. Throughout the rest of the fifth chapter, the phrase "sons and daughters" is repeated several times in giving the descendants of Adam. So most of the descendants of Adam before Noah had rather large families. But after Noah, the average number of offspring is around four. So even as far back as Noah it does not seem that people were having uncontrolled numbers of offspring, and there were methods of contraception available. In her book, *The Intercourse of Knowledge*, Athalya Brenner writes, "A number of plants in the Songs of Solomon were used by women in the ancient Mediterranean world as contraception and abortifacients. These include pomegranates, wine, myrrh, spikenard, and cinnamon." So there were options for contraception available. Of course there were exceptions; after the death of his first ten children, Job had ten more and King Rehoboam had eighty-eight children (eighteen wives/sixty concubines). For the most part though, we see just average numbers of children being born in the Bible and not the high figure you would expect without some sort of birth control. Another scripture used to denounce contraception is Gen. 38:8–9. This involves Onan who was instructed to take his dead brother's wife to father a child with so that the brother would have offspring. Since the child would not be considered his, Onan did not ejaculate into Tamar during sex but onto the ground. This displeased God who then killed Onan. Again, this is taken out of context. The issue is not birth control, and it is also not masturbation (also discouraged with this scripture). The problem was disobedience that is the reason Onan's life was taken. Of course, these examples do not prove that birth control was used, but they do show that the wrong contextual application is in place here.

One of my favorite examples of "clouding" is found in Psalm 105:15, "Touch not my anointed and do my prophets no harm." It is famously used by clergy to portray themselves as protected by God. It's as if God himself is warning us against disrespectful treatment of his very special men. As if they are untouchable and we the laity are never to question or dispute them. It is one of the tools used to assure obedience and control. It gives the impression that we are in danger of the wrath of God if we at any time or in any way fail to be subservient to them. It sets up the idea that no matter what members of the clergy do wrong and no matter how guilty they are, it is totally inappropriate and disrespectful for anyone but God to say anything about it. So not only is a contextual mistake, it's a failure to recognize that the thought should be left in the OT and, if valid, would be found in the NT (recurrence). So what is the context? It's a poem. It is not from God at all but from David. It is an exhortation by David encouraging Israel to worship, praise, obey, and seek the Lord because of his role in their lives. One of the things he did was to protect them from enemies to whom he said, "Touch not my anointed and do my prophets no harm." So the anointed was Israel and his prophets were the prophets of that time. And he would have been talking about true prophets of God not just anyone who calls him or herself prophet. Scriptures like this are not meant to have an active part in our daily lives as directives and it is tragic that when taken out of context, they can have such a powerful negative impact. There are millions of people who truly love and try to sincerely serve God that have swallowed the wrong meaning of this scripture hook, line, and sinker.

Another clouding example is from Galatians 7:1, "Be not deceived; God is not mocked: whatsoever a man soweth, that shall he also reap." This is a very popular scripture and one of the few that is used to convey two different ideas that are both contextually wrong. One idea is that of retribution or retaliation. All of us who love the Lord and are trying to live more righteously struggle against fleshly thoughts and attitudes. Lust, greed, jealousy, and envy are just a few of the areas that we battle. Forgiveness is also on this list and is sometime a very, very difficult thing to do. There is a quote by an unknown author, "We are most like beasts when we kill, we are most like men when we judge, we are most like God when we forgive." Many times in our lives we are victims of terrible hurts, and we often suffer for years with the wounds inflicted upon us. At other times, we are the perpetrators of these dastardly acts and in some cases suffer for years as well. When we are the victim, we often find ourselves waiting for the day when "they get theirs." There is that inner, if not outer, smile when the person who has hurt us falls onto hard times. The phase "I hope you rot in hell" is meant quite literally by thousands who have been hurt to the core of their emotions and hold a deep dark place of sadness and anger for the deeds done to them. I must admit that I am guilty of causing such pain, and even though I have asked for and received forgiveness, I still struggle with the pain that I have caused and need to forgive myself. But these are the feelings that prompt the response, "You reap what you sow!" Other responses are "That's good for ya," "God don't like ugly," "What goes around comes around." It is very difficult to teach the principle of forgiveness to someone who has this "payback" mentality. But when the scripture is not taught correctly, the principle of forgiving suffers in that person's life. Fuel is added to the fire when the OT seems to support this idea in Leviticus 24:19–21 (eye for an eye). This scripture is not suggesting the OT law, which was literally applied as punishment for crimes, but a spiritual law that applies to the next life. Our eternal life. This scripture does not give license to vengeful hearts! To take the meaning of this scripture as "you'll get yours" is to totally misunderstand it. Furthermore, this mistake can be avoided if we simply take the time to reflect on the general principles of the NT that exude the opposite frame of mind. For example, one-third of "the fruit of the spirit," love, peace, and longsuffering seem to fly in the face of payback. And if you are unable to recognize Jesus as full of grace, forgiveness, tolerance, and understanding, 1 Peter 3:9 tells us "not to render evil for evil." So payback is definitely not the thought here.

In our present climate of the "Prosperity Gospel," this scripture is also used as a principle of giving. It is a wonderful and spiritually significant verse that has been bastardized into the rhetoric of money grubbing and greed! It is another tool in the arsenal of the shepherds who fleece instead of serve the sheep. They preach, "You reap what you sow; god loves a cheerful giver; you can't beat God giving." The idea is that God blesses us according to how much we give him. You reap what you sow. If you sow sparingly, you reap sparingly! If you give a little, you receive a little! If you give a lot, you receive a lot! In our present economy, there are few people who would say they have everything they need, bills all paid on time, no debt and savings in the bank to carry them through a period of unexpected financial turmoil. There are probably more people that have just a very little who are in desperate need of quite a lot. But according to this principle, God will not supply the needs of the ones who need him most because they don't have enough to sow in the first place. This is likely the source of the concept of "seed faith." So again we are being suckered by lines that sound good appeal to and take advantage of our needs and our failure to study the word for ourselves. In a way, we deserve this abuse because we don't make use of the Bible so that we know what it is really saying. Before we get to reap what you sow of chapter 6, chapter 5 of Galatians ends listing the "fruit of the spirit." There is a definite connection between these two passages, but since we seldom read the chapters together or as a continuation, we miss it. Galatians 5:16 says, "Walk in the spirit and ye shall not fulfill the lusts of the flesh." In short, the way to produce the fruit of the spirit is to walk in the spirit. Relating this to chapter 6, our walk is our sowing. Chapter 6 begins talking about the restoration of a person who has fallen into sin. This is an example of what happens when we fail to walk in the spirit or when we sow to the flesh. We are encouraged to support that person in love and the understanding that we to could fall to temptation if we are not careful. Another reason that we fall is having false confidence in our strength against temptations and Galatians 6:3 says when this happens, "He deceiveth himself." We then get to verse 7: "Be not deceived…whatsoever a man soweth, that shall he also reap." But it is verse 8 that nails down the true meaning of the passage. But most people probably don't know this verse exists. This verse says, "For he that soweth to his flesh shall of the flesh reap corruption; but he that soweth to the spirit shall of the spirit reap everlasting life." If we replace the *soweth* from chapter 6 with the *walk* from chapter 5 we get, "He that walks in the flesh shall reap corruption but he that walks in the spirit shall reap everlasting life." So this passage is not about giving but about getting, getting everlasting life. It is not about "seed faith" but about salvation and grace. Reap what you sow is not about vengeance and payback but about victory and paying it forward. It is about reaping a harvest of a new righteous character because you have sown the seeds of walking in the spirit and abiding in God's word. It is about becoming a new creature because you have gotten past the old things. It is about being caught up in the rapture and not being left behind in someone else's mess. Of course it is not difficult to manipulate the meaning as we saw above by tying it to other scriptures. But I would not want to be the one having to come up with an explanation to God for twisting the meaning of his words. As you can see, if we take more time when studying the scriptures, it is very clear in most cases what the word is trying to convey. It does not make us sinners or disobedient when we dig deep into the meaning of the word. This is exactly what we should be doing!

For the last example of clouding, I'll use Matthew7:1, "Judge not, that ye be not judged." Taken alone, this scripture seems to reflect a general Christian principle that cannot be denied—compassion. It is no secret that Christians are expected to exhibit this quality.

Nonbelievers take great pleasure in pointing out when we fail in this capacity. It is in this climate that this scripture is embraced though again in error. It usually goes something like this. Mr. Jones sees Mr. Smith in a situation that does not reflect godly morals. Let's say he is seen coming out of a bar. For a denomination that teaches against drinking alcohol, this would at least raise an eyebrow. But let's not judge, there could be other reasons he was in the bar. But if this happens on a regular basis, does that become a cause for concern? Perhaps, but in the spirit of "judge not," Mr. Jones would not say anything to Mr. Smith about it. That would not mean Jones wouldn't say anything to anyone else. But speaking to Mr. Smith would be accusing him of wrongdoing, it would be judging him! The idea is that we don't point the finger at anyone because you don't want a finger pointed at you. But actually we should want a finger pointed at us. If Mr. Smith is doing something he shouldn't, Mr. Jones is doing him a service by pointing it out. Smith may tell Jones to mind his own affairs, but he has been made aware that he has been seen. Smith may explain to Jones the reason for his being there, which may be totally above board in which case Smith keeps Jones from becoming a gossip. This is exactly what Matthew 18 directs us to do when we see another taken in a fault, go to him. How do we detect the fault? We "judge." Judging is nothing more than discerning, recognizing the difference between one thing and another. As usual if we just read further into the chapter verses, 16 and 20 make this clear. Those verses tell us to test prophets (judge) because some of them are false and come to us in "sheep's clothing." Verse 16 says, "Ye shall know them by their fruits." When we see apples on a tree, we know this is not an orange tree or a pear tree or a lemon tree. We know it is an apple tree because of the fruit it bears. This is judging, calling a spade a spade! Matthew 7: 1 is not telling us not to judge. It is telling us to be careful of the way we judge. Verse 3 gives the example of seeing the mote (speck) in the eye of someone else but not seeing the beam (log) in our own eye. It is teaching us to be sure we are as quick to recognize our own flaws as we are to point out the flaws of others. We are not being taught to ignore those flaws as many in the clergy tend to use this scripture to protect themselves. If we are the light of the world, there must be a difference, and we must be able to recognize and point out that difference when the situation presents itself.

It seems that because "we walk by faith," many people think that logic and reason have no place in the exploration of God's word. Some feel that we are not meant to know everything, that some things are mystery and should be accepted by faith. This is true. There are some things we will not know the answers to in this life. But there are many others that simply have not been explored diligently. Some people feel that when you question God's word, you are questioning God! But these are two different things. It is one thing to question God, that is, to second guess him as if maybe he doesn't really know what he is doing. It is quite another to ask a question of God or his word. In the latter case, we are looking for understanding. We are seeking knowledge, we are seeking to know God better, we are striving to become more like him. We can't do his will if we don't understand what his will is or what his word is saying. God wants us to choose the right from the wrong, the good from the bad, and he wants us to choose it freely with a clear understanding. We can't serve God to the best of our ability if we don't understand his directions. That is why rightly dividing this and all other words of truth is so important.

Fractured Fairy Tales

A VERY POPULAR CARTOON from the sixties is *Rocky the Flying Squirrel*. He and his pal, Bullwinkle, had adventures during the course of a half hour TV show. A show within the show was a piece called *Fractured Fairy Tales*. These were five-minute shorts that were based on classic, well-known fairy tales but with a twist. The story never went the way it was originally written. Either the main character did not act the way you expected or the plot was changed or the ending (most of the time) went in a different direction. Because of all the changes, the plot found in the original story was fractured. Because of the fractures, the original story was sometime barely recognizable. Over the years this has also happened to scripture and this is another source of our failing to understand it. Some scriptures have been misquoted, a word missing here or there or a word added. In some cases what we believe to come from the Bible does not exist there at all. Let's look first at some of my favorite passages that are misquoted and the problems related to them.

"Money is the root of all evil." The correct quote is from 1 Timothy 6:10, "For the love of money is the root of all evil: which while some coveted after, they have erred from the faith, and pierced themselves through with many sorrows."

This phrase is so ingrained in our culture that there are probably many people who don't realize it has a biblical origin. The World Wealth Report of 2013 gave a figure of 12 million HNWIs (high net worth individuals) worldwide with their combined assets growing to 55.8 trillion by 2015. Of course, the US topped the list with 3.44 million millionaires. In 2015, there were 290 new billionaires added to the world list of a record 1,892. One of those newcomers was Michael Jordon. Oprah Winfrey is also a billionaire. While Michael and Oprah are nowhere near the top of the list (Bill Gates, 67 billion; Warren Buffet, 53.5 billion), they represent a special demographic. No, not their race. Though they are the only black American billionaires, there are nine other black billionaires around the world, and Oprah is not the only female on the list; there is one other. To me what makes Oprah and Michael special is their origin, their backgrounds. They are both from working class families, laborers. They were not born into money, they did not come from influential families, and neither of them won the lottery. They made their money the old-fashioned way, they earned it. They both used a talent, worked very hard, and fulfilled a lifetime of personal expectations. They are the epitome of the American dream! They finally got a piece of the pie! They will serve as motivation and inspiration for many to continue the pursuit of a dream and their own piece of pie. Unfortunately, there are some pursuing "pie" that are willing to do anything to get it. Those in larcenous endeavors extend from cyberspace to the pulpit. But in all these cases, it is the love of money and not the money itself that is the problem. It is when we allow the desire and pursuit of possessions to be the driving force of our lives and that force leads to illegal activity or activity that takes advantage or hurts others that money takes on an evil aura. This is much like the rational of "guns don't kill, people kill." But in this case, it is not only what is done with the money but how the money was obtained in the first place.

It has become very clear in my experience that many, perhaps most charismatic Christians, base their experience with God on how they feel. They sincerely love and desire to please God, but the active pursuit of the knowledge and understanding of his word is greatly lacking. That is why phrases like this can so easily be taken for scripture. Instead of looking into them, we allow them to hang around until they become a part of our theology. When our theology is flawed at some point, it will have an impact on our lives perhaps in stunted growth, perhaps in bondage to sin. That is why it is so important to get a clear understanding of what the Bible is saying to us.

A commonly quoted scripture from my childhood is "God will cast your sins into the sea of forgetfulness." I heard this quoted often when I was growing up. This is thought to portray God's forgiving nature and the extent to which his efforts to forgive us reach. However, I encountered a problem when searching for this "sea" to find out if it was a metaphor or an actual geographical location. With this being one of the first "investigations" I embarked on, I was stunned to find that there is no such scripture. It does not exist at all. This was very surprising and also very unnerving. How could they have this wrong? How could they have this so wrong? There must be a reason. They can't be just making stuff up! My faith, not in God, but in leaders began to falter. So as I searched, I found something very interesting. There were two scriptures that if read one behind the other might sound like the fake scripture. The first is Micah 7:19, "He will turn again, he will have compassion on us; he will subdue our iniquities; and thou wilt cast all their sins into the depths of the sea." The second is Hebrews 8:12, "For I will be merciful to their unrighteousness, and their sins and their iniquities I will remember no more. Micah says sins will be cast into the sea and Hebrews that they will not be remembered or "forgotten," sea of forgotten or forgetting or forgetfulness. So here we have an example of a fake scripture that was likely the offspring of two actual biblical verses. How could this happen? Well, a guess is that some preacher speaking about God's forgiveness used both the authentic scriptures together and began to elaborate with the colorful phrases that some are able to rattle off. The sea of forgetfulness was likely one of those phrases, and let's face it, it sounds good! Unfortunately in the charismatic churches, we have not yet learned that because it sounds good does not mean that it is good for you or correct. So, this phrase that is so appealing to the ear was probably used by another preacher and another, etc., and before you know it, it's taken as scripture. Now some might say well, what's the big deal? It is conveying the same message as the actual scriptures so what's the harm in turning a more colorful phrase to get the point across? The harm is in the word *forgetfulness*.

In the scripture from Hebrews, the phrase is "remember no more," not forget. While in English to say "remember no more" and "forget" seem to say the same thing, the Greek word for remember does not have the same meaning. The Greek word is *mnomai* and it has reference to recalling, reminding, or making mention of. This is not the same as forgetting. To forget in this sense means the items (in this case sins) are no longer a part of stored memory and therefore cannot be recalled. This is not the case with God since he is omniscient and knows all things, it is impossible for him to be unable to recall anything that has ever happened. That is to say in our common use of the word, God can't forget! So God is not saying here that our sins are wiped from his memory, he is saying that he won't bring them up or mention them anymore. The use of *forget* here also places a fracture in our practical theology. If the word *forget* is used with forgiveness, it implies a colloquialism that is also not biblical, "forgive and forget." If we are expected to erase events from our memories as a part of forgiveness, then a great number of us will be on the losing side of this equation. An example of this can be seen in the shootings that occurred in the South Carolina church in 2015. Several family members of victims extended forgiveness to the shooter, but I dare say they will never forget him! Many loving, caring, sincere people are kept in bondage when they are told, "If you don't forget, you haven't forgiven." If we can recognize the fallacy in these ideas and where they come from, we can begin to repair some of the damage that has been done for so many years. When a criminal is granted amnesty for his crime, the crime is not reversed. He still has a conviction but for whatever reason he is pardoned and released. The crime is not erased from the books, but he is released as if his debt to society has been paid. He is given a clean slate (in theory). In reference to forgiveness, God requires amnesty, not amnesia. We should stop treating offenders as if a crime were committed, and while it may be a good thing if you are able to forget, it is certainly not a requirement.

I think most of us have heard the verse "Where two or three gather touching and agreeing." This is used in the context of prayer and the strength of partnering in prayer. It lets us know that prayer is more powerful when there is a group focused on a matter than when one is praying alone. This is certainly the case as is evidenced in Acts 12 when Peter was imprisoned probably to face beheading. While he was in chains, verse 5 says the church prayed for him without ceasing and Peter was released. So yes, there is great power in numbers when it comes to prayer but that scripture is not talking about prayer. First looking at the scripture in Matthew 18:19, "Again I say unto you, That if two of you shall agree on earth as touching anything that they shall ask, it shall be done for them of my Father which is in heaven." So we actually see touch and agree in this scripture, but not prayer, so where does that come from? It probably comes from "anything they shall ask." Well, that seems reasonable, after all when do we usually ask anything of God but in prayer? Our concept of prayer is generally just a time to present our needs, wants, etc., before him. So it is not much of a stretch to see this as relating to prayer. But of course, I would not mention it unless there was a fracture and there is. If you read from the beginning of chapter 18, it is clear that Christ is not talking about prayer. If you read past verses 19 and 20, it is not talking about prayer or anything related to prayer. This should give the reader cause to ask, where is the prayer? Well, it's just not there! This chapter and these verses are not about prayer, they are about dealing with sin in the church. In verses 6–10, it talks about the drastic steps we should be willing to take in order to keep sin out of our lives, i.e., pluck out an eye or cut off a hand or foot. We should also be willing to take these measures rather than causing someone else to sin. Of course, it doesn't mean literally pluck out an eye but not allowing yourself to see or visualize anything that would lead you or anyone else into sin, especially those new to the church. Plucking out an eye would equate to doing all things possible to avoid pornography when you know this is a problem for you. Cutting off a foot to avoiding at all costs places that hold particular temptation for you. Verses 15–18 directs in how to deal with the open sin of another starting with a private attempt one-on-one. If the offender will not repent, he is to be approached with a witness present. If that fails, they should be taken before the church. This is when the two agreeing and touching anything comes in. It is talking about agreeing upon the disposition of an offending member not about a prayer request. Some might say, "What's the big deal? The idea is still correct about prayer. It is better when two or three come together."

Yes, that it true, but I think the problem is that if this scripture is applied to the wrong thing, it will likely not be applied to the correct thing—church discipline, which is so sorely needed today.

If we were to compile a top ten list of biblical/theological ideas that are fractured one of the top three would probably be, "He won't put more on you than you can bear." At first glance this seems to be a very comforting thought. After all, God knows everything right? So if he knows how much we can handle and would never give us more than we can handle, we can be confident that whatever we have to handle we can handle it, right? Well, not quite. This is fractured in two ways. First, there is no scripture that says this. This phrase is likely a product of 1 Corinthians 10:13, "There hath no temptation taken you but such as is common to man: but God is faithful, who will not suffer you to be tempted above that ye are able; but will with the temptation also make a way to escape, that ye may be able to bear it." So now that we see the actual scripture related to this idea, we can see that again context rears its head. The popular phrase is generally used in the context of human suffering. We most often hear it when someone is going through what we would call trials or tribulation as the suffering experienced by Job. It is used when a person is suffering the loss of employment or some other extreme financial disaster. We hear it in the face of family crisis such as a teenager falling into gangs, drug culture, or pregnancy. We hear it when a doctor announces the finding of a terminal illness or with the unexpected death of a loved one. This is meant to be consoling and to show support, but at best, it applies a very small bandage to a very large wound. At worst, it can lead to spiritual confusion, discouragement, and even a turning away from God instead of toward him. Of course, Satan is very pleased with this, and this is one of the reasons he continues to foster the perpetuation of the use of such phrases in the Christian vernacular. If we look at just verse 13, one word should jump out at us even without the rest of the passage, *temptation*. If we read this verse with the sole purpose of understanding it, the focus is the avoidance of temptation. If we take the time to read verses 1–12, we see that Paul is recounting the failures of the Israelites in keeping the law while in the wilderness. He spoke of their idolatry, debauchery, and fornication noting that in one day twenty-three thousand of them fell to sin. He continues in verses 14–22 to remind the Corinthians that they are now members with Christ and should not be partakers of evil things. When verse 13 refers to being able to "bear it," it is referring to the ability to stand firm in the face of temptation without sin.

Proof that we sometimes experience more than we can bear is clinical depression. This is more than just a deep state of sadness. And for those who think that God's people don't or shouldn't suffer with this problem, there were plenty of God's chosen in the Bible with this issue. Probably the most obvious example is Job. If you are saying, "But Job was fine, he made it through the trial," so it was not more than he could bear. But if you read the whole account, he was likely in his depressed state when God slapped him around and snapped him out of it. So he didn't bear it alone, he had help. How about Elijah who after calling down fire on a soaked altar and killing four hundred prophets of Baal, turned tail and ran from one woman, Jezebel. In 1 Kings 19:4, he basically requested suicide. I would say that he was not bearing this situation very well. Again it took God stepping in to help him bear up under the weight of his circumstance. An angel was sent to feed him and get him back on track. King Saul's depression basically led to madness in his misperception and pursuit of David. And speaking of David, let's not forget the numerous lamenting Psalms that were written in sadness and despondence because of the many sins he had committed and the effect they had on his life and his relationship with God. Once again it was God's forgiveness and restoration that brought David out of his depression. He did not get back into the game on his own. Of course there are things we are not able to bear that's why Psalm 55:22 tells us, "Cast your burdens upon the Lord and He shall sustain thee: He shall never suffer the righteous to be moved." If we could bear them, if they weren't too much for us, there would be no reason to cast them onto the Lord. Peter also tells us in 1 Peter 5:7, "Casting all your cares upon Him for He careth for you." He does know how much we can bear. He knows everything about us, our strengths and weaknesses, our hearts' desires. So what does he gain from our suffering, what does he learn? Nothing! It's we who learn, if we open our minds long enough. If we learn to examine ourselves with truth, no holds barred, we stand to learn that our biggest enemy is self. Paul tells us in Galatians 6:2, "Bear ye one another's burdens and so fulfill the law of Christ." Paul is encouraging us to share the burdens of our brothers and sisters to help and support them in times of trouble and dismay. If God never gives us more than we can bear, why is there a need to support one another when the going gets tough?

Another fairy tale is the idea of losing your salvation. I can call it a fairy tale now but growing up that was what I believed. That is what I was taught, and that is what was in my heart. Once an idea gets into your heart and becomes a part of you, it can be difficult if not impossible to extract. The idea of "once saved always saved" was scoffed at ridiculed and seen as nonsensical. I was taught that salvation came in steps. You were saved (accepted Christ) sanctified (process of self-cleansing) and then the Holy Ghost would come into your life. It was possible for the HG to come as soon as you got saved, but this was rare and normally the above sequence was the way things would proceed. The way I understood salvation was as long as I was free from sin I was saved. If I committed a sin, I needed to repent. If for whatever reason I failed to repent, I was no longer saved; my salvation was gone along with the HG. If I remained in that state for a significant amount of time, I was now in a backslidden state. I would need to go through the whole process all over again if I decided to get saved again. As a maturing Christian adult, I have to ask God's forgiveness several times a week, sometimes per day. It is very likely that there are times when I should repent of something that I just don't realize. If my childhood concept were true and I lost my salvation every time I committed a sin, then regained it once I repented, that would be like constantly jumping in and out of a tub of bath water and expecting to get clean. The HG leaving us because of sin is like running from our friends as kids because they had "cooties" or had stepped in dog poop. I had a picture of the HG jumping into me and staying for a while, but as soon as I committed a sin, it would jump out again. If I repented immediately, it would return immediately. If I failed to repent immediately or committed another sin, the HG would distance itself from me more and more. ("The HG will not dwell in an unclean temple.") The time between the initial sin and becoming a backslider was rather arbitrary and probably related to many factors, like was the sin public or private. With this model in place, I can understand why so few people are able to mature in the faith. The cycle of sin and repentance must seem a hopeless task to someone exposed for the first time to so many failures and the feeling that they can never be good enough no matter how hard they try. It doesn't help when they are exposed to people who act as if they have never sinned a day in their lives. I'm sure that many just give up out of the frustration of messing up over and over as they try to "sanctify" themselves. So before we look at a couple of scriptures, consider a couple of observations.

To lose your salvation can be equated with backsliding as was suggested earlier. If that is the case and we let the Bible guide us, we should be able to find an example of losing it and regaining it somewhere in scripture. But guess what? There is no such example to be found. In fact, the term *backslider* does not appear anywhere in the NT. It is of course present in the OT but usually applied to Israel as a nation and not to individuals. With this wonderful gift of salvation being paid for and only requiring that we receive it, you would think that one of the NT writers would address what we should do if we lose it, but they don't, not even once. There are scriptures that may seem to insinuate backsliding and Matthew 7:23 is one of them. In this verse, Christ responds to some who are trying to enter the Kingdom of Heaven with "I never knew you." He is rejecting those who in verse 22 proclaim the miracles they have done in his name. It may seem that these who have done such great works as prophesy, casting out demons, and healing had at some point turned away from God. The key to understanding the passage is in the Greek word used for work in verse 23. The word *ergazoai* refers to occupation as in livelihood or profession. In other words, he is talking about someone who did these things outside of the power of God (iniquity) and for their own gain. So this is not a picture of someone who once worked under the power of God but somehow turned away and is now a sinner again. This is a person who is deliberately and intentionally using God's word for profit. They may have performed miracles, but

Christ is saying not by his power. So they either did things to make it appear that a miracle had occurred or they were powered by Satan. This sort of thing went on in the Bible so it is not talking just about future events. The sorcerer Simon in Acts 8:9–24 tried to buy the power of the HS. In Acts 19:11–20, the Sons of Sceva tried to invoke the power of the name Jesus without the HS in their lives, but none of these indicate backsliding. The term is not used in the NT. So why do we use it? Is it another term erroneously pulled from the OT and applied to what we believe? Is this another example of letting what we believe explain what the Bible is saying instead of letting what the Bible says dictate what we believe?

The other observation is the plan of salvation itself. This plan was put in place because of the fall of man, and if we just listen to what the Bible is saying and not what we believe we will see, that it's a perfect plan. Here's why. Man fell because Satan deceived Adam and Eve then tricked them into disobeying God. This disobedience separated man from God. So now God had to put a plan into action that could repair the damage that was done much like the repair that must be done on an auto after an accident. If your fender gets smashed or the hood crushed a good auto body man can make your car look like new. The problem is that you can drive out onto the street in your newly repaired vehicle be hit again and need the same repair all over again. Wouldn't it be wonderful if when you had an accident in your car once the repair was made, you could never have another accident! Somehow all the other cars would avoid you or be repelled by you like you had a force field. No more accidents ever! Well, think for a minute, doesn't it make perfect sense that if God was to repair something that Satan was responsible for breaking he would repair it in such a way that it could not be broken again? If God is doing the repair, you would think it would ever have to be repaired again? That makes so much sense even before applying any scriptures to the idea but for clarity let's do just that.

In chapter 10 of St. John, Christ paints a picture of himself as a shepherd. It is very important to get the significance of this picture if we are to really understand what Christ is trying to say. The metaphor of shepherding is used throughout the Bible. It is used famously in Psalm 23 and by Jacob on his death bed in Genesis 48:24. In Revelation, John doubles up on the motif in 7:17, "For the lamb in the center of the throne shall be their shepherd and shall guide them to springs of the water of life and God shall wipe every tear from their eyes." Being a shepherd was a very common occupation in the Middle East, one that everyone could relate to and understand if not appreciate. The fathers of the Nation of Israel were shepherds. Moses was a king who became a shepherd. David was a shepherd who became a king. It is very safe to say that the people Christ was talking to had a very good working knowledge of what it meant to be a shepherd. But because we don't we miss the essence of the message these words bring. To be a good shepherd, the flock had to come first at all cost. Their food, guidance, and safety were all the responsibility of the shepherd. Without his caring hand, the flock would wander aimlessly and end up in dangerous if not life-threatening situations. Protection was probably the most important thing supplied by the shepherd. When the flock was away from home, a makeshift temporary shelter would be erected, called a fold. John 10:16 says, "And other sheep I have which are not of this fold, them also I must bring." Because of the climate, many times grazing animals would have to be taken to the grass in order to feed. This meant sometimes the flock would spend the night away from home. The fold was a makeshift enclosure that would take advantage of the natural terrain as much as possible using the side of a mountain or hill and rocks, branches, or shrubs that were available. Many times the enclosure would be in a U shape with the entrance at the open end. This allowed one way in and one way out. Thorns and thistle could be place on top of the other material to keep the sheep from jumping out and predators from getting in. The shepherd would position himself in front of the opening again to protect the sheep from wandering out and anyone or anything from getting in. Notice that the shape of a U can be made with your hand. Place your palm up and hold your fingers together. Hold your thumb at a 90 degree angle as in prep to make a gun with your fingers. Now point your fingers and thumb upward, capital *U*. The shepherd getting a good night sleep was not as important as the safety of the sheep. The shepherd would sometimes put himself in harm's way for the sake of the sheep (1 Sam. 17:34–36, David speaks of killing a lion and a bear). We can see then that the shepherd's job was one of great responsibility. In fact, one can assert that if the sheep were not his own, his reputation as a shepherd was on the line whenever he was out with them. It was the responsibility of the shepherd to see that all the sheep came home. In chapter 34 of Ezekiel, he expounds on the failure of the leaders of his day. In verse 2, he bashes the "shepherds of Israel who feed themselves" (much like many leaders today). In Jeremiah 10:21, he says the leaders have scattered the flock because they are stupid (the leaders are stupid, not the flock, well at least here not the flock). Using the shepherd motif as a contrast to the character of the selfish leaders of that day, God was able to present a very plain picture of how he saw these self-centered leaders. Further in chapter 34, God tells the prophet that he will one day deliver the people from the clutches of these bad shepherds into the hands of one who is to come, that is the good shepherd whom Jesus introduces himself as.

In John 10:11, Jesus states the fact, "I am the good shepherd." He is not just saying he is "a" shepherd but that he is a very special shepherd one spoken of in the past. He is one that the people have heard alluded to in scripture, one they have been anticipating. They would have understood that he was not just telling a story using cute little sheep. With the same confidence David expressed in facing Goliath, Jesus announces his infallibility in this job. It is impossible for him to fail in any capacity as a shepherd! Whatever is required of him as a shepherd, he will live up to! In 10:29, he says, "My Father which gave them me is greater than all." It might be mistaken that the phrase "gave them me" refers to Jesus being given to the sheep and in a sense this is true. He was given as our savior to die for our sins, but that is not what is being said here. The Greek word used for gave in this scripture is *didomi*, which has a meaning of committing as in committing troops to a battle or money to a project. It is a pledge or binding of someone or something to a particular course of action. In other words in giving the sheep to Christ, God is expecting a pledge from Christ to bind himself to the sheep with the task of bringing them home to heaven. They are not being given to Christ in the sense of a gift but as a task of responsibility. In 10:16, he says, "And other sheep I have which are not of this fold, them also I must bring." The phrase "I have" indicates acceptance of the task given to him. He has taken the responsibility that God has given him. He further acknowledges this responsibility with the words "I must bring." The sheep are not responsible for themselves. It is not by their own efforts that they get home but those of the shepherd. Even if they stray from the fold, the shepherd must bring them back. Notice that even a sheep that strays still belongs to Christ (other sheep *I have*, which are not of this fold.) Even one that has somehow left the fold Christ still claims possession of. The coup de grace seems to come in 10:28–29 where Jesus says, "Neither shall any man pluck them out of my hands." Verse 29 says, "And no man is able to pluck them out of my Father's hand." This has to be the most definitive statement of protection and security in the Bible. We are the sheep! Jesus the Christ is holding on to us! God the Father is holding on to us. If you make both your hands in the shape of a U as earlier and place one on top of the other, we get a picture of their joint protection. It is a "twofold" protection. If they are both watching us, protecting us, guiding us, how could we ever be lost!

It is very difficult to read chapter 10 of St. John completely and come away with the idea that salvation can be lost. In verse 28, Jesus says, "And I give unto them eternal life and they shall never perish." If it can be lost, it is not eternal. If Christ says it's eternal and we say it can be lost, are we calling Christ a liar? If there seems to be confusion about this issue and the scriptures are clearly saying something, who do you think is confused? Losing our salvation is like losing our connection with Christ. It's like losing the relationship that he bled and died for. It's as if the bleeding and the suffering and the dying were not able to get the job done. Many church doctrines and traditional attitudes about this issue teach and encourage the idea that salvation can be lost when scriptures don't seem to be saying that. Scriptures do seem to be saying that we should be confident and secure in the fact that eternity has already begun for us once we accept Christ, and we never have to worry or wonder whether we are going to heaven or not. It's a done deal!

One reason I believe it is hard for some to embrace the idea that our salvation is secure is that it is hard for us to think like God. First Timothy 2:4 says that God would have all be saved and come to the knowledge of the truth. The truth is that God could easily have made us his servants. He could have just willed it be so. But he loves us. He loves with a perfect love that desires our love in return. But just as Adam and Eve chose to eat the forbidden fruit, God wants us to choose him of our own free will. Adam and Eve were never meant to be separated from God, but when they were, he made a way possible for their return. I admit that this is a difficult concept to grasp especially if you have grown up trying to "earn" your salvation. If you could just be good enough or change enough. If you could stop doing the bad and do more of the good, maybe then you would be worthy of salvation. But you can't earn it and even if you could, no one could afford the price. You can't earn it, no one can buy it. It is a gift and if you can't do anything to get it, how can you do anything to lose it? It is difficult for us to think that anything could be so easy, that there must be a catch. Things that seem too good to be true usually are. But that's by man's standard, not God's. The thinking is that if we can't lose our salvation, then people could get saved and go back to all the sinful things they were doing without the fear of going to hell. There are a couple of problems with this line of thinking. Galatians 6:7 says, "Be not deceived, God is not mocked. Whatsoever a man soweth that shall he also reap." When Christ grants eternal life to a person, he knows that the person is sincere. He knows the intention of the person is to walk with him and to be guided by him. It is not possible to "trick" Christ into giving us eternal life and then intentionally going back to a life of sin. In 2 Corinthian 5:17, we read, "Therefore if any man be in Christ he is a new creature: old things are passed away; behold all things are become new." When we truly accept Christ into our lives, we are changed! Our very nature is changed so that it would be impossible to feel that way about sin, to feel comfortable pursuing it and having it as a regular part of our lives. Light and dark cannot exist in the same place and neither can the heart of a person who has been truly born again and one who is seeking to satisfy a sinful nature. If it is indeed possible to lose one's salvation, it must be under some very, very special extenuating circumstances. The image portrayed in St. John 10 just does not fit the profile of something that is easily lost.

God cannot lie! Think about that for a minute. *God cannot lie!* If you believe in God and what he says about himself and what scriptures say about him. If you believe in who he is and what he is and what his personage and character are, his righteousness and unchanging essence, then you have to believe that God cannot lie. In St. John 14:16, Christ promised to pray for the HS to come to those that love him and keep his commandments and that HS would abide with them *forever.* How do you lose something that is abiding with you forever? How can something abide with you forever if it can be lost? These two concepts cannot exist together it is impossible! It would be like mixing dark with light or letting east meet west. When we try to understand these ideas, it is important to keep in mind that God is not a man that he should lie (Num. 23:19). God is not a man and there are things about him that we just cannot understand, but it is important to try understanding the most important ideas. Sometimes that means trying to think outside "our human box" or box of traditional thinking. God and his son want us to be confident about our salvation. Satan wants to keep us guessing. If he can keep us guessing and hoping, we are saved; he can continue to use guilt and doubt, disappointment, and discouragement as major weapons in his arsenal in the war that we face daily.

The charismatic movement has fostered the use of spiritual, mystic, almost magical insight as the primary means for our understanding of God and what he wants for us and what he wants to say to us. Discernment is seen primarily as a spiritual gift that only certain people are blessed with instead of the everyday ability to "rightly divide truth" that comes from studying and understanding God's word. Unfortunately, this has caused analytical thinking and everyday common sense to sometime, maybe most of the time to be placed on a back burner. We do ourselves a great disservice and many of us walk our Christian lives in defeat for years because we are looking into the sky and waiting for a feeling instead of looking into the Bible and understanding it's meaning.

So now we have looked at several examples of things that cause misunderstanding of the scriptures. But why do these things persist? Why do they flourish and continue to be passed from one generation to the next? Of course there are many contributing factors, but one very common denominator is the clergy! There are many things about the way that clergy operate in charismatic circles that perpetuate misinformation, misconception, and therefore misunderstanding. Some are as childish as wanting to have your own way all the time. Some are as complex as interpersonal relationship issues that should really disqualify a person from serving in that capacity. Some are as sinister as a con man that comes off the street only to run a new con from the pulpit. No matter the source the result is the same, God's people suffer. They are stuck in the quicksand of half-truths and misinformation. They are trapped in prisons of tradition and conformity. They are caught on the hooks of prosperity, healing, and bountiful blessings that in many if not most cases never materialize. Let's begin our look at "The Mand of God."

We Don't Need No
Stinking Papers

A FAMOUS SCENE IN the movie *The Treasure of the Sierra Madre* shows
the star Humphrey Bogart in a confrontation with Mexican bandits.
The bandits are pretending to be Federal police. They are pretending
to be authorized. They are pretending to be the real deal. Bogart is
savvy enough to request authentication and asks, "Where are your
badges?" The leader replies, "We ain't got no badges. We don't need
no badges. I don't have to show you no stinkin' badges!" They are
pretending to be authorized; they are pretending to be qualified.
When questioned, they became angered and indignant. Sadly, they
bear a striking resemblance to many charismatic clergymen. In fact,
if you were to ask about their qualifications, you might get something like "I'm authorized by God and qualified by the Holy Ghost.
We don't need no stinkin' papers." But papers are exactly what they
need! Educational certificates, college degrees, maybe some still need
high school diplomas. Remember, clergymen are "called," and this
calling is by way of the Holy Spirit. This is a wonderful thing if the
HS is really involved but only the called knows for sure. And sometimes that is not true. I'm sure there are many who sincerely think
they have been called by the Spirit, but they are listening to something else, at best themselves and at worst demonic forces. There are
all sorts of possibilities in between, parents and loved ones, natural
abilities such as speaking, singing, and photographic memory. Some
people have gifts of a spiritual nature that are not powered by God,
i.e., prophecy, foreseeing, fortune-telling, soothsayers, etc. Many of

us are duped because we assume anything that happens in church is from God and that simply is not true. Let's take a logical look at this situation.

I am a podiatrist, a foot doctor. This required a four year bachelor's degree (from an accredited university), four years of training in a podiatry school (again accredited), and two to four years of additional training as a resident under doctors who have been working in the field for many years. That's just for feet. The more complicated the body part, the more years required for training in the medical field. Once the schoolwork is done, there is a license exam that has to be passed before you can work in the chosen area. There is usually a national exam and then some states have their own exam that must be passed in addition to the national one. All this is done to assure that people who are serving in this capacity are actually qualified to help people and not hurt them at least not because of ignorance. No one being treated by a doctor would consider this amount of training unreasonable. So doctors are subjected to all this training and the rigorous testing because they care for our natural, physical bodies. Our bodies are real, tangible entities. There is no mistaking when something goes wrong because of a doctor. In the natural world human life is the most precious thing we have and so it is protected by our society through regulation of training and licensing. But as a Christian and Bible believer, our souls are more precious than our physical bodies because they are going to last forever. So, the watchmen of our souls, the shepherds of our spirits, the keepers of our eternity should be experts of the Bible. Yet our churches are filled with pastors and other members of the clergy that are completely authorized by their organizations but are totally unqualified to occupy these positions. There are no requirements for theology degrees or degrees of any kind. In some cases, there is not even a high school diploma.

The charismatic movement was founded on spiritual experience. Being touched by the Holy Spirit was the most important characteristic of the new religion. Feeling the spirit in or on your body, speaking in tongues, jumping around the floor doing a holy dance, rolling around the floor spitting, snotting and foaming at the mouth were all signs that a person was full of the Holy Ghost. The shudders and quaking, the trembling, and the crying are all indicators today that the Spirit is upon a person. These are the kinds of tangible indicators of the presence of an intangible Spirit dwelling inside you. But what makes a preacher different? What qualifies him to stand in the pulpit and speak to God's people about his word? Well, in my church, until recently the biggest factor was the pastor. Usually what the pastor looks for is dedication, submission, and loyalty and that is to the pastor not God. I'm not saying that dedication to God is not important but the more dedication to the pastor is shown the better qualified a candidate will be deemed. Paying tithes, giving generously, and attending services regularly are all a part of the invisible résumé that a pastor considers. A recent trend in my church is the position of "armor bearer." This is a position mentioned in the Bible (1 Sam. 31:4, 2 Sam. 23:37, and others). It was a person who carried the large shield and other weapons for the king. I'm sure there is a clear and probably legitimate job description for the position, but it seems to be primarily a gentleman's gentleman. He carries the pastor's Bible and briefcase into and out of the church. He carries the pastor's coat or other garments and helps him change as necessary. He seems to acts as somewhat a bodyguard in many cases. I have known in the past and seen recently pastors that are older and could use this help but most of them that have this help are young, strong, and healthy enough to carry their own Bible. This seems to have trended from bishops getting this kind of treatment, but what's wrong with their hands? I'm not trying to say that these are the only things considered, of course candidates have to be able to read (in most cases) and share thoughts on a scripture. But in my experience, the factors that could be considered "brownnosing" seem to have as great an influence as anything else in the selection of a good candidate for ministry. So, these watchmen should be experts about the Bible. I am not suggesting they all have PhDs in theology or divinity though that would be wonderful, but they should be experts relative to their congregations. This is the twenty-first century and the general population is a lot more educated than at the time the charismatic movement began. In 1910, only 19% of fifteen to eighteen year olds were even in high school and barely 9% of those graduated. By the 1950s, about ten years before the charismatic movement (Pentecostals already in full swing), only 34% of people twenty-five and older had HS diplomas. So as recent as the fifties, church congregations were filled with people who had little education and probably didn't read very well, if at all. In that climate, a preacher who could read was probably one of if not the most educated person in the church. Just on the basis of a lack of understanding, how many would have even been capable of questioning the preacher? Today things are different. From the year 2000 to 2014, the number of people age twenty-five to twenty-nine with HS diplomas increased from 86–91%. In 2000, one-fourth of the people in the US had a BA degree vs. one-twentieth in 1940. The congregations today are much more educated as a whole than when the movement started. Therefore, it is imperative that the preachers are more educated, first to serve God's people with the quality of leadership they need and also so that they need not be ashamed, rightly dividing the word of truth. How embarrassed I have been personally, for my home church and for my denomination at some of the things I have heard over the pulpits in many different places. The simple things that preachers don't know like the OT books that are poetry vs. history, major vs. minor prophets? One of my favorites is the fact that so many bishops, pastors, elders, and ministers will call your attention to the twenty-fourth division of Psalms when there are only five divisions. The saddest thing is that I have personally pointed this out when teaching SS and elders who have heard it continue to make the mistake. With the things going on in the world that seem to be pointing to the end times there is very little understanding of eschatology, the rapture, and the millennium and these are things people have questions about but can't get answers from the ones who should know best. To compound the problem, instead of admitting not knowing and going home to study, some give off the wall answers that make them look foolish to those who do know and under minds the confidence that was once there. Then we wonder about the Exodus that seems to be taking place from some Pentecostal to nondenominational churches.

Something that you hear very often from clergyman is that they don't prepare their sermons in advance and many that do only prepare overnight. Those that don't prepare "say" they rely on the HS to literally word their mouths as they speak. This of course gives the impression that what is being said is directly from God. This is very disturbing to me. As I said earlier, our souls are our most precious possession. The delivery of God's word has eternal ramifications. Our understanding of the word has a direct effect on our success in the Christian walk. If the word we are fed is tainted, so is our understanding and therefore the rate of maturity we exhibit as God's children. It should be the goal of everyone who stands before God's people to be absolutely accurate in everything they say whether talking about the Bible or something that helps to make a point. It is very difficult to do this when talking off the cuff. There are people who are gifted to speak this way but not all gifts are from God or fueled by the HS and con men sometimes move from one con to another. When we fail to give accurate information and the flaw comes to light, the credibility of anything we have said or will say becomes questionable. An example comes from Bishop T. D. Jakes who is probably the most well-known preacher in the US, if not the world. He is a dynamic speaker and prolific author but gave misinformation on the Dr. Oz show when talking about his most recent book, *Destiny*. In the segment, the bishop discourages listeners from allowing themselves to be influenced by the past. He points out the difficulty of leaving our past and walking into our destiny. To illustrate this, he gives an example of a squeaking step and states, "The step doesn't make noise until you leave it." In other words, when you land on a noisy stair, it isn't noisy until you step off. Unfortunately, this is not true, and I know because I recently tried to fix some noisy stairs in my home and they squeak when stepped on and off. Maybe there are some that squeak only when you come off but not all, and that's what his description implied. Now this may seem trivial to notice, and it certainly doesn't take away from the point he was making. In fact, the audience erupted with epiphanic approval, and I believe there were some amens voiced at one point. But the issue is that this great speaker and author who has worked not only in television but film and stage gave out the wrong information. It may seem like small potatoes, but it's just the kind of thing that a cynic would use to cast doubt. "If he got that wrong, what else is he saying that's wrong?" So it is a very dangerous practice to preach without preparation, by the seat of your pants if I may. Having said that, I'm sure it's possible for the HS to use someone regularly in that off-the-cuff style but the spirit is not going to bring to your memory on a regular basis something that you have not stored there already. If that were the case, there would be no need for Timothy's admonition to "study to show thyself approved."

When we come before God's people, it is a great responsibility, but I think many times we miss the importance and the significance and the repercussions that are hinted in James 3:1, "My brethren, be not many masters, knowing that we shall receive the greater condemnation." Masters here, meaning anyone who gives instruction in or about God's word. When we come before God's people, it should be with the attitude of a master chef preparing a meal for the president and a room full of kings and queens. We should want only the finest ingredients, the recipe should be very familiar and comfortable to us, and it should be something we have already eaten ourselves. Instead for too many it is like stopping by Burger King or having a pizza delivered, very little effort. My mother used to recite a poem called "If Jesus Came to Your House." I wonder how preaching would change if the speaker knew Christ would be in the audience? How much more careful and precise with information and preparation? It's funny because all of them would tell the congregation he is there but not all their sermons reflect that belief.

It seems to me that the delivery of God's word in some churches is more about presentation than it is about content. In these churches because the Holy Spirit is thought to physically move us, a physical response is significant to most speakers. The spontaneous shouts of amen, hallelujah, glory, etc., are indicators that the speaker is reaching the congregation. These are taken as signs that the people are paying attention to what is being said. The call and response nature of the churches is such a driving force that congregations may be accused of being dead if there is no reaction from the crowd. The preacher may give notice that he should not have to pump up the group if the HS is in them and then he proceeds to pump them up anyway. If the church is quiet and not easily excited, it is inferred to be dead, and of course, "Anything that is dead should be buried" is what the preacher says of them. In many ways, this style is more about the preacher getting positive feedback and reinforcement than it is about God's people being fed. Because this is what we are used to and what we've grown up with and what we expect, when someone comes along with a beneficial style we miss what is being said because "He can't preach." Over the years, I've seen several types within this general style and here are a few.

There is the "high priest." This is a person who portrays what he thinks is the appearance of holiness. His walk is holy as if looking up to God with every step. His mannerisms are holy as in raising his arms to God or opening his arms wide as if receiving the crowd unto himself as Christ is often depicted in paintings. He may dress in holy garb like a robe. His speech is holy, slow, and deliberate pronouncing certain key words with exaggerated piety, i.e., "mand for man, gawd for God." The prayers of these men are usually very long and inflated with very large words used primarily for impression sake. This person will very often present him or herself as if in a perpetual state of communicating with God and or the HS. No matter where you meet them, they are found somehow in the Spirit.

Then there is the "professor or scholar." This person uses the intellectual approach to impress. He/she has often accumulated vast amounts of knowledge and information, large words, and famous quotations. But when you pay close attention to what they are saying, it becomes apparent that they are focusing on their particular area of knowledge and not really shedding light on the scripture. This presentation becomes very similar to a card trick or other slide of hand deceptions. By drawing in and impressing the crowd with this new information, then connecting any scripture that seems relevant the sermon takes on the aura of some new revelation. This approach might sound something like this from a preacher:

"Genesis 1:3, 'And God said let there be light and there was light.' Yes, we all know God created light but most of the time we take it for granted. It is an amazing thing and only an amazing God could create such a wonderful thing. So let's look at light for a minute. We often talk about things happening in the blink of an eye or as fast as lightning. One of the first things you notice about light is speed. Nothing travels at the speed of light but light. That speed is 186,000 mi./sec. That means, if you could travel at that speed, you could circle the earth 7.5 times in one second. Look at God! The distance light travels in one year is called a light-year and it is a distance and not a time and that distance is 5.8 trillion miles. Because of the size of the universe, it is easier to measure distances this way because the numbers in miles would be too large and hard to handle. For example, the distance between the sun and the earth is ninety-three million miles and that is called an astronomical unit. But if you measure the distance from our galaxy, the Milky Way, to our nearest neighbor galaxy Andromeda in miles, we are talking about 10.5 quintillion mi., that's eighteen zeros. Amazingly, if you divide one astronomical unit (93 million mi.) into the distance covered in a light-year, you get 63,000 and this is the same as the number of inches in one mile. So God took a cosmic ruler the (light-year) and an earthly ruler (mile) and gave them a common unit (63,000). Who coordinated all this? God! No not a coincidence, a "coordinance." So God made this amazing thing called light but then in Matthew 5:14, he said, "Ye are the light of the world," so we are like the light! But how? Well, we just saw how fast light is so we have to be fast and James 1:19 says be swift to hear! So we are to be swift to hear his word and his voice and his leading. Light is also bright it shines and Matthew 5:16 says, "Let your light so shine before men," and Matthew 13:43 says, "The righteous shine forth as the sun." So we are to be happy and full of joy! It's time out for God's people to always be such sour pusses and grumpy old men and women. Light also gives off warmth. The temperature at the surface of the sun is 10,000 degrees and a bolt of lightning holds 1.21 gigawatts of power. That's very, very hot and God wants us hot as well. Revelation 3:15 says, "I would that thou wert hot!" So he can't use you if you are cold; he'll spit you out. So you've got to be on fire for God and look at you. Some of you are still sitting on your seats.

So this is an example of how the scholar might present God's word. We can see that he does give some good information but the points he makes about what the scriptures are saying do not correlate with the actual meaning of those scriptures.

There is the "Mr. Trump." This one is similar to the high priest in that he sounds as if he is more holy than everyone else. His method is to talk loudly, openly, frankly, and graphically about sin or sinful things. In many cases, he borders on being obscene and abusive in his language. The tactic is to say anything no matter how vulgar (within reason) to get a response and keep the attention of his audience. He is very much like Donald Trump was in his bid for the Republican presidential nomination 2015–16.

The last category is the "rock star." These are individuals who have gained some level of celebrity status in either their denomination or Christian circles in general, and they don't have to be a T. D. Jakes. These are preachers who require being prepaid before they will grace you with their presence. They need hotels and living expense and a cut of the "take" (any money raised in offerings) during their visit. I wonder how many times Jesus's accommodations were prepaid? They can get away with this because they draw large crowds that can be manipulated to give huge amounts of money. The sponsor is easily willing to share the proceeds because "the take" will be so great. These people travel the country spending days to weeks in one place and moving on to the next town many times with several engagements each year. They seem to fall into at least three groups: singer, comic, or prophet. The singer is usually a person with a very good voice. They may have been a singer professionally at one point or just a person that has always had a gift of music. Whatever the case, singing is a large part of what they do in the pulpit and they usually incorporate several "numbers" into their preaching. Then there is the comic. With this person, you spend half the time laughing at the things he says. Not that there is anything wrong with laughing or injecting a little humor at times. Frankly, I don't think there is anything wrong with "Christian comedians" and that is something that has become popular in recent years. But the pulpit is not "Def Comedy Jam" and if that's what they enjoy, maybe they should try their hands at stand-up. Some would make better comics anyway. Lastly, there is the "prophet." I have a real problem with these guys, so much so that I'll come back to them later. Prophets are all the rage today. There are a great many men and women who travel the country with this self-imposed title! Unfortunately, probably 90 percent of them are either abject phonies or powered by something other than the Holy Spirit. Think about this, in the Old Testament there were six major prophets and twelve minor prophets. Depending on the source, the New Testament has eight to fifteen people who were or acted at least once in the prophetic realm. That's a total of thirty-six prophets in the entire Holy Bible. I am quite sure that we can find thirty-six people calling themselves prophet just in the state of New York! These people don't even have to be decent speakers because the crowds come to hear them prophesy! They come hoping the Great Prophet will have a word for them that he will "minister" to them. Usually this involves the laying on of hands by the prophet in a very holy and pious way while he says something very personal to the individual that he supposedly gets from God. At these services people line the aisle or pack the altar waiting to hear from God. Or the prophet will call individuals by pointing them out or by calling out specific names. The latter has great wow factor until you realize the amount of this kind of information that is available on the Internet! So these are a few of the characters we run into in our services and our pulpits. There are those I'm sure who know exactly what they are doing, but I think the saddest thing is there are those who don't know and really believe they are doing God's work because they are following the pattern of the leaders that have gone before them. But that is no excuse because James 3:1 lets us know there is a greater responsibility for those who hold these positions. Probably the best thing some people could do is to step down from these positions and admit they should never have been in them in the first place. But of course, that will never happen.

I think one of the biggest problems with these preachers is the failure, over the course of many years, to really understand what the term *preach* meant in the Bible. As with many of the things I've mentioned, over the years this term has taken on a meaning that is different from what was being done by the Apostles in the New Testament. For that we need to look at the Greek language once more. Webster's dictionary defines the word *preach* as: "delivering a sermon or religious address to an assembled group of people typically in a church." That is very close to what most people would say if asked to provide a definition. The Bible uses the word *preach* about fifty times. That does not include the use of the past participle. Of these fifty only three are in the OT. The book of Ecclesiastes uses the word *preacher* seven times and the Hebrew word used there is *qoheleth*, but as we shall see it does not have the same meaning as the NT word. In the NT, there are five different words used all of which are translated to *preach* (*diaggello*, once; *laleo*, once; *kataggello*, four times; *euaggellizo*, eighteen times; *kerusso*, twenty-two times). So we see here of the forty-seven times the English NT uses one word, there are actually five different words used in Greek. That can be very dangerous in our quest for understanding if all five have very different meanings and we apply the same meaning to all. That is why understanding the difference in some Greek versus English words can be very important. In this case however, there is only a slight difference between these five words. The meanings are as follows: *diaggello*, to herald (thoroughly); *laleo*, to talk, utter words, tell something; *kataggello*, shew, declare, report (firmly, with conviction); *euaggellizo*, announce good news, bring good tidings, bring glad tidings; *kerusso*, to herald as an official messenger. As you can see, these words are all conveying the idea of sharing information that the recipient has not heard before. The words are referring to news! They are referencing the sharing of sudden and perhaps even emergent information. This is especially clear with *diaggello* and *kerusso* both of which use the word *herald* in their definitions. *Herald* is defined as: "an official messenger bringing news or a person or thing viewed as a sign that something is about to happen." The important focus here should be news. When we act as heralds or something is being herald, it is an announcement of something that did not exist or was not present in the past. For example in the announcement of the birth of Christ, Luke 2:10–11, the angel said, "Behold I bring you good tidings of great joy," from which a songwriter penned, "Hark the Herald Angel Sing." The angel was a herald. In American history, there is a very famous herald in Paul Revere as he rode the county side crying, "The British are coming."

Also from the colonial period the town crier who walked the streets announcing news or proclamations is another example of a herald.

The point is that the original or the NT idea of preaching was the spreading of the gospel message, a brand-new message to people who had not heard this message before. Note that the difference between the words *heard* and *herald* is only one letter but that one letter difference clarifies what preaching should be. If something has already been heard, it is not possible to herald it. You cannot herald information that the hearer already has. There would have been no need for Paul Revere's famous ride if everyone knew the British were on the way. Therefore, it is almost impossible to herald or preach the good news from the pulpit every Sunday because most of the congregation already knows that good news! It is possible if someone walks in from the street with no prior knowledge of Christ, him crucified, and raised from the dead. But the speaker would then have to be talking specifically about the birth, death, and resurrection in the hearing of this person for the very first time. Let's step back to the OT at this point. As stated earlier, the OT (Hebrew) word for preacher is *qoheleth* and is found in Ecclesiastes seven times and is also translated as teacher. In fact, it is only found in Ecclesiastes. *Qoheleth* is from a base word *qahal* that means "a summoned group, they who are called out, or to assemble." So it is taken to mean one who assembles to teach. The Septuagint word (Greek translation of the OT) is *ekklesiastes* from which we get the English Ecclesiastes. So *qoheleth* = Hebrew for preacher = Septuagint for teacher = English Ecclesiastes. So the book of Ecclesiastes is a series of teachings by a well-known public speaker usually thought to be Solomon. So when Solomon is referred to as preacher in Ecclesiastes, the word is more closely related to teacher or lecturer. This is a better description of the writing in Ecclesiastes than to call it preaching or heralding. So what Solomon did in Ecclesiastes was not preaching in the NT use of the word. He was sharing the wisdom of his experience, not sharing or announcing good news. Since the NT is the basis for Christianity, that is where we should take our definition from. It may seem to some that focusing on this point is unimportant and grasping at straws. But it is the failure to understand this point that proves to be the "straw that broke the camel's back," the camel being God's people. They suffer because what they are getting from the pulpit in a great many cases is not what they need for growth and maturing as Christians. When we fail to provide the correct food in the early stages of spiritual life, the growth process is stunted sometimes irrevocably. Just as poor neonatal nutrition prevents the development of a strong body in an infant, babes in Christ develop spiritual rickets, scurvy, and anemia without the proper spiritual diet. I would venture a guess that many church leaders who fall into sin (some over and over) are themselves victims of this spiritual malnutrition. If these clergymen were presenting the kinds of messages that nurture the flock, they would likely at some point feed the areas of their own weakness. But then that is hard to do when you are focused on offerings, titles, and doctrines instead of what the Bible really says.

It is really amazing to me and embarrassing at the same time that in the last five or so years, I have learned and understand more about the Bible studying on my own than what I learned in the previous fifty-five years. What I speak of here is foundational and fundamental knowledge versus information. For example, it was my own study that opened my eyes to the importance of the "armor of God" in our daily lives. I never heard a sermon or a series of messages on this subject that can make such a difference in a successful walk with God. Yet there is so much information available on this subject. In fact, several different authors have written entire books on the subject. One author wrote a book three hundred pages long and then wrote a second to cover what he left out of the first. But it is something that would take more than one sermon to attack and most Pentecostal preachers don't do series. What is it that they do? Well, I've been trying to answer that for a while, and it has been very difficult but let's give it a shot.

This is not meant to ridicule or belittle the clergy I've been exposed to. As I have said, I love my church and have great respect for its foundation and forefathers, but this is my experience and I am very sure that there are countless many who will agree. Most Pentecostals have heard the joke where two people are talking after Sunday service and the conversation goes (1) "We suuuure had a good time in service this morning!" (2) "Yeah? What did he preach about?" (1) "I don't know, but we sure had a good time." I don't know what he preached about! This is a very sad commentary, but unfortunately, it is too often true that people come out of a sermon and many times can't tell you what the speaker was talking about. They may be able to quote a few things that he said especially comical things. They may be able to quote the scripture that was used for a text but many times they are unable to give a general topic, theme, or point the speaker was trying to get across. It is not because they weren't listening but because the speakers in many cases are so disjointed in their presentation that it is hard to follow the line of thinking. Or that the style used does not lend itself to the subject or even the speaker. Perhaps the saddest part of this situation is that people are so indoctrinated by this style that when someone does not use it, "they can't preach." I have come to the conclusion that many if not most Pentecostal preachers engage in what I will call "spiritual cheerleading." Anyone who has attended a football or basketball game will recall seeing cheerleaders on the sideline or courtside. These young people parade up and down yelling, rhyming, dancing, and doing all sorts of acrobatics in an attempt to excite the crowd to root for the home team. Sadly this is much of what happens in many pulpits every Sunday all over this country and probably the world. That is the nature of the Pentecostal sermon. It is geared for the most part to excite not to explain. In most cases if the crowd is not loud and active, the speaker will begin with some remark about how dead they are or he shouldn't have to pump them up, which he proceeds to do. No matter what the sermon is about, it is seems more important that the "joy of the Lord" is expressed or the speaker has not been successful. This makes sense when you remember that the Pentecostal movement is based on the presumption of the presence and activity of the HS. So if that presence is not manifested by activity during the services, the gathering was for naught. There are some contemporary theologians who feel that Pentecostals place the HS above Christ but that is not the case. It is not that the HS is above or more important than Christ in our lives but that the HS is an indication of Christ in our lives and these outward expressions are thought to be evidence of the inward dwelling. Therefore, the attitude "no joy, no Jesus; no speaking in tongues, no Spirit." Thus the great premium placed on the holy dance, tongues, and any other ecstatic expressions seen in our assemblies. So the mark of a good sermon is that it "tears (rips) up the church." That is, everyone jumping and screaming, dancing, speaking in tongues, and praising the Lord when he is finished. Most of the time, however, nobody is more enlightened in their understanding of God's word.

So what I mean by "spiritual cheerleading" is that most sermons are exhortations of some sort or in some area. Whatever the chosen subject matter or scripture, the audience is encouraged to do or not do something as the case may be. For example if speaking on the virtue of loving your neighbor, several scriptures on this subject would be employed along with everyday examples that people can relate to showing the positive and negative aspects of this topic. What's wrong with that? If done occasionally, nothing. We all need to be encouraged about one thing or another at different periods in our lives, and if loving your neighbor hits you at the right time, great. The problem is that this is usually the norm, so it happens all the time. Also in this style, one or two scriptures are chosen because of their relationship to the subject matter and used as a jump-off point for this matter. In many cases, they do not end up being the primary focus of the sermon. There are two major problems with this. One is that using just a couple of lines from a passage, the lines are often taken out of context and therefore misrepresented as in some of the earlier examples of misquoted and misunderstood scriptures. The other is that using just two or three verses of a passage does not allow you to develop the whole idea of the passage and again the context and the essence of the passage go undiscovered not only by the audience but by the speaker. As a result, the true meaning of many very famous and frequently quoted scriptures are mysteries not only to many Pentecostals but to their leaders. Some of these scriptures have insight and meaning that is vital to Christian maturity but remains unharvested by the clergy and unused by the parishioners. This becomes apparent when leaders are asked very basic questions and they give the wrong or no answer at all. Questions like, how many times was the temple destroyed in the OT, or who are the major versus minor prophets? Make no mistake, I am not exaggerating; and when simple things like these can't be answered correctly, it is obvious that more important things are out of their scope and who suffers, the people. Paul speaking to the carnal Corinthian church in 1 Corinthian 3:2 says, "I fed you milk and not meat because you were not able to bear it." Many Pentecostal churches are being fed milk not because they can't bear it but because the preachers don't have the meat! They dance around superficial or contemporary ideas that tradition has brought to scriptures missing most of the meat and never getting to the bone! How can a new Christian successfully fight the battle against sin if they are never trained in the weapons of warfare? (The armor of God.) How do they know what to look for as signs of change without understanding the Fruit of the Spirit? How are they to have confidence in their salvation when they are trying or hoping to make it to heaven? How can they effectively commune with God if never taught to pray? So, preaching in this way is like a bowl of "Jambalaya." You get a very unique flavor from all the different ingredients combined but it's hard to tell what any individual item tastes like.

Over and over I have talked with people who are no longer going to church or have left the Pentecostal church because they were not being taught. Of course, pastors who hear this will likely reply, "You can't be taught if you don't come." Certainly, that is many times the case but just as many if not more times they are just not getting anything when they are present and as time goes by they get tired of the monotony and the wasted time and slowly fade into memory. You can be sure that Satan puts his two cents into the pot every chance he gets, but in many cases, he doesn't have to do very much because the clergy is doing so little. My cousin Kathy said in a Bible study once, "It seems that pastors (clergy) have lost interest in being shepherds." I think she was right. Sheep are totally dependent upon the shepherd. One of the reasons that Christ used the shepherd metaphor was to relay the character of this relationship. The sheep will eat whatever the shepherd provides. But as dumb as they are portrayed being, if he doesn't provide enough, I'll bet they wonder off to find something more to eat. You will never hear a shepherd blaming the sheep for not getting enough food because he knows who is responsible for the food. The shepherd would never blame the sheep for not getting enough water or for being caught by a predator. If not fed, it's the shepherd's fault! No water, shepherd's fault! Caught by a wolf, shepherd! All too often though you will hear clergy blame the sheep for not growing, for immaturity, for habitual sin and failure to thrive. Really? In actuality, in many cases, it is the clergy who should be charged with neglect! Recently in my hometown news, a dog named Jada was rescued from a neglecting home. After being examined, it was found that she had cancer and not long to live. The workers at the shelter along with the community decided to make a "bucket list" and provide the things that appeared on the list before Jada's death. This sounds like a very sweet and kind gesture, and I'm sure the dog enjoyed most of the things she experienced. But well-wishing as it seemed, nothing on that list came from Jada's own requesting. It was all surmised! The shelter workers guessed at what Jada might like and proceeded to supply those things on the list. This is the kind of method that many clergy use in deciding what to "feed" their flocks. They decide what is needed.

In most cases they will say something like, "This is what God has put on my heart for you" or "the Holy Spirit wants us to study this" or "this is where we need to be for a while." After all it must always come across that God is making the choice. That way if it fails, it is not the pastor's fault and it is certainly not God's fault, so again it falls on the sheep and something they are doing wrong. But many times it's just a comfort zone especially when the same or similar material resurfaces over and over. Or, it may be that some colleague has suggested a particular area or material because it worked for them especially if the colleague is a superior. It may be a particular leadership desire such as church growth or financial increase. But not everything requires our being taken by the hand step by step in everything we do by the HS. I know some will say, "Well I don't know about you, but I want the Spirit to guide me every step of the way." Well if you are stuck with a flat tire in the middle of a snowstorm with three to four inches falling per hour, you had better be doing something other than praying. The point is that many of the needs of God's people can be found out if the shepherd would simply ask the sheep. Unlike Jada, people can actually tell you what they need, want, etc. Of course, we want the HS to guide us and in the most important things we should always rely on him, but we can get pointed in the right direction in other ways as well. Naturally there are some things that are common requirements for all sheep to flourish but unlike the four-legged kind, some human flocks have very specific needs not shared by others. What better way to discover these needs than—Oh, let's see…Hmmmmm…How about ask!

Why don't leaders ask what the people need? One possibility is the comfort zone. We all operate there as much as possible. It's a very special person who is always trying to get out of their zone. When the church is asked what some of their concerns, issues, questions, etc., are there are bound to be a few areas that the pastor is not knowledgeable in. This is true for any pastor. Even a pastor who holds a PhD from an accredited university would find areas he's not a master of in this scenario. I think what comes into play here is confidence at least to some degree (no pun intended). In this situation, the reaction of the PhD holder would likely be to recognize the unfamiliar areas, study to become familiar, or get someone who is familiar with the material. The PhD has enough confidence in himself and his degree that he is not threatened by the need to study or relinquish time to an expert. He recognizes that no one knows everything and that no one expects him to know everything. However, when there are no credentials, there is nothing that qualifies you. Though spiritually you may feel qualified by the HS; actually in many cases, there is nothing to qualify the position of pastor but a reputation for giving large, a large aspiration to greatness, and a big mouth. And if people would really learn to listen, many times that big mouth would betray him.

Unfortunately, I think too often this has more to do with pride than anything else. The pride, the prestige, and the power associated with being a pastor can be quite an ego boost when the best of intentions are the reasons for being there. But when motives for being in leadership are not pure, these three *P*s can be an intoxicant that leads to many unsuccessful and failed ministries. In the worst case, it can lead to the spiritual downfall through sin on the part of the intoxicated leader. We are all well acquainted with the many public humil-iations of pastors/preachers over the last few decades. Personally I feel sorry for them and as a man can understand the temptations that can occur. But in many cases if leaders were really focused on the good of the sheep, what is best for the sheep, how will what I do help or hurt the sheep, it would be much harder to do something that was totally selfish and exploitive. So to admit that there are things they don't know, they don't have all the answers, or God forbid that someone else in the congregation might know more would be to weaken the force of all three *P*s, or so it would seem. The almost comical irony of this is that in fact it is the opposite that is true. To admit his deficiency can actually be beneficial. By this admission, he shows his people how important it is for him to get things right. They don't focus on the fact that he doesn't know something but on the fact that he takes the time to get it right. Remember, these people know that he is not a graduate of Divinity School, and they don't expect him to have all the answers but they do expect that he can get them. This admission can bring confidence to the people in what the leader says off the cuff because they can trust he would not give them something he was not sure of. Of course these benefits can be negated if the leader is in the habit of repeating things he's heard and not researched. Also if he is just totally inept scripturally (which does happen) and relies on theatrics more than facts; eventually, he will begin to come across as a buffoon or a clown and the level of respect will decline no matter what he does. That doesn't mean he won't have a congregation but the congregation will be terribly underfed and malnourished spiritually speaking.

Not having credentials is not an excuse for "slipshod" treatment of God's word and his people. The Internet makes available a vast wealth of information at the touch of a button. Of course you have to learn what sources to use because unfortunately not everything is accurate. There are also educational opportunities online. It is pos-sible for a pastor/preacher to become credentialed from the comfort of his own home and at his own pace. As with anything, the quality of these online degrees vary and institutions should be researched and degree programs compared because some of them are just out to make a buck. Some will promise a BA degree in a few months when it normally takes at least four years. But even if you don't want a degree, there are plenty of books clergy should have in their possession. One is a good Hebrew/Greek concordance. This one book will open the understanding of scripture like never before. Another is something about the history and culture of the biblical period and of course a good English dictionary. Many times we use a word in a certain way with a certain meaning that is totally incorrect and leads to misunderstanding and misconceptions for example the word argument. Because we typically associate this word with anger, it keeps us from deep discussions that could serve to open the eyes of our mind to very important ideas and concepts. Most important is a sincere desire to please God and a heart for his people. If you are not in this business for God, then you're just giving people the business and you should probably get out of the business!

Follow the Leader

DICK BUTKUS IS A former member of the Chicago Bears of the NFL. He is regarded as one of the best linebackers of all time and was named the most feared tackler of all time by NFL.com in 2009. I reference him at this point only because of his name and state categorically that my use of a similar sounding name in this chapter is in no way meant to reflect upon him in any way shape or form. However, there is a practice among members of the clergy (at least in my church) that is best described by the name that I will use for any clergymen that engage in this activity and that is Mr. Buttkiss. This term will apply to the many preachers who seek to be elevated to elders, elders to pastors, pastors to superintendents, and superintendents to bishops but who employ this tactic. I am in no way suggesting that all who desire these elevations engage in this practice. I am sure there are many who are qualified and deserve to be in these positions. It is the very character that clergy has taken on that has led to and fosters this behavior. One of the problems with Mr. Buttkiss however is that many times he takes the place of a person who should be elevated and this is only possible because leadership makes it so.

As mentioned earlier, we are living in the age of televangelism, an age where there are many millionaire preachers. Preaching the gospel is no longer just a calling, it has become big business. I would not be surprised to see the Prosperity Gospel as a commodity on the NYSE or NASDAQ before long. As I said before, I realize there is a financial aspect to the successful functioning of even a small neighborhood church. And of course, there is a responsibility of church members to support the church. But in my mind in many cases, there is a very thin line between responsibility and extortion! Extortion may seem a bit extreme at first but bear with my line of thinking and see where it takes you.

Financial responsibility for the local church is any financial obligation that is placed upon a church member for the support, maintenance, and general functioning of a church. This includes tithing, free will offerings, benevolent giving for special needs and occasions, etc. But it also includes financial support for the pastor. This usually includes a salary, an annual pastoral anniversary celebration, appreciation celebrations for the pastor's wife, excuse me (first lady), and any other perks that are supplied by the church members. Certainly church members should provide the financial support for church operation, and it should be a joint effort, but it is not always possible for it to be an equal effort. In Mark 14:7, Christ noted, "The poor you will have with you always." Most churches (at least most urban churches) are likely to have populations that represent many different financial states. Some families are able to meet any monetary request without a second thought. But there are others for whom just paying tithes is a struggle. So, what do they do when there are several bills that are behind but bombarded with phrases like "God loves a cheerful giver" (2 Cor. 9:7), sacrificial giving and seed faith. Extortion is the practice of obtaining property, services but especially money through force or threats (coercion). In other words, the use of pressure or intimidation to force someone to act in a certain way. This was a practice commonly used by the "mob" or organized crime in the days of racketeering during the 1920s. Neighborhood shopkeepers and business owners would be forced to pay protection money to keep the very people they were paying from coming in and tearing up their store or hurting them and/or their families. With extortion, there is a threat that something bad would happen (or something good won't happen) if this money was not paid. This is exactly what the prosperity gospel does, and it is in this climate that many if not most churches function in my denomination. In teaching that blessings are directly related to giving the threat is implied that failing to give will prevent your being blessed. That is, blessings will be withheld if you don't give, as if what is being given is being given directly to God. Now of course I must qualify this statement because it is certainly true that we are blessed for our giving but not always in an "eye for an eye" manner. For example, if I give ten dollars, it does not mean that God will bless me with ten dollars. If I give someone a suit, I won't necessarily be given a suit. And it doesn't matter that the preacher prays that God bless some twenty, some thirty, some sixty, and some hundredfold. God's blessing is determined by what we need before what we want and God himself makes that decision. God wants us to be prosperous but that prosperity is based on the parallel prosperity of our souls (3 John 1:2) not on how much we give. In other words, as our souls grow, mature, improve, do well, the other aspects of our lives will follow suit. And it may be that as we grow spiritually, these physical things become less important. So, even the words used in praying over offerings can dishonor God, because the person praying is trying to convince us that this kind of giving honors God. If the phrases and terms thrown around while collecting money are not accurate and biblical that is like taking money under false pretenses. That is why I use the term *extortion*! People are being convinced to do things based on at best misinformation and at worst outright lies. Look at this example and see what you think.

An evangelist comes to town with a "reputation" for prophesy of great financial blessings and or miraculous healings. He will be playing, uh, preaching for two or three weeks and advertising goes out to the community well in advance of his arrival. The word is spread and the church is packed the very first night. People come from miles around, why? To hear this great speaker and to be fed by the wisdom of his God-sent message? Well maybe a few but most come to get a blessing! People come hoping, praying that he will call them out of the whole crowd, single them out, and present them with a special word from God. And he may do just that! He may call a woman who has just lost her job and tell her that she will get another in a certain number of days. He may tell some man that he's been diagnosed with a certain illness but that God is going to heal him. He may say that someone has legal papers in their pocket or purse and that a case will be decided in their favor. Someone may be in desperate need of a new car, and they are told they will have it soon. He may call people up and share knowledge of physical illness that presumably he could know nothing about or people in wheelchairs on canes or crutches to pronounce healing upon them. Anyone who has not been called up is now waiting, praying, hoping that they are next. When he is finished "ministering" to the crowd he, not the deacons, raises an offering. He may raise it with a specific blessing attached for example the "you won't bounce another check" blessing. But these blessing always have a specific amount attached to them—$52.50, $37.72, $119.02, etc. What if you don't have the particular amount requested? You can get with someone else who doesn't have it all and bring it together. You can write a postdated check; you can bring it in the next night. Some churches are even equipped to allow your swiping of a credit card. So throngs of people fill the aisles, desperate for a blessing, a breakthrough, a word, deliverance if they have the price! It's funny but in the Bible I don't recall any situation where Jesus healed or provided any other miracle (water to wine, feeding the multitudes, Lazarus raised) that required any monetary contribution on the part of the recipient. These people are coerced into giving an offering that they are made to believe is somehow connected to that blessing. In other words, if you don't give this offering, I can't promise that the blessing you seek will be granted. In this scenario, it is very likely that the person who needs a blessing the most would be the least likely to be blessed because they don't have the price of admission!

This happens on a lesser scale in the weekly services. Our holiness or how much or little we please God is often insinuated to be connected to how much we give. How regularly do we pay tithes? Do we pay 100 percent? How much do we give in the offerings? How many churches begin the giving portion of worship with "Will a man rob God"? So using this phrase out of context with the wrong meaning, to get people to do something particular is extortion! Many who read this (or hear about it) will say, how dare he say such things? Who does he think he is? But if your desire is to sincerely serve God, it might be a good idea to at least think about this idea. As I suggested, this extortionist attitude extends from the Prosperity Gospel and the lucrative salaries and lavish lifestyles of many of the world's most popular and successful television preachers. So, it stands to reason that many young men and women who have grown up in or around church or have been recently exposed to it, might develop the desire to work in this capacity. Not because of a deep and sincere desire to serve God and do his will, but because of the associated perks. This is what I believe motivates Mr. Buttkiss. He is or wants to become a member of a group we might call "The good Old Boys." Though not necessarily white or southern, they do "share a strong sense of fellowship to other members of his peer group." This group is usually made up of the most prominent leaders of the organization starting at the national level. Many times they are jurisdictional bishops and as such have the power to elevate and depose, to appoint, oppress, and abuse with that power. Some of them are very successful pastors of very large churches with very large congregations and thus very large influence. Some of them are elders who are successful in business outside of the church and therefore highly sought after for his ability to be a benefit either to a group or an individual. These are all men who usually have at least one of three things: power, prestige, or money and usually if you have one it will probably lead to at least one of the other two. They think alike, act alike, and have common goals; and many times it's because they learned how to "play the game." The name of the game, "Ecclesiastical King of the Hill."

Most of us, boys at least, probably played the childhood version of this game at some point in our lives. One person stands on a small hill or raised mound of dirt trying to remain atop while others charged up and tried to wrestle the king off the hill. Usually it was the strongest, most athletic person who could occupy the top for the longest period. The ecclesiastical version differs in that those at the bottom are not trying to remove the one at the top but to join him. Even better than joining him is to acquire their own personal hill, which a reigning king can provide or assist in attaining depending upon his own level of power. So how does this work? First Mr. Buttkiss decides on an objective. He may be a young man who wants to be a pastor or a pastor who wants to be a bishop, the same mechanism applies. Mr. Buttkiss has to get noticed. The best way to get noticed is to impress! In a perfect world where the primary purpose for being "a man of the cloth" is to serve and to please God, those in leadership would be most impressed by those who are most like Christ. Those who love the word and study the word and live the word, those whose lives have been transformed to reflect the word and who have developed the "mind of Christ," these are the men and women who should catch the eye of those in leadership. Dedication to God and his ultimate truth and a sacrificial servile attitude toward his people are definite earmarks for someone to be considered a servant of God. Unfortunately, most of the time it's those who love the pastor or bishop, those who study him and learn to please him, those who have been transformed to reflect and regurgitate "the pastor said this, or the bishop said that," those who can read the pastor or bishop's mind and present him with tokens of love that touch his heart, these are the people who are noticed by leadership. Now I am not saying that everyone who sincerely loves their pastor or bishop is seeking "reparation." Those who truly love their leader usually become very apparent to everyone in the congregation. I'm not saying it is wrong to do these things when the motive is pure, but when there are ulterior motives, usually Mr. or Ms. Buttkiss are in the room.

Though this name is fabricated, the character it portrays is not and it is likely that anyone reading this knows someone who fits the description. Let me share one of the many that I have experienced. When I was very young, a group of students who were going to college in my town started coming to our church. They were already saved and were looking for a holiness church to attend while going to school. They were members of our organization but from a major city and brought a different level of enthusiasm and dedication as young people than I had seen in that age group. As they attended services with us regularly, they became part of our church family and were embraced as sons and daughter by all. There was only one male in the group, but he was very respectful, courteous, and pious for such a young man. All in all, quite charming! Everyone loved him and before long he had people eating out of his hand. I don't believe there was unscrupulous intent in the beginning, but after a time, the young man changed. He began to get closer and closer to our pastor. Their relationship seemed to get stronger and closer by the week. I seem to remember him having a mother in his life but not a father, so perhaps that was part of it but it continued to intensify. Before long you could say that he revered our pastor! He talked about him publicly during testimony services, how much he loved and respected the pastor, and wanted to do something special for him. Then one Sunday he announced publicly that he wanted to shine the pastor's shoes! It seemed he had shined shoes as a child to make money and had become quite good at it. Being a college student and not having much money, he wasn't able to purchase anything, but he suuuuuure knew how to shiiiiiiiine some shoes. Well, pastor swallowed it hook, line, and sinker and from then on the young man could do no wrong and could get anything he wanted from the pastor. A short time after that it became noised about that the young man wanted to preach. He felt the call of the Lord and declared himself for the ministry. Normally, it would take a while for someone to prove himself worthy of a trial sermon, but in the very short time, this young man was allowed to preach. After just one sermon the young man was granted a license by our pastor. Finally, a short time after that the young man announced he was leaving school and returning home. It seemed that the pastor at his home church had passed away and since he was now a minister, he would be in the running to become the next pastor. He left and I do believe he became the pastor eventually if not immediately. At any rate, we never really heard from him again. Some of the other young ladies have kept in touch over the years, but not that young man who loved our pastor sooooooooooooo much! This is not an uncommon scenario. Some are more subtle, some are more blatant, and some are even more extravagant. There are even instances where blackmail may be a part of the plot but unfortunately these soap opera–like situations are all too real.

One of the reasons Mr. Buttkiss can be successful is the susceptibility of those in power. Most of us have personal emotional baggage some more than others. If we are lucky, we are able to make it through life reasonably well despite the load we carry around. If we are real lucky or (blessed) we somehow get therapy in some way shape or form. Sadly, most do not get help with these issues. Some do not even know there is an issue! Issues like child abuse (physical, emotional, and sexual), poverty, neglect, abandonment (intentional or not). All these things leave wounds, and if the wounds are not treated, they may form ulcers. An ulcer is an open sore that for one reason or another is usually very difficult to heal. The longer an ulcer is open, the more likely it will become infected and of course with infection the wound becomes "susceptible" to even greater problems. For example if someone grew up in an impoverished environment and never experienced economic stability but was then exposed to the financial gains possible through pastoral leadership, they might easily become susceptible to a very generous Mr. Buttkiss. What about a person with deep seated emotional needs for affection, someone who missed out on the love of one very special person? This could make them susceptible to the Mr. Buttkiss who just looooooooooooves the pastor sooooooooooo much! That person who would walk through fire for the pastor, never disagrees with the pastor, and thinks the pastor can do no wrong. That is until things don't go the way they want them to. It is also possible that there are undiagnosed psychological problem such as paranoia and delusions of grandeur that are undetected and the reasons that some clergy find themselves in bondage. One of these problems is bad enough but suppose someone is burdened with more than one? If it seems I'm blowing this out of proportion, I once heard Dr. David Jeremiah on the radio speaking about a friend who is a member of a famous and accredited theological seminary. His friend had been keeping a list of graduates from seminary who had fallen into sin of some sort or another and the list had topped 100! The point is there is not enough effort made in screening the members of a group who are supposed to be the guardians of our souls.

In certain occupations or professions, particular qualities are essential for success. It would be very difficult to be a firefighter without a certain level of courage. Conversely, if someone is known to be a pyromaniac, you might question his reporting that he was on the scene trying to put out the fire. In the last few years there has been a surge of questionable shootings by police officers all over the country. At one point it seemed to be racial but that is not entirely true. In my opinion these shootings reveal a problem in the screening system that is used to psychologically evaluate candidates for law enforcement positions. It may be that the system is failing to pick up characteristics that make some officers susceptible to firing weapons prematurely. I have heard of an appeal process that allows a rejected candidate to fight a negative decision and have it reversed. There is something wrong with the process, but at least there is a process. Candidates are exposed on some level to a psychological evaluation. This has not been the case in the Pentecostal church in the past. With all the sexual indiscretions of church leaders in recent years some organizations may be initiating these safeguards but what about those that are already installed as leaders?

It is very obvious that many of those in ministry do not belong. Look at the scandal of the Catholic Church and the priests over the last few decades. As religious organizations go, the Catholic Church is second to none in terms of credentialing and administration. Yet even in this great religious machine predators have slipped through the cracks. How much greater is the chance that ill equipped not to mention outright dangerous people are sitting in leadership roles in churches where the primary qualification is one man's perceiving of another man's Holy Spirit. It is very often these leaders who cast a negative shadow on the "true" church. Not only are they potentially dangerous to the physical well-being of church members but more importantly to the spiritual well-being. Many times after being exposed to the wiles of such leaders, people are left confused, deluded, and even resentful. After such a great letdown, many people change their way of thinking about religion and about God. CNN recently ran a special that looked at the lives of some of the survivors of the Jonestown massacre. One lady and one gentleman no longer attended church anywhere. They continue to believe in God and in Christ, but they no longer think it's necessary to attend a particular church on a regular basis. Another man has turned completely away from Christianity and now acknowledges many gods from many religions and has covered his body with tattoos to commemorate them.

I am certainly not condoning the choices made by those survivors, but from a human standpoint, I totally understand. When we commit ourselves to a Christian philosophy, the backbone of every doctrine is faith. Faith makes it all real, makes it all worthwhile. Hebrews 11:1 says faith is the substance of things hoped for. Hebrews 11:6 says we can't please God without it. In John 20:29, Jesus called those who believed without seeing (signs, wonders) blessed, also expressing faith. When we finally accept this biblical principle, we commit our lives to it. This is part of what giving ourselves to Christ means. But in doing so, many of us also give our lives to the shepherd, the pastor, the leader. Consciously or subconsciously over time, we develop faith in the man of God. We begin to trust him more and more. This happens on a different scale for different people, but I think it happens to all on some level who have any long-term relationship with a church. As this trust develops, we can become "brainwashed" to a degree. This is not as bad as it may seem; after all, that is what should happen according to Philippians 2:5 (let this mind be in you which was also in Christ Jesus) and 1 Corinthians 2:16 (having the mind of Christ). So we should become brainwashed by God's word. We should develop a new way of thinking, feeling, and acting that is all based upon the word of God. But depending on the level of trust that develops for the pastor, we can sometime be brainwashed by him as well. If he is not totally and completely dedicated to God and God's truth, that's where we get into trouble. When we sincerely give our lives to Christ and join a church, we also give our lives to the pastor. We assume that he has done the same and that he is even more committed and dedicated than we are. He is assumed to be on a completely different level than we are. When leaders fall, they are not taking just themselves down a dark and disgraceful path, but they are also taking many who have put their total trust in someone who has now let them down. This can be a very lonely and confusing time. You now have to figure out where things went wrong and how or if things can be repaired. Are you just stupid and gullible? Was all that stuff you bought into just a bunch of lies and all part of a con game? Or is the word of God true and that pastor or preacher or evangelist was a fake or weak or just never really got it! Recovery from such a devastating experience can take years and in some cases never happens.

Being a leader is a grave responsibility that all too often is taken for granted in church circles. Some men and women seem to be drawn to ministry for the glitz and glamour more than for God and his Glory. Like so many unsavory things that have been allowed to creep into the church, a distorted financial focus has found its pew! In an effort to build financial stability and allow churches to run more efficiently, adopting the business model has become a tool of Satan in many instances. The financial crisis of 2007–08 has been called a global event and considered by some the worst financial crisis since the Great Depression. But it is an even greater crisis that the church has allowed even condoned and that is the prosperity ministry. While bailouts allowed big business to stay afloat, many Americans were evicted or foreclosed. Where some CEOs were fired and given million dollar severance packages, many retired Americans lost much of if not all their retirement funds and were forced to go back to work. Business moguls go on with life as usual while "Joe the Plumber" loses his life savings. With these same models entering the church infrastructure, many of the same attitudes precipitate from it. When there is more focus on what the pastor "gets" than what the church "gives" there is a problem. This is not conjecture but conclusion drawn from Christ himself in the Bible. As our example, Jesus was always serving others always doing something for someone else. In Matthew 20:28, he says, "The Son of man came not to be ministered unto but to minister," or serve. In fact, I believe the only instance of Jesus being served (other than a meal with everyone else being served as well) was the woman with the Alabaster Box who washed Jesus's feet and anointed him with oil (Matt. 26:7, Luke 7:38). In many (if not all) of our churches, there are people living on fixed incomes who are just barely able to make ends meet. People on Social Security Disability, Public Assistance, Social Security Retirement, and other very limited retirement incomes and in many cases they are made to feel guilty if they fail to pay tithes and give offerings regularly. I have never heard of a pastor who relieved the elderly from certain giving responsibilities. There may be one somewhere, but I have never heard of one. I'm sure the argument from the clergy would be "Who am I to deprive these of the blessings they get form the giving?" I am also sure there are those who would not want to be relieved for the same reason. The point being that very few leaders ever seem to think about the hardship that giving can put on some people. Very few leaders ever think about taking some of that money on a regular basis and giving it to a family or a person in need or meeting a specific need that is made known without any questions or talk of repaying. After all, that is the reason that the early Christian church often pooled their resources not for the temple and there were no churches yet. It was to make sure everyone had what was needed to survive.

The activity of Mr. Buttkiss and the King of the Hill gang basically boils down to a favoritism program: "You wash my back, and I'll wash yours." This is in direct disobedience to the Bible where it says, "God is no respecter of persons," that is God doesn't show favoritism at least not in that way. God's favor is shown toward those that serve him versus those that don't (Acts 10:34, Ro. 2:10–11). If we try being simple and honest, there is nothing easier that describes this practice. And even though everyone else in the congregation can see that the pastor has favorites, it is so difficult if not impossible to get some leaders to see this sin in themselves. I have personally tried on more than one occasion and failed and have been told by others that they had failed as well. When the people see this favoritism, it leads to a couple of different responses. One is to join the club. Some people will just get on the bandwagon and do what they see being done. If it's working for that person, why not me? So it can lead someone else into sinful behavior. Since the leader is involved, this will keep some from ever considering that there is something wrong with it. Now this man who is supposed to be a guiding light is guiding someone down the dark road of sin. Few if any will see it that way and you will never be able to convince the others that you are acting out of anything but jealousy and so it continues. However there are those who when confronted with this dynamic fall into a sort of limbo. There is the feeling that something is wrong but because the leader is involved they cannot fathom that he could possibly be guilty of wrongdoing. They languish in a state of confusion and their great respect and trust in the leader prevents them from ever being able to question what is going on. If per chance they were to ask the question they would likely be made to feel foolish because they gained such a wrong perspective from what they observed. This state of limbo keeps that person from growing, maturing as a Christian. But that personal failure to thrive also deprives the church group as a whole. It may as well deprive the pastor access to talent or gift, spiritual or natural, that this confused person now fails to operate in.

Some people will recognize that this behavior is wrong, that it is not biblical. This person can also end up in a state of confusion. This time the dilemma is a bit more complicated. If this behavior is not biblical, then the pastor/leader is wrong. Or there is something wrong with the Bible or their understanding of it. If they decide that the leader is wrong, they will likely lose faith in him. If they are no longer able to trust him, they are likely to eventually leave his congregation and go to another church. However, if the level of trust was very high, if there was great confidence and esteem, if this was developed over a long period with a longstanding relationship, then the loss may be greater. This person may look at this situation from a different perspective. Perhaps it is the Bible that is the problem. Perhaps the things in the Bible are just a collection of stories meant to be a guide for a good life. Something to help provide a moral compass to those interested in travelling life's road with consideration for their fellow man. After all, if this stuff were real, how could any preacher dare live this lie in the face of the God that the Bible talks about? He would have to be crazy or just not really believe it himself. So this person would likely leave the church as well but more likely to avoid all churches as a result.

I think the most insidious potential danger posed by Mr. Butkiss is to the general membership of a church. As mentioned earlier, some perpetrators are not thinking about serving God; they are not thinking about serving the people, and they are certainly not thinking about serving the pastor they are kissing up to. They are only thinking of themselves. They are the most dangerous because they will do whatever is necessary to achieve their goals, and in most cases, the goal centers on money! They will play any game they will play any part they will "play" any individual if it gets them closer to their goal. They know what to say and how to act, and when a pastor is duped by one of these, it's like inviting a wolf into the sheepfold. It may seem hard to believe I'm talking about a preacher, a man of the cloth, the man of God! But believe it or not, it's true. Most of them will probably deny it and a small group may not even recognize it, making the situation sadder. These people are capable of presenting themselves in whatever form a group is most susceptible to much like the serpent in the Garden of Eden. When a leader allows himself to take part in these relationships, it exposes aspects of his character that should automatically disqualify him as a shepherd. He loses his objectivity and his ability to react in an unbiased way because now his decisions are influenced by Mr. Buttkiss rather than what's best for the group. More importantly, he exposes the fact that he is not led by God or even godly principles. While in the pulpit he seems full of the love of God and driven by the power of God, he is actually full of the love of money and the power of the almighty dollar. Perhaps you think I'm being judgmental, some in church leadership may think, "Who do you think you are making these statements?" But it's not who I think I am, but who the Bible says you are if you are Mr. Buttkiss. The principles of the Bible are very clear and no matter what business, financial or even spiritual model you try to present it in, *greed* is *greed*!

A favorite poem of my mother was written by Lois Blanchard Eades and asks the question, "If Jesus came to your house…" I suggest that this poem is not only speaking to us as individuals in our homes but to pastors and church leaders in the business offices and the financial records of their churches. Apportion of the poem says:

> If Jesus came to your house to spend a day
> or two, if He came unexpectedly I wonder what
> you'd do. Oh, I know you'd give your nicest room
> to such and honored Guest, and all the food
> you'd serve to Him would be the very best, And
> you would keep assuring Him you're glad to have
> Him there, that serving Him in your own home
> is joy beyond compare.

But when you saw Him coming could you
meet Him at the door, with arms outstretched in
welcome to your heavenly visitor? Or would you
have to change your close before you let Him in?
Or hide some magazines and put the Bible where
they'd been? Would you turn off the radio and
hope he hadn't heard? And wished you hadn't
uttered that last, loud, hasty word?

Unfortunately, as the poem suggests, most of us would not pass
a spot inspection in our homes. I wonder how many pastors could
stand to have Jesus show up and go through the church's financial
books. But oh, if you believe what you preach (and even if you don't),
he's looking at the books every day!

Satan's Ace

HAVE YOU EVER TRIED to picture what the Garden of Eden must have been like? Maybe you have seen one of the famous artist renderings of this idea. *The Garden of Earthly Delights* is a painting by Hieronymus Bosch of the Netherlands. It is a set (triptych) of three separate paintings attached together the first of which depicts God presenting Eve to Adam. This happened in chapter two of Genesis after the rest of creation had been completed. With Eve being the last thing created, we might look at her as the crowning glory to an astounding series of events as if God saved the best for last. She was truly magnificent in so many wonderful ways. For example, she was the only part of the earthbound creation that did not come from the dust of the ground. She was created form Adam's rib. Seems we've been chasing after that rib ever since.

Yes, men loooooooooove women! (Well, most men anyway.) And why not? What's not to love? It's just a natural attraction sometimes to a fault. Think about the fact that of all the instructions given to Adam, he didn't have to be told what to do with Eve! The one thing a man really doesn't need the directions for (well, many anyway). Let's face it, sex is an "earthly delight" and God intended it to be just that. First Corinthian 7:3, "Husband and wife render due benevolence to one another." Verse 4, "The wife hath not the power over her body but the husband, and vice versa." Ephesians 5:22, "Wives submit to your husbands." Verse 24, "In everything." Hebrews 13:4, "Marriage is honorable...the bed is undefiled." It seems clear to me that scriptures like these are trying to make it very plain that the sexual relationship between a husband and wife is not only sanctioned by God but encouraged. There are those who suggest that sex is only for procreation and if you're not planning to have children you should not get married. These people obviously have no idea what the "Songs of Solomon" are singing about! Here are a few verses and some possible interpretations from David Hubbard's Song of Solomon, Tom Gledhill's the Message of the Song of Songs, and Jodie Dillow's "Solomon of Sex":

- 1:6—"My own vineyard" refers to her body
- 2:3—"Shade," "fruit," and "apple tree" are all ancient erotic symbols; fruit and apples are symbols of male genitals possibly hinting here at an oral caress.
- 2:15—The meaning of the whole verse is: Let us give full expression to our love now while our bodies (vines) are young (tender grapes) before aging (the foxes) takes its toll on our bodies (spoil the vines).
- 4:5—"Thy two breasts" ??????
- 4:10—"The scent of your perfumes" refers to fragrances she naturally produces.
- 4:11—"Your lips drip with honey" speaks of the sweetness of her kisses.
- 4:11—"Honey and milk are under your tongue" points to the depth and fullness of the kissing.
- 4:12—"Garden" refers to her vulva and vagina. When the lover says it is locked up, he is saying it has never been entered; she is a virgin.
- 4:12—"A spring shut up" refers to precious liquid reserved for private use.
- 4:15—"Rivers of water" refer to a picture of the abundant moisture produced by her excitement and anticipation of the long awaited consummation.
- 4:14—"Let my beloved come into his garden." The Hebrew phrase (come into or go into) is used frequently of sexual penetration (Genesis 16:2).
- 5:2—"My head is covered with dew" refers to pre-ejaculation fluid that drips from the lover's penis.

- 6:11—"Garden," "vine," and "pomegranates" all occur most frequently in sections where the man is speaking. He uses them to paint poetic pictures of the woman's erogenous zones.

There is nothing in any of these passages that suggest babies or family, just pleasure. There are commentators who find spiritual explanations for these words, but they are really grabbing at straws. How else can you logically interpret "Thy two breasts"? You don't need a PhD or an understanding of Greek or Hebrew to get the sexual overtone of this book. Sex was meant to be and still is a beautiful and wonderful experience free from guilt and shame. Remember, Adam and Eve were initially naked in the garden the way God made them, uncovered. So, God meant for men and women to enjoy each other's nakedness (in the confines of marriage). It always has been and was always meant to be a pleasurable experience. So how did something given by God come to have such a bad reputation? Satan of course! And of course it started in the Garden of Eden.

Until we ask them, we can only speculate about the natural state of Adam and Eve, but there must have been some level of great intelligence along with a childlike innocence. Adam was intelligent and creative enough to name all of creation but not wise enough to decline Eve's invitation to eat the fruit. Their trust and obedience to God may have been related to the absence of guile in their existence to that point. They may not have been able to conceive the idea that anything spoken to them was anything but true because everything God said had been true. To that point God had only said don't once. When Satan introduced his suggestion this must have been the first time they questioned either God or their own understanding. After eating the fruit, the statement "I was naked; and I hid myself" may represent the tip of the iceberg that was Adam's new awareness. His nakedness may have also represented the uncovering of his innocence naturally, physically, and spiritually. This may have been the very first time that Adam realized, "I have options," and it is this realization that Satan has relied on ever since.

Dr. John Macarthur calls Satan the "Ape" of God. This means that Satan seeks to mimic God and mostly in a mocking, irreverent, or opposite way. For example, the Godhead consists of the holy trinity (Father, Son, Holy Ghost). In the book of Revelation (chapter 12 and 13), we see the unholy trinity (the beast, the Antichrist, and the false prophet). When it comes to sex, Satan's plan is again to encourage sexual activity that is opposite to God's design, will, ideas, word, etc. When it comes to sex, he is pleased with anything that is opposite what the Bible says about sex. If we look at today's society, adultery, fornication (intercourse where at least one of the participants is unmarried), pornography, and homosexuality all seem to be the norm; and these are all things that are promoted by Satan. It seems that these activities, which were once kept behind closed doors because they would be met with disdain and disgust in the open, are now met with nonchalant indifference in the case of adultery and applause and cheers for being courageous in the case of homosexuality. And just as Solomon sang the praises of this God-given pleasure, he also noted, "There is nothing new under the sun." Satan has used sex to cause problems for mankind for a long, long time and the Bible is full of examples. Let's stay with Solomon for a moment.

Solomon has been called by some the wisest man ever to live. He is even found on some current lists of the smartest people in history. This is certainly reflected in his early years as ruler of Israel with the building of the first temple and unification of the northern and southern kingdoms. The Songs of Solomon are thought to be written in his early years as ruler and the Shulamite lover in that probably his first wife. But as time passed, he became more and more focused on material things and less focused on God. By chapter 11 of 1 Kings, we find him with seven hundred wives and three hundred concubines. This means that even if Solomon tried to make love to each of these women at least once a year, he would have to be with 2.7 of them each day. If he just slept with a different one of them each night, it would take 2.7 years to get around to all of them. Many of the wives came from other countries and therefore religious backgrounds. He allowed himself to be caught up into idolatry, which led to his drifting away from God. Samson had a similar problem.

Though he loved only one woman, she was also a foreigner and this led to his demise. This powerful judge who once killed a thousand men all alone fell to the hand of a weak, soft, beautiful woman. The great things he had done and all he was capable of doing came to a screeching halt when she cut his hair, thus breaking the Nazerite vow. While with Solomon and Samson a case can be made for love being at least partially to blame, that is not likely the case for Hophni and Phinehas. These were two sons of the judge and high priest Eli. The priests were always from the tribe of Levi, and as such, Hophni and Phinehas were also priests. But they seemed to put their own twist on the work they did and how they performed their duties. There was a certain portions of the offerings and tithes to the temple that were allowed for the support of the priests. These brothers evidently decided they would take more than the prescribed amount. They also engaged in intercourse with the temple servants (clearly a perk not listed in the job description).

As with Solomon and Samson, we can see how drifting away from God just a little in one small area can often lead to sailing into the deepest unchartered waters of sin and depravity. This might be the case with Lot's daughters. After the destruction of Sodom and Gomorrah, Lot took his two daughters into the mountains as directed instead of a nearby city Zoar. Why the mountains? Zoar apparently was not very far from the "twin cities" and perhaps their influence had already traveled there. Perhaps being in the mountains, he finally took a good look at himself and realized how far he had fallen. Maybe there in the mountains he could find himself and repent, but it seems it was too late for his daughters. It looks like the influence of Sodom and Gomorrah had already had an effect on the sisters. In verse 8, Lot refers to his daughters as if they are virgins. In Genesis 19:30–38, we see Lot's daughters willfully intentionally plotting to have intercourse with him. This does not sound like the actions of a virgin. If he was mistaken about their virginity, the older sister may just have been full of sexual desire and her father was the only option. In verse 31, it sounds like the older sister thinks the world has come to an end and that their father is the last man on earth. We don't know how much time has passed but likely a good amount because verse 33 says, "They made him drink wine," and they didn't have wine when the angels took them from the city. No matter what the reason for the action of the daughters, it sound like the bottom line is that the influence of the city had taken its toll on the girls. Probably the most well-known case of sexual impropriety in scripture is in 2 Samuel 11 with David and Bathsheba. We have in this case not only sexual sin but murder. David embodies the adage "Power corrupts and absolute power corrupts absolutely." Because of one selfish act, David took away Uriah's life and destroyed Uriah's family as well as his own. The repercussions of his decisions in this matter followed him for the rest of his life. And just like Lot, his children were affected too. The emotional pain and destruction of lives that occurred because of David's selfish act plays out all too often in our society today. Adultery, pornography, homosexuality, and sexual abuse are all very prevalent today; and they can all be found in some way tied to many of our churches.

For its ability to influence people to do things that are out of character, sex is probably second only to drugs and alcohol. This seems to be Satan's "ace in the hole." He can count on it to work on some level most of the time even in God's servants as we see from the examples above. And as in the examples from the Old Testament, we have many examples in our society of godly men falling to the temptations of sex. The Catholic Church is still dealing with the aftermath of the multiple sexual improprieties unearthed among the priesthood over the years. Many of the different Protestant denomination have a representative of this unfortunate state of affairs. As noted above, sex is a natural part of our human character. It is not something that has to be learned. Sexual feelings and attractions are in our programming; it's how we are wired. Some of us are wired more or less than others, but it's there in most cases. I can remember having sexual feelings as early as kindergarten though I did not understand what I was feeling. I remember it was pleasant, and I welcomed it whenever it occurred. When it had passed, I could remember how it felt even though it was over. I can remember! I believe it is our ability to remember that helps to make sexual temptation such a formidable and successful weapon for Satan. We can at any given moment access any memory from any time in our lives no matter where we are or what we are doing. At work, at school, at church, or even at prayer, sexual thoughts, pictures, and memories can invade our minds even when we are not trying to bring them up. This is one of the reasons Philippians 4:8 tells us, "Think on these things," that is things that are pure, honest, and virtuous to name a few.

Pornography is a tool that takes advantage of our capacity to remember, and it is one of the things that Satan has used in recent years to win great battles against Bible-based morals and a society with clear ethical views. In March 2016, *Playboy* magazine began its first non-nude monthly publication. This is an amazing turn of events from the magazine that has been the leader in that industry at least in terms of being most well-known. No, they have not developed a new sense of dignity or moral conscience. The fact is that other modes of dispensing pornography along with the more explicit presentations possible elsewhere have cut into its circulation. At its greatest popularity, *Playboy* sold seven million copies per month. Now the monthly circulation is around 800,000. As mentioned before, it's everywhere! And the best thing about that (depending on your point of view), nobody has to know you are looking at it. No bulky magazine, no special hiding place, no worry about being seen going into the adult store. A 2014 survey of Christian men sponsored by a Bible based organization called Proven Men Ministries revealed some alarming statistics. The survey was conducted by Barna Group and used a sample of 388 self-described Christian men. For the age group eighteen to thirty years old,

- 77% looked at pornography at least monthly
- 36% viewed pornography on a daily basis
- 32% admitted to being addicted to porn (another 12% thought they might be)

For middle-aged Christian men ages thirty-one to forty-nine,

- 77% had looked at pornography while at work in the past three months

- 64% viewed pornography at least monthly
- 18% admitted being addicted (another 8% thought they might be)

For married men,

- 55% looked at pornography at least monthly
- 35% had an extra-marital sexual affair while married

According to an article in the *Christian Research Journal*, "Darkening Our Minds: The Problem of Pornography Among Christians":

> During the month of January 2002, 27.5 million internet users visited pornographic web sites.
> Americans spent an estimated $220 million on pornographic web sites in 2001,
> In a national survey polling 1,031 adults, Zogby International and Focus on the Family found that 20 percent of the respondents had recently visited a pornographic website. Over 18 percent of the Zogby/Focus survey men identified themselves as Christian.

Another survey cited:

> Half of all Christian men have some sort of problem with pornography
> 50 percent of men admitted viewing pornography within one week of attending a Promise Keepers event
> 54 percent of pastors admitted viewing pornography in the past year

47 percent of respondents in a 2003 Focus
on the Family poll said pornography was a problem in their home.

As I stated earlier, pornography exploits the memory. Now if
you are lucky and your exposure to porn is accidently finding your
dad's stash or the one time your uncle or a friend shared a book you
are talking about one instance. But with the amazing capacity of
the brain to store and recall not only images but feelings and even
smells, over the years different things can trigger these images and
feelings to jump into consciousness. I remember my first glimpse of
what we called "a girly" magazine. At that time in my preteens the
pictures were mainly women in bikinis with a lot of cleavage and
maybe buttocks here and there. But all these years later I can still
remember those images and of course the more explicit images I have
seen since. Now just imagine the person who deliberately and continually seeks out pornographic material and over and over restocks
the memory banks with fresh images. The ability to recall becomes
boundless. And I believe it is this recall that is the basis for the devastating effect that pornography has on marriages. Let's return to cakes
for an analogy to show what happens. Suppose you grew up with one
dessert in your life. A delicious, rich, moist, buttery, golden pound
cake. No frosting, no glaze, no whipped topping or fruit, just a wonderful pound cake. Every time there was dessert or a special occasion
where a sweet was required, you had that pound cake and you loved
that pound cake. Now suppose an evil grandma who loved to bake
moved in next door and every week she baked a new cake and sent it
to your family—yellow cake with chocolate frosting, coconut cake,
red velvet, German chocolate, pineapple upside down, angel food,
devil's food. Eventually you might find one of those cakes that you
enjoy more than any other and you might wish to have that one
whenever given a choice. Or you might find that you like having all
the different cakes rather than the pound cake and lose all interest in
that old staple.

This is a very crude comparison, but I think it paints a picture
of what happens with exposure to pornography. This is especially

dangerous for the married man as men seem to be especially sensitive to visual stimulation. So now you have access to hundreds even thousands of women (or men) anytime you choose and you will never, ever be turned down. So now all these women of all colors, shapes, and sizes become your wife's competition. She's in a battle, and she doesn't know it. Even if she is a very adventurous wife willing to dress up, role play, and try anything you want, she is still just one woman; and it will be very hard for her to win the competition against all the others. This is probably what happens in many cases of men who are no longer aroused sexually by their wives, but they are aroused by other women. Then they blame it on the wife who maybe is not the same size or has let herself go in some or all ways. But he could still be in love with her, but now he has ruined their intimacy because he has let other women into his mind, not his bed but his mind. This is part of what Christ meant in Matthew 5:28, "But I say unto you, whosoever looketh on a woman to lust after her hath committed adultery with her already in his heart"—heart adultery.

Heart adultery is a very interesting concept. At first glance it seems rather abstract as if this is another metaphor used by our Lord. But if we pay close attention to what is meant in the following verses (1 Cor. 7:3–4, Eph. 5:22–24, Heb. 13:4), we come away with an understanding that the husband no longer has ownership or control over his body, it belongs to his wife (and vice versa). This is not in a malicious or dominating way but in a loving, submissive way. With an attitude that desires to please the partner in every way, shape, and form. Every part of one partner's body becomes the property of the other. When it comes to sex, that includes the brain or more precisely your thoughts. So your sexual thoughts belong to your spouse. Dreams about sex should be about the spouse. Fantasies should be about the spouse. Whenever you become aroused, it should be because of the spouse. If any of those areas are given to someone else, that is heart adultery. Keeping all these areas focused on your partner may seem like an impossible task to some and as with all shortcomings I'm sure Christ understands. But I think he lets us know the high standard he places on the marital relationship and how far we are from meeting his expectations. Ephesians 5:23 says,

"For the husband is the head of the wife even as Christ is the head of the church: and He is the savior of the body." Many times when this verse is addressed, the focus is on leadership and the role of the husband as the one in charge. But as the theme of this book points out, many concepts are lost when we fail to read the entire passage. Reading further, Ephesians 5:25 says, "Husbands love your wives, even as Christ also loved the church, and gave himself for it." If we are to act in accordance to this scripture, our wives should be treated in such a way that our every waking moment as husbands would be split between "How can I please God?" and "How can I please my wife?" We should be willing as Christ was for the church to sacrifice anything for her happiness. I am not suggesting that we drain the family bank account to buy her unnecessary gifts. Remember we are pleasing God first and he desires that we be good stewards with our money. Also if you have a wife who would be pleased with you making such a move, you have a bigger problem than pleasing her and you really need to seek God's guidance. But Ephesians says love wives as Christ loved the church and gave himself for it. The entire three years of Christ's ministry was spent working toward the redemption of the church. Everything he did was for the benefit of the church and he ultimately laid down his life for it. I think Ephesians is saying that in our capacity as husbands we should always be focused on what we can do to benefit our wives and our relationship to the point that we sacrifice in the sense that we no longer think of ourselves first. Surrendering, sacrificing even our thought life to be possessed by our spouse seems to be in line with these scriptures and can decrease and perhaps eventually prevent heart adultery. I know, some men will say, "Well, my wife doesn't deserve to be treated that way and when she acts better or treats me better, I'll treat her better." But remember if you are in sincere service to God, your job is first to please him and that means obey his word, which means please your wife. I think one of the saddest situations to witness is a church leader or pastor who regularly and publicly speaks sharply or harshly to his wife. So pornography can lead to heart adultery, and if left unchecked, that can lead to the real thing.

With adultery being such a big *don't* in the Bible, how does it become such a big *do* among clergy? I once asked a brother how he could continue to fall to sex over and over, and he answered, "I guess I don't try hard enough." I realize now he just didn't get it. I think a lot of clergy just don't get it. I think the most important reason for falling is failure to "practice what you preach." I think many times they just fail to do what the word says, put on the whole armor of God, let this mind be in you that is in Christ, whatsoever is true, etc....think on these things, flee fornication, abhor that which is evil, cleave to that which is good. Most of the above portions of scripture are familiar to the average churchgoing Christian and certainly to the clergy. But they are just that, portions. When the entire passage they belong to is not as familiar, then the power and meaning of that passage is lost. We are taught in Pentecostal circles to speak the word of God against Satan as Christ did when he was tempted in the wilderness. But Christ spoke those words not only as the Son of God but as one who had full understanding of what was being said. Those words spoken by Christ were not just verbalizations of language. They were verbalizations of concepts and principles that were a part of who Christ is. It would not have been enough for Christ to say the words, if he didn't fully and truly understand their meaning and also believe what he was saying. The power of those words were active in his life on a daily basis. And remember, these were God's words!

Think about it! God's words! The very God who said, "Let there be light," and there was light; who said, "Let the waters under the heavens be gathered together unto one place and let the dry land appear: and it was so"; who said, "Let the earth bring forth grass, and herb yielding seed, and the fruit tree yielding fruit after his kind, whose seed is in itself, upon the earth: and it was so." All this and all of creation was done with his words. Now he has given us his words that in most cases we use haphazardly and in worse-case scenarios not at all. Because many if not most Pentecostal/charismatic clergy tend to preach using one or two verses they often miss the true meaning and power of passages and probably that which is most important. This type of preaching is usually "topical" preaching, that is to use a scripture to support the idea or topic of the speaker (eisogesis).

While there is no guarantee that this style will lead to confused or inaccurate teaching, the chances are very high. So if this method is used in preaching odds are this method is used in studying. It is very unlikely that a person can use inefficient or incorrect study methods and come to correct conclusions. Therefore with a flawed method of studying the word leading to flawed understanding of the word, it is understandable that there would be a lot of flawed application of the word to their lives. As was said before, if you don't use the recipe correctly, the cake is not going to come out the way you expect it to. For us to have such a powerful tool at our disposal and be inept in its use is really tragic especially in the present climate of apathy and apostasy. We spend so much time focused on feelings, but we don't "feel" the need to devote time to truly understand God's word. I would never be so bold as to suggest that I have the complete answer to the problem of infidelity among the clergy, but I am quite sure that the failure to understand the word and the subsequent inability to accurately and efficiently apply it in to their own lives has to be a part of the puzzle.

I dare not leave this subject without talking about a couple of the victims. The recent scandal involving Bill Cosby paints a clear picture of one aspect of the victim's suffering. For decades, these women nursed a wound that could not heal, these emotional wounds remain open because the situation was never dealt with. Not even an apology. You might say, "But the Cosby cases are technically rape, that's not the same as a preacher having a consensual affair." Well, in a way it is. Make no mistake here, in many cases the women are the pursuer, but even if a woman consents to the relationship, a rape occurs. She is raped of the perception of the preacher being that righteous hand of God on earth. She no longer has the confidence that the man of God is the honest, trustworthy shepherd we expect in the pulpit. There will always be that doubt for her with other clergy who will have to go a little further to prove themselves. But what about the woman who's pursued by clergy without her encouragement? She suffers with a bigger can of worms. The first woman who is as interested in the clergyman as he is with her recognizes her own guilt in the situation and whatever happens as a result of the affair, she is at least a contributing partner. Not so with the second woman. She didn't ask for this attention, she did not ask to be put into this situation, and now she has several issues to deal with and all on her own.

(1) What should she do? Should she tell someone that this clergyman, possibly the pastor, has made or is making inappropriate advances toward her?

The Bible is very clear about actions to be taken in cases of sinful activity among the brotherhood and this applies to the clergy (pastors included). Galatians 6:1 and Matthew 18:15–20 direct us to confront the person about the sin (lovingly) encouraging them to repent of the sin. Matthew outlines further the steps to be taken if the person denies or refuses to repent including expulsion from the church.

(2) If so, who does she tell? This is one of the most difficult things to decide and of course should be driven by the Holy Spirit's guidance. If the guilty party is not the pastor, he should probably be the one to confide in. If it is the pastor things become more complicated. Do you tell his wife, another clergyman, a close friend? As before the choice should be guided by the Holy Spirit but someone should be brought in as a witness if he denies or refuses to repent.

(3) If she decides to tell someone, will they believe her? This is probably the driving force of all her action in this situation. As with the Cosby case, many of the women when asked why they hadn't come forward before now, replied, "He's Bill Cosby, who will believe me?" As this is the case in the secular world, this effect is magnified greatly in the church world because clergy especially the pastor are shown great respect and reverence. Little Miss Nobody seldom feels anyone would take her side against a man who most likely has been in service for many years and has a great reputation with his people. If she gets the courage to say something, she will likely ruin her own reputation as well. For everyone that believes her there will probably be two that don't. Her name will be dragged through the mud, and she will be treated as a harlot or a home wrecker and will probably end up leaving a church that she may have great love for and a great desire to stay in.

(4) Who else will be hurt? As this innocent young woman con-
templates doing something that may change her life forever, she has
to consider that other lives will be affected as well. What about his
wife and children, how will they take it and what will be their reaction? Will they turn on him causing the family to be torn apart, or
will they support him and come to his rescue turning instead on the
young woman? What about other church members? These are people
who have likely developed a loving and trusting relationship with this
man, a man they have served, supported, and sacrificed for. In many
cases, they have submitted to being treated like children and endured
embarrassed in public out of obedience and respect for this man and
who he represents. There might have been times when against their
better judgment, they followed his direction and leadership and were
not comfortable or happy as a result, but they trusted him they had
faith in him and his God. Most will likely lose faith in him but some
will also lose faith in God.

Let's call the innocent woman along with the wife and children
of the accused primary victims because their lives will be changed
outside the walls of the church. This scandal will follow them in
some way, shape, or form most of if not the rest of their lives. It
will influence family interpersonal relationships as well as mental
and emotional attitudes, not to mention the blow taken by their
faith in God. Let's call the church members secondary victims. They
are secondary because outside of the church their lives are generally
unchanged. One reaction by members is to believe the scandal react
with anger and disgust then to leave the church. This may be one
who will not be associated with a leader like this for righteousness
sake or it may be someone who is just not able to forgive for that
offense. Another reaction is to believe the scandal and forgive but
expect some sort of punishment be enacted. Both are understandable, but the second is more what the Bible teaches. Another is to
deny, deny, deny that the pastor could do such a thing; and if he
did, the woman lured, tempted, seduced, or raped him. This is the
kind of reaction that keeps the sinner from recognizing the issue here
and that maybe there is a deeper problem to be dealt with. The most
dangerous reaction is the person who wants to pretend that it never

happened. Of course, this is totally understandable but is also very detrimental on a couple of levels.

Of course the Bible calls for repentance from sin, but when the clergy fall short of God's glory, usually we want to keep it as quiet as possible, brush it under the rug, describe it in words that are soft, loving, and tender and let the man get back to the pulpit and do the work God called him to do. This is not so bad for the first offender, or is it? Speaking of preachers/leaders caught in sin, 1 Timothy 5:20 says, "Rebuke them openly that others might fear." A rebuke in these cases could come in many forms. The guilty party might be removed from his position temporarily or permanently depending on the offense or the number of offenses that have occurred. In my opinion if clergy, he should be removed from the pulpit for a time and not allowed to function in that capacity during the prescribed time. I find it amazing that someone guilty of sin would have the guts to stand in God's holy place knowing what they have done. But I guess that speaks to how insincere some people are about ministry or that the ministry is just a game to so many. The higher the office or position held by the offender, the longer the time of sanction should be just like a prison term correlates with the crime. A rebuke should be obvious. It should stick out like a black eye and everyone should know exactly where that black eye came from. If some who have become repeat offenders had been rebuked as the Bible directs, perhaps they would not have committed a second or third or more sins.

Then there are those "mega church" leaders who answer to no one. They are independent of any organization and therefore have no leadership above them. When they fall, it's as if a judge committed murder and then presided over his own trial. They make the decision about their situation, they decide if they will speak on it and when as well as what the ultimate punishment will be (usually none). There have been a few that at least tried to appear repentant most notably Jimmy Swaggart. Most others just denied the allegations and/or made them quietly go away somehow. In these cases, rebuke will not happen. Most of these guys don't have the humility it requires to have someone in the church act in the capacity of judge but that is exactly what the Bible says. Matthew 18:19–20 teaches where two or three touch and agree…ask and it shall be done. This verse is often quoted as relating to prayer meetings or particular prayer requests as stated before. But this is talking about church discipline. In verse 19, Jesus says, "Again I say…two or three again," indicating his saying it before and that is in verse 16, "But if he will not hear thee, then take with thee 2 or 3 more," and these two or three are witnesses to the conversation about the sin in question. So we see again that the Bible has given us clear instructions about many very important issues but we fail to follow them partly out of ignorance. When we fail to understand that the two or three gathered is not talking about prayer we miss that we are being told to pursue and handle these cases with conviction and purpose. They are not to be spirited away as if nothing has happened and hope that people will just forget about it.

As I said earlier, some people just refuse to believe a beloved leader/pastor would be capable of such improprieties. This attitude is often encouraged by the silence of the accused. By not saying anything, he gives the appearance of one that is being falsely accused and unfairly treated. With certain subtle remarks, he can even come across as the victim yet he won't even fight to defend himself. That is one of the reasons it's so important to admit our offense of another and in a case where it is a public infraction it keeps the innocent from bearing undue burden. This is another reason that open rebuke is important; it brings the facts to the forefront and clears any doubt about blame. Because of the love that some have for their leaders even when it is clear that he is guilty, the loyal followers often exhibit another pattern. They don't want to talk about it. Any conversation in this area is dissuaded under the guise of "forgive and forget" or "digging up old dirt." This is also a problem for victims of abuse who are counseled by those with this method of dealing with emotional issues. The guilty will often hide behind forgiveness. In a case where the wife is a primary victim, she may also hide behind forgiveness to avoid her own pain. Forgiveness is used to squelch guilt and embarrassment, pain and disappointment. But because there is so much love or some other need to hold on to the relationship, it is easier to let go of the crime than to let go of the criminal.

For example look at a wife who has a guilty husband. On the one hand she recognizes his wrongdoing but on the other she loves him dearly and wants to protect him. Even if she realizes she may be hurting herself, she can't help supporting him out of love. So in the name of "love," she stops talking about it, and she won't tolerate anyone else talking about it. She uses the idea of Christian love as a reason that others should not talk about it. As people stopped talking about it, the assumption of healing is made, and the Holy Spirit has healed the wounded heart. The love of Christ has renewed a right spirit. The problem with this line of thinking is that it ignores Matthew 5:23–24, which teaches the law of reconciliation. It says that if I have wronged my brother or sister that I have no communion with God until I go back to the person I've wronged and ask forgiveness. And we are not talking about a quick unfeeling "sorry." It should be totally sincere and should be recognized as such by the victim. Let's face it, when it comes to apologizing, people can usually tell when we are sincere and when we are not. I have been in the position of begging forgiveness, so I know it is a hard thing to do. And even though I have asked I still have not been able to forgive myself for the damage that came at my hand. I am pummeled by it regularly and will be for the rest of my life. And some victims may not forgive right away or ever and to be honest there are things that are humanly unforgivable. But that is another problem because God wants us to forgive. But that is also where the Holy Spirit comes in, to help us with these unforgivable deeds. Nevertheless, the victim is owed that apology and request to be forgiven. So, it is not therapeutic and it is not Holy or righteous, for a victim to be encouraged toward silence if that victim wants, needs to talk about it. Because people are silent about it, because they seem to be okay does not mean they have gotten past it. It does not mean they are healed. In this example, this wife is acting as an enabler of her husband. By failing to require some sort of recompense, she leaves the husband with the feeling he's gotten away with it. Even though he has sinned and been found out, the results were not so bad. In the supposed name of Christian love and forgiveness, people are often convinced to keep silent; but in doing so, it may keep the victim from healing, especially if there has been no request for forgiveness from the perp. This failure to rebuke openly is probably one of the reasons there are so many repeat offences in the sexual sins. The inherent power that sex exerts on our nature along with a failure to react to this sin in the way the Bible directs is a recipe for "Let's do it again."

Victims who can't let go are often painted as being "weak, hateful, holding a grudge, won't let it die." They are painted as being of or influenced by a demonic force. They are seen as having a spirit of division or confusion instead of crying out for healing, understanding, and reconciliation. The truth of the matter is that Christians who fail to recognize the needs of the victim in these situations are probably more likely the one that is demon influenced. Satan is always very happy when we get something wrong whether intentional or not. Demonic forces are likely the driving force behind the perpetuation of these misdirected feelings and attitudes. Because we fail in so many cases to look directly to the Bible for our guidance and course of action in these things, we end up wandering down the road of "I think this and I feel like that." Unfortunately, God's will is never based on our feelings and neither should our theology. Many times religious judgments are made that are based not on scripture and a clear understanding of it but on what we feel or believe.

One biblical principle that cannot be misunderstood is that "God is love," and he wants us to treat each other with love. When a woman (or a man) is victimized by a church leader, sometimes they are totally innocent and need to have someone put their arms around them and support them instead of dragging them through the mud. When a fallen member of the clergy does not have the guts to stand up and take his or her licks, does the innocent have to suffer a second humiliation? Not if we would follow God's book and his direction for handling such things. But in many cases those in authority have so many skeletons in their own closets they fear retaliation if they were to "do the right thing."

Preachers who fall into sexual sin do a lot of damage to a lot of people in a lot of different ways. Oddly enough, it is not single preachers that are the biggest problem in this area but those that are married. Statistically, there are just about as many divorces among

Christians as there are in the secular world. That seems amazing when you think about it! Christians are God's people. God made man and woman and God instituted marriage. God gave a recipe for how relationships in general and marriage in particular is to work. You would think that the man of God being so close to God, knowing the most about God and being guided by God would have the best marriages in the world. And in some cases that is true. I know retired Pastor Barkins and his wife who seem to have one of those special marriages. They have always seemed to be very much in love publically and those closest to them seem to say the same thing about their private lives. But for every set of Barkinses there are two or three that you would not know were married if it weren't mentioned publically. As I grew up and began to notice all the older couples that did not really seem very happy it was a real puzzle. As I understood more about what the Bible says about marriage, I became even more puzzled. Here were two people who love God and are living their lives for him. They say they love him and would do anything to please him. They say they love each other or did at one point. Why can't two God-loving, God-fearing people be happy together? Yeah, the Barkinses seem to have the recipe. But there goes that word *recipe* again. Unfortunately, that's a big part of the problem, not that there is a recipe but that usually we don't follow it.

Like so many of the things I have mentioned, marriage is very important to God and this is made crystal clear in the Bible. But as I've pointed out in many areas, we just don't seem to follow the recipe God gave us. And as before, it happens because we fail to fully understand the word because we fail to read in context and fail to read entire passages. I have often been in discussions concerning man being the head of the household or heard preaching that portrays this point. This premise is from Ephesians 5:23, "The husband is the head of the wife," and most who use it focus on the power issue here. They will then reference an instance in the Bible that seems to support it, as when Sarah called Abraham lord (Gen. 18:12). But of course this does not strike a pleasing note for most women. Who knows a woman in this day that would willingly call their husband lord? (I think I know just one) but thus the debate begins. The man is seeking to be honored and respected and points out that this is what the Bible directs women to do. The women wanting to be loved say that if he would treat me in a certain way I wouldn't mind calling him lord. I think one of the saddest things to see happen in a church is for a godly man to treat his wife like an old bar of soap or a woman to treat her husband like a child. This does happen all too often and anyone reading this can probably think of at least one example in each category.

Ephesians 5:22–33 paints a clear picture of what the godly marriage should be like. Amazingly each partner is directed to give the other exactly what they want and need most. That is to say, every man wants one thing more than anything else in a relationship (not sex). Women want something different but they also want it more than anything else in the relationship. It's amazing because you don't usually find couples bending over backwards trying to please one another. Frankly it's quite the opposite, most of the time it seems couples are trying to "one up" each other each trying to stay one step ahead of the other. In that Ephesians passage, wives are told to "submit" to their husbands but husbands are told to "love" their wives. While growing up and reading this passage, it was always puzzling. Paul is teaching about the marriage relationship, two people coming together in an equal partnership to spend the rest of their lives together. If it is an equal partnership, why aren't the two partners given equal directions, the same directions? Why not wives submit to your husbands and husbands submit to your wives? Or wives love your husbands and husbands love your wives? Why different instructions? The reason was beautifully explained in a book by Dr. Emerson Eggerich called *Love and Respect*. In it Dr. Eggerich explains the reason for the different ingredients in God's recipe. He explains that men and women need different things. The Greek word for submit in Ephesians 5:22 speaking to wives is "hupatasso" and means to obey, to be subject to, to be subordinate. Dr. Eggrich described this as respect but not just any old respect, unconditional respect. Likewise in verse 25 when he tells husbands to love their wives he's talking about unconditional love. Unconditional love is not a difficult idea to embrace after all doesn't everyone want that? The point is that this is the "most" important thing for most women. They want to be loved for themselves not for their beauty or because they are sexy. They want to be loved the same way before and after the baby fat. They want us to love them the way they love us with bald heads and beer bellies, unable to bend over to put your own shoes on. They love the Homer Simpsons and the Archie Bunkers and they love them with all their heart and without reservation. This is an easy enough concept to understand. Unconditional respect however is a little harder to grasp because we are used to the idea that respect is earned. Only certain people in certain circles or positions seem to garner automatic respect, i.e., religious leaders (the pope, church bishops). Even the highest office in our nation has lost the automatic respect it used to command. How many times have you heard the media refer to the former president as "Obama" or "Bush." It is very difficult to show respect when you do not feel respectful toward someone. It is hard to show love when you do not feel loving. But there are two points to remember here. First, this is a command through the mouth of Paul but from the mouth of God. This is a directive not a suggestion and not something we get to choose how to enact. The second point is that both these words are actions in this passage not feelings. Like Nike says, "Just Do It," we are told in this scripture to do something and that something is not based on whether the people deserve it or if we feel like doing it at the time. Just do it!

Of the two directives I think the wife has the more difficult task. Taking the meaning of the Greek *hupatasso* as "being subject to," this by definition is to be under someone's control or jurisdiction. That is to, in some way and on some level, relinquish your independence to another. In a very real way, a woman is directed to allow herself to be subordinate to her husband. This is not suggesting that a woman become a puppet or that she doesn't think for herself or doesn't have good ideas. She may actually be more intelligent than her husband and more talented in many ways but he should always feel like "The King of the Castle." When asked, his children should respond with "Dad is the boss." I should add here that we are talking about the man being the head or leader primarily in spiritual things. "As Christ is the head of the church." Even when he is not working, when the wife is providing for the family, he should always be lifted up as the leader of the household. Of course, I'm talking here about a father/husband who has lost a job not one who has never had a job. Treating a man this way may seem silly or unreasonable to some. Why shouldn't the wife take credit for her provision in this case, shouldn't she be proud that she was able to hold things together on her own? These are all valid points and sure there is a sense of pride that should exist for a woman in that situation. But there is a bigger picture to have our eyes on, God's design! We should be following his pattern, his design.

There are aspects of being a husband and father that supersede his ability to supply for the family. I am in no way diminishing the importance of a man being a provider but a good man is not less a man because he has less money. Things like love, support, protection, encouragement, and of course a heart for God are all priceless commodities. The effect of these intangibles cannot be measured quantitatively but the difference is very obvious in homes with a stable male head of household. I am not suggesting that any man is better than no man. But it is very, very difficult for a woman to teach a boy how to be a man. Without a father in her life, it is very difficult to influence a girl toward the kind of man she should be interested in. With a real dad in the home, she can see what a real man looks like. It is easy for a boy to become a man when he sees a man who acts like a man get treated like a man. I admit this is not always true. There are some men that are better for their children when they live on another continent. But mostly dads are a positive not a negative despite what some psychologists are saying. This is all inherent in God's design. There is a different character to a home when there is a strong positive husband/father in the picture.

The idea of the husband as "King of the Castle" does not mean that he is a harsh ruler that reigns with an iron fist. It should be more like Christ's description of himself as a shepherd, loving, caring, and sacrificing. He should be revered as a king but should not act like a king. As I suggested, I think loving is the easier of the two directives. It seems a lot easier to treat someone with love even if there is no love than to give respect to someone who really doesn't deserve it. That's why it's so easy for guys to take advantage of women. They treat them with love in actions and words until they get what they want whether that is sex or money or whatever else. Showing love can give you a good feeling even if it's not genuine so in this case it can be a win-win for the giver. You would think the love directive given in Ephesians 5:22 is romantic love since it is between a husband and wife but that is not the case. The word used for love there is *agapao* and does not relate to Eros or sexual love at all. *Agapao* means to love in a moral or social sense, and if you notice, it looks a lot like agape and in fact it comes from that very word. Agape is godly love, pure selfless sacrificial and unconditional love. This is not a love that takes advantage. It is not a love that abuses or speaks harshly or embarrasses or ridicules or belittles or betrays. It is as Christ loved the church (agape love) that men are to love their wives. So it is Eros that would drive a man to say sweet nothings into one ear and goodbye into the other. It is Eros on some level that draws most of us into relationships. It is Eros that fuels the fire of romantic love and the ringing of wedding bells. But is also Eros that leads to the decline of most if not all relationships in some way, shape, or form. How then could I possibly say that of the two directives love is the easier because agape love can only be accomplished with Christ.

So this problem is the same as all the other topics we have touched on. Because the "recipe" is not being followed, most marriages problems can be traced back to this. We don't read entire passages so we miss the context. We focus on one verse so the meat of the word is never taken in not to mention digested. But again this is a problem that the clergy must take much of the responsibility for. In most cases, there is premarital counseling done by the minister who performs the ceremony. It is in these sessions that these things should be addressed. But I have found that most cases where there is counseling it is woefully inadequate in terms of time spent, the material or areas covered are off the mark and if the minister has a rotten marriage himself what possible good could he be to anyone else?

So like everything else we have covered, the clergy take another hit for poor preparation, information, and presentation. But how on earth do we ever get them to listen?

Prophets for Profit

WE ARE LIVING IN a tumultuous time in American as well as world history. Civil Rights have taken on new meaning with the LGBT community in the forefront. America, a country that was founded on Christian ethics, is fast becoming a humanist or existential nation with Christians in the category of aliens or minorities. Economic unrest and uncertainty in different countries is having a ripple effect in the US and other major financial markets. Just as our economy seems to be recovering from 2008 the European Union experiences discord. Tragic natural disasters like tsunamis, earthquakes, and sink-holes are becoming commonplace. Gun violence is no longer an inner city phenomenon and we thought the Taliban was bad, enter ISIS. People are afraid. They are looking for answers to many important questions and help to find a way out. Government can't help because it's run by politicians. Politicians can't help because their focus is their party and not their people. We have more millionaires in the US than any country in the world, seven times our nearest competitor but people are hungry right here in America. To live comfortably, most households require two incomes and very few people have adequate savings to carry them through a financial emergency. People are hop-ing, praying for some financial windfall like the lottery in which the US posted its first billion-dollar-plus jackpot in 2016. Everyone would like a piece of the pie and one group has found an ingenious if not insidious way to get their cut, the modern-day prophet.

Of all the areas I have broached in this book, this is the one for which I have the most disdain. In most of the other areas the argu-ment can be made for innocence and the "I didn't know" defense.

And there are instances where some level of ignorance can be the crutch to lean on in this case as well. But for the most part I think (based upon scripture) that most of these guys are primarily "con artists." Again, this is not meant to be disrespectful, but it is simply lining up what I have been exposed to with what the Bible says about prophecy and the two just don't mesh. These men make the circuit to cities across the country year after year in revival and crusades and they draw large crowds who gather not so much to hear God's word but to see and hear the prophetic work that is advertised. People flock to these meetings out of their need and desperation hoping that the Man of God speaks a word of prophecy into their lives. Some are seeking financial blessing, some physical healing, others mental or emotional. Some are present for themselves and others for a loved one. But all are reaching, seeking, hoping, and praying that tonight is their night, the night the prophet will "speak a word" into their lives. They come by the hundreds all denominations all races all colors. After an exhilarating praise period, the prophet goes to the word of God and preaches. After the sermon, it's time for the main event. There are a couple of methods used at this point. Some prophets will look the crowd over, choose selected individuals and begin to prophesy to the person selected. Another will publicly announce particular information about an individual appearing not to know their name just this information that identifies them specifically, like an address or a phone number or that they have a particular document on them or that they recently saw a doctor about a particular part of the body or illness. Another method is to simply ask anyone who wishes to step into the aisle forming a line and come forward to the prophet who then "ministers" individually to all.

Prophesies can cover any number of categories from totally material to totally spiritual. One person might be told they are going to get a new car, another, a new home, another healing from illness, someone else a promotion at work, still another a deeper relationship with God, yet another an elevation in ministry. The feeling in the room is like everyone is waiting for a baby to be born or while opening a gift on Christmas morning. The anticipation of who will be called can be seen on every face in the room. Everyone is disappointed when they are not chosen but immediate anticipation swells as the next selection is made. Everyone wants to be the next contestant, uh participant. There is a catch, however, one thing we can't forget, all these prophesies, all these blessings, all these wonderful proclamations have to be purchased. Not by love or prayer or fasting but by cold, hard cash. You see, the word from these prophets, the great blessing everyone hopes to hear requires an offering. No money, no blessing, no prophesy, no miracle. They don't actually say that but that's what it boils down to. Here's how it works.

Once all the prophecies are issued, it's time to raise the offering. The first problem is that it is normally outside procedural etiquette for a speaker to raise his own offering. They get around this however by making it sound as if the offering is to benefit the ministry of the host church when in most if not all cases the prophet is getting a large cut of all the money raised during his visit. This is much like the procedure for the presentation of a rock concert or some other theatrical event where the performer gets "a percentage of the gate." So it benefits him to raise as much money as possible every night. He does whatever he can each night to ensure the gate uh crowd will be larger the following night. A frequent tactic is that each night a specific dollar amount is requested. The amount often seems to be an unrounded figure like $37.35 not always but quite frequently and usually the amount gets larger each night. Not only does this practice smell similar to running some sort of numbers game but it actually contradicts what 2 Corinthians 9:7 says about giving, "Every man according as he purposeth in his heart, so let him give: not grudgingly or of necessity for God loveth a cheerful giver." So in doing this, these prophets of God, supposedly called by God and sharing a prophetic word that is supposedly coming from God is not obedient to God's written word. Intuitively, many people probably recognize this fact but we fall for it from several levels. Firstly this is a prophet, a man with a special relationship with God and likely has God's permission to breach the 2 Corinthian verse, and they do make it sound like God has sanctioned the amount. Secondly, everyone else is doing it so it can't be wrong, especially if the pastor and all the clergy are involved. And ultimately, I want to be blessed like everyone else.

The prophet insinuates that receiving the fulfillment of the prophecy is based on the recipient's faith and that faith is demonstrated by giving the requested amount. Often the persons receiving the prophecy will be directed to get into the offering line first stressing the vital importance of their participation to the point that if someone does not have the requested amount they are directed to borrow it from someone or to pledge it or to write a post-dated check. I have even seen two people who did not have the money told to gather the amount between them. Those who did not receive a prophetic word are encouraged to participate in the offering with the designated amount pointing out that anyone who participates will be blessed uniquely. The money is always the most important thing with these guys. But then, money is important! As noted earlier, it is the importance of money and the lack thereof that makes this operation successful. I admit that I have fallen for this game like so many others believing, trusting, hoping this man was what he said he was and had the promise of God as he claimed. But there was nothing! No miracle, no blessing, no change in any area of my life that could be a result of the words of this "prophet." But how did I let myself get caught out there, I'm intelligent, educated, there must be something more, a hook that I was caught on like a big mouth bass but what? That hook or ploy used by most people seeking to raise money especially these guys is "seed faith."

Seed faith is a phrase or concept first used by Oral Roberts in the 1970s. Because of public response, it has flourished and is very alive today and is the source of the multimillion dollar success of so many televangelists currently on our airways. This is the method that many of these prophets use in extracting funds from their pigeon uh participants. The idea is that the money requested by the prophet is a seed, giving it to him is sowing and when your request is granted that is reaping the harvest. It all sounds very biblical, right? And actually there are several scriptures that seem to support this scheme:

- Genesis 8:22, "While the earth remaineth seedtime and harvest...shall not cease."

- Matthew 17:20, "If you have faith as a grain of mustard seed you shall say unto this mountain remove hence to yonder place and it shall remove, and nothing shall be impossible unto you.
- Luke 6:38, "Give and it shall be given unto you good measure, pressed down and shaken together, running over shall men give into your bosom. For with the same measure that you mete withal it shall be measured to you again."
- Matthew 13, Mark 4, Luke 8—The Parable of the Sower
- Proverbs 11:25, "The liberal soul shall be made fat and he that watereth shall be watered also himself."
- 2 Corinthians 9:6, "But this I say, he that soweth sparingly shall reap sparingly and he which Soweth bountifully shall reap also bountifully."

Of course these scriptures are in no way suggesting, encouraging, or supporting the seed faith sham. They are simply fiery darts used to bring a pretense of legitimacy to this game, but they are all either misquoted or taken out of context. The Genesis scripture as seen above is missing "and cold and heat and summer and winter and day and night." In Genesis 8:15–22, Noah and his family are leaving the Ark after the flood. In verse 21, God promises never to "curse" the land again for man's sake (or because of man). That is, the earth would never again suffer for man's sin and as long as the earth exists there would always be the changing of the seasons and all the related cycles including seedtime and harvest. Reading the scripture to support seed faith means there is either a purposeful misrepresentation of the scripture or someone's reading comprehension is somewhere in the first or second grade level. Matthew 17:20 is probably the most well known of these scriptures because of its frequent use referencing faith in a general sense. But this verse is a metaphor and not meant to be taken literally at all and certainly not for support of seed faith. As real as it is, faith is an intangible commodity. As he did with most other metaphors, Christ is using the qualities of a tangible mustard seed to bring understanding to the concept of intangible faith. There was no need to elaborate on the seed's qualities (very small size of the seed growing to a very large plant or tree) because the people he was talking to would have been well acquainted with them. He was not suggesting that with the right amount or kind of faith any of us would be able to cause Mt. Everest to go sailing through the sky and be dropped into the Pacific. It was a proportionality comparison Christ was making. The very tiny mustard seed relative to the very large mountain they were near. In verse 20 Christ charged the disciples with unbelief and in verse 17 he called them faithless and perverse. We know the disciples had some faith or they would not have been there with Jesus in the first place. So why did Jesus call them faithless? It probably reflects the idea that the amount of faith they did have was so small as to be almost nonexistent. Note that Christ said "If you have faith as a grain of mustard seed" suggesting that the disciples lacked even that small amount. He was talking about personal mountains, emotional, spiritual, relational, and even financial. I'm not denying the ability of faith to influence the physical realm, but this scripture is misunderstood if taken literally and is not meant to support seed faith. The Parable of the Sower found in Matthew 13, Mark 4, and Luke 8 is another scripture used to support the seed faith idea. A parable is again a tool used to convey better understanding of something Christ was talking about and seems to be one of his favorite methods. This parable is talking about the sowing or sharing of the gospel and the different ways people will respond to it. Word sown by the wayside and eaten by fowl is those who heard the gospel but were tricked by Satan did not understand and rejected the word. That sown on stony ground those who believed but did not allow the word to take root in their heart and later fell away. That sown into good ground represents those who allowed the word to germinate, grow, and ultimately produced fruit or changed lives. The only thing even remotely related to the phrase seed faith is the word sower.

Unlike the other scriptures noted 2 Corinthians 9:6–15 is actually talking about giving but that's the end of the correlation. This scripture is dealing with the condition of our hearts when giving. Verse 7 of this passage gives us "God loveth a cheerful giver," which is a concept that is greatly exploited in church services. A recent trend has the congregations cheering and clapping with joy as if rooting for a favorite sports team when an offering is "taken." One problem with this is that loud noise does not ensure there is true joy in our hearts when giving. Another is the idea that when giving in or to a church we are giving to God. That may seem intuitive at first but consider this, what does God need with your money? We always hear, "Let's bless God with an offering," but really how does the offering bless God?

Jesus answered this question in his conversation with the rich young ruler in Matt. 19:16-22 (Mk. 10:17-27). This young man came to Christ asking what "good thing" he could do to have eternal life. His great wealth was of course known by the Savior and he immediately went to the "heart" of the matter. After telling him to keep the commandments and then listing a few the young man reported he was already doing these. Jesus then hit him where it hurts. The young man was told to sell all his possessions, give to the poor and then follow Christ. The young man walked away dejected because he was not able to give up his riches. Two important issues here. 1- The condition of our heart is always of the utmost importance to our relationship with God. The Father wants to be the most important thing in our lives, number one, numero uno! More important than mom, dad, wife, kids, job and money. It is apparent that though the young man was keeping the commandments it wasn't being done from a heart that was sincere and dedicated to the God of the commandments. Being a cheerful giver doesn't mean we whistle and cheer when it's time to give an offering in church. It means our love for Christ leads to love for our neighbors and strangers and leads us to look for opportunities to give to those in need as we encounter them in our daily lives. It may lead us to even sacrifice something that we truly need in order to help someone else in need. 2-Notice that Christ told the young man to give to the poor! Not to the synagogue, not to the Temple and certainly not to him. He was directed to help the less fortunate which until recent years was one of the primary functions of the church. In fact, that is why churches are not taxed by the government. Historically the church has been such a benevolent force in most communities that they were not taxed probably as a courtesy for all the good they provide in their neighborhoods. That was of course when the men who ran the churches were men of God who had hearts that reflected God and focused on doing for others instead of themselves. So, can an offering really bless God?

Well of course it can when it is used as in 1 Corinthian 13 with true and sincere agape love. In Matthew 19:16–30, Christ tells a rich young ruler to sell all he has and give it to the poor as an expression of his commitment to the Savior. Giving to and caring for those less fortunate is demonstrated by Christ throughout scripture and we are commanded to do so (Ro. 12:13, Heb. 13:16, Lk. 3:10–11, Eph. 4:27–28, Matt. 5:42). This can also be accomplished by "ministries" that spend the money raised truly ministering the gospel message outside the confines of the church. But how many offerings collected in churches are actually used to benefit the needy? Of course there are great examples of churches living up to this standard and some denominations do a better job in general than others. And I know that churches have expenses. But if there is not a large proportion of annual church income going to benefit others in a godly and righteous way is that church not similar to the rich young ruler who walked away from Christ? Is a church in that position really blessing God? So again a scripture is being used to manipulate people into nonscriptural behavior. In essence, God's word is being "bastardized" with these practices by men who portray themselves "called of God."

Speaking of sacrifice, that is also something that is encouraged by the seed faith mongers. The idea of sacrificial giving is a very important aspect of the ploy and of course again, many scriptures are used errantly to support the fact that you will be blessed if you give until it hurts! For example, the incident of the Widow's Mite (Luke 21:1-4; Mark 12: 41-44) is often used to show the importance of sacrificial giving. This very poor widowed woman is observed by Christ giving two mites which equaled a farthing. A farthing would have been worth one fourth of a penny. Christ stated that she gave more than all the rich givers because she presumably gave all she had. Christ comments are taken to mean that we should follow her example and be willing to give sacrificially. Statements like "giving out of your need, you will be blessed", meaning those who have a need should be struggling to give more, or "God can't put anything into your hand if it's always closed", meaning God can't bless you with more if you hand is always closed holding onto what you have. But as usual, if we look closer at this passage it may be saying something a little different. In both Mark and Luke this takes place in the Temple. Jesus often went there to teach and as was his habit to notice the people and comment on their activities as related to salvation, sin, righteousness etc. In this case, he is sitting near the treasury. The treasury was a set of thirteen chests that were located in the "court of the women." The chests were called trumpets because of the shape of the opening where offerings were placed by temple worshippers. Many different offerings were placed into these chests; money-tribute, sacrifice-tribute, money gifts instead of sacrifice; freewill-offerings for wood, incense, temple decorations and burnt- offerings. In both gospels in the verses before noticing the widow, Christ observes the scribes parading through the temple in all their splendor. He notes their attire and comments how they dress to be seen, how they live for the attention they get from the commoners who look up to them with great estime and respect. They look for and expect the best seats whether in the synagogue or at feasts and are known for the great long prayers they made in public. But both scriptures say they "devour widows' houses." Then he sees the poor widow put in her two mites. He lashes and trashes, verbally ridicules and humiliates the scribes for efforts on every level to appear better than anyone else and in Christ's sight they are outdone by a poor widow. But Christ never said the woman was blessed for doing it, he never suggests that we emulate her actions. It could indeed be a further slap in the face of the scribe because if they did not devour widow's houses she may have had more to put into the treasury. Again, it is quite ironic that a scripture used by a few to take advantage of so many, may actually be a scripture that is meant to reprimand a few who take advantage of so many.

There are several implications that seem inherent in embracing seed faith that like the above scriptures just do not line up with the Bible. (1) God sent this man (the prophet) and God directed him to ask for this particular seed amount. When we allow ourselves to operate under the seed faith premise, we are operating as if this is God's guy. As with most things, I've discussed the Bible speak directly to the issue of verifying the credentials of these men but because we are usually in such a hurry to get a blessing we pay little attention to what the word says about this. And because of the way they operate, it can be difficult but that is where leaders come in and should take that responsibility. In Deuteronomy 18:15–22, we are given directions on identifying a false prophet and 1 John 4:1 tells us, "Try the spirits whether they are from God." More on Deuteronomy 18 shortly but 1 John is talking about discernment. He's not referring to some spiritual second sense where you go off into a trance and your eyes roll back or a voice comes into your head to tell you this guy is a fake. Discernment is simply knowing and understanding enough scripture that applies to the situation that enables you to say yes it is or no this is not of God. Yes there is a spiritual gift of discernment but not all of us have that and 1 John is talking to all of us about something we should all possess. (2) Giving the seed is a gauge of the strength or amount of your faith. This is rarely said outright, but it is always implied. "If you trust God, you will find a way to come up with that seed." "Show God how much you want that blessing." (3) The seed somehow jump starts or initiates the process of your request being fulfilled. It is almost as if the clock is running on a timer and the blessing can't begin to materialize until the seed is sown. Sometimes the timer is implied to have almost life-threatening importance. (4) The seed is implied to give God evidence of your faith. But if God knows everything, he knows your faith level so why would he need evidence? He wants us to believe without seeing (St. John 20:29). He can see into our hearts but he needs evidence? Pundits will say, "God required a show of faith in the Bible, look at Abraham being told to sacrifice his son." Yes, God asked Abraham for a sacrifice which is what the prophets do. But God was testing Abraham's obedience and he was not promising to give him anything in return. (5) Giving a seed seems to override God's will. Again this is never stated but God's will in the matter is never addressed. Suppose you give your seed, but God does not want you to have the request you made do you get it anyway because of your seed? Of course not but that is the way the seed is portrayed. And if you give a seed but don't get a blessing (which happens most of the time), shouldn't you get your money back? I'd like to see that happen, a money-back guarantee.

It seems to me that the seed faith idea blatantly contradicts a very important scripture about faith. Hebrews 11:1 says, "Now faith is the substance of things hoped for, the evidence of things not seen." Faith: complete trust or confidence in someone or something

Substance: the real physical matter or material of which a person or thing consists and which has a tangible solid presence.

Substance (Greek: *Hupostasis*): support, essence, a foundation, a source of confidence, beginning.

So faith is complete trust and confidence in God and I'll add and his ability to handle whatever problems, questions, issues, etc., we throw at him. Further it is the understanding that he is omniscient and knows all about all these things before we come to him. Faith is intangible. You can't touch, taste, see, smell, or hear it. It exists only in the spiritual realm is not subject to any laws of the physical world and is therefore not restricted by any of these laws. Even though we can experience the emotion or sensation of having faith, there is no hands on recognition of faith is here or faith is there. Our desires our hopes our needs are also intangible and exist in the spiritual realm. Take for example a financial need. We may be able to verbalize and even visualize it in our minds. We know how much is needed so we are able to rationalize it relative to what it is needed for, but it has no substance so we cannot touch or feel it. But somehow being in the same realm or dimension or plane as our faith and the Holy Spirit that financial need is transformed from the spiritual to the physical by manipulation of space, time, or materials as is needed by the power of the Holy Spirit. In other words, at God's direction the spirit and/or angels manipulate people, places, situations, or things to bring our supplications from the spirit realm to reality.

As you can see, there is no great difference between the English and Greek definitions of substance that being foundation, that which something is built upon or the essence that of which something is made. So in the spiritual realm, faith is the matter or material that is used by the Holy Spirit to take our needs from the spiritual to the physical realm. So faith connects the spiritual with the physical world. This function of faith is probably why those two words feel so intuitively right together. Seed faith would have us believe that the seed, money (always money), is somehow able to influence the spiritual realm when money is physical and the spirit realm is not. In essence, seed faith would have us believe "seed" is the substance of things hoped for. Interestingly enough, I think a lot of what I have covered here is in the back of many minds when faced with the seed faith proposition. They have doubts and questions but instead of looking for answers they succumb to the idea I don't want to be the only one missing out on a blessing. Another attitude is probably, what harm could it do to give the seed? It's a lot like filling out the Publisher's Clearing House entry forms. They say no purchase required but most people probably feel they have a better shot at winning if they buy something. Ironically, giving the seed may be a greater indication of a lack of faith than it is of abundance. We are physical beings and as such we identify with physical actions. That act of giving may serve to bolster the faith of the giver even as the giving is in process. The concept of seed faith giving boils down basically to a psychological tool used by these so-called prophets to swindle desperate people out of hard earned dollars; dollars that in many cases they can ill afford to lose. This is another reason that studying and understanding what the Bible really says is so important on an individual level. Let's now talk a little more specifically about these "pulpit pirates."

Having touched on the practices of many who call themselves prophet today, let's compare these with the function of God's prophets in the Bible. The dictionary defines a *prophet* as "a person regarded as an inspired teacher or proclaimer of the word of God." A more biblical definition however is a person chosen directly by God to whom God speaks directly with usually very specific instructions concerning very specific situations. The dictionary definition could apply to anyone who preaches God's word but the biblical characterization is that of a much more direct and active relationship. Deuteronomy 18:18–22 speaks about this office, in verse 18 God says, "I will raise them up a Prophet from among their bretheren, like unto thee, and

I will put my words into his mouth, and he shall speak unto them all that I shall command him." According to the dictionary, in a general sense, a prophet is someone who preaches, teaches, expounds on the word of God. But Deuteronomy makes the relationship more specific. The idea is that the words you hear from this "prophet" are not his words but words directly from God as with the frequent announcement of a prophet in the Bible, "Thus saith the Lord." God says he will appoint the prophet. In most cases this call from God is known only to a select few other than the prophet himself, i.e. Eli and Samuel, so how do we know a prophet has really been called by God and was not self-appointed? Deuteronomy 18:22 tells us, "When a prophet speaketh in the name of the Lord, if the thing follow not, nor come to pass, that is the thing which the Lord hath not spoken, but the prophet has spoken it presumptuously: thou shall not be afraid of him." He is basically saying that if a prophet predicts something that does not come true, that prophet is not from God. According to this scripture, there is no prophet of God who is not 100 percent accurate in making predictions, which is the bread and butter of most so-called prophets today (Jeremiah 28:9). There is no such thing as 95 percent accuracy in God. If a prophet has ever been wrong or the prediction was not fulfilled, it is not because of your lack of faith and if there is sin in your life that would deter the prophecy the prophet should know this and make you aware of this issue as a part of the prophecy. God would not send you a word without being very specific about any small details related to the outcome. That is what happened in the Old Testament (2 Chronicles 24:19).

Dennis Bratcher questions the use of this scripture as the primary test of a true prophet making a very important and valid point in agreement with what I have referred to several times, context. His point is that the context of Deuteronomy 18 is teaching against syncretism (the merging of different religions). Deuteronomy 13:1–5 and 17:2–6 deals with this, and Jeremiah 27:9 also specifically mentioning prophets, dreamers, diviners, and sorcerers because some of these were using their craft to draw the Israelites to other religious practices. When people saw these signs and wonders (likely by magic of demonic source), they took it as verification that this was a true servant of God. But their teaching was contrary to God's and would draw the people away from the truth. So in the light of the general dictionary definition of a prophet I would agree with Mr. Bratcher, as far as teaching God's principles and foundational truths a true prophets must stay true to God's word. In his opinion as long as a prophet stays in line with the truth of God's word he should be considered a true prophet. He feels Deuteronomy 18:22 should not be taken "as the primary, only and absolute validation of a prophet" based on these grounds. Deuteronomy 18:9–14 takes great pains to list the several "abominations" (diviners, sorcerers, etc.) that the Israelites should avoid but prophets are absent from this grouping. Then in verses 15–22 God's description of "his" prophet is laid out. Bratcher notes that "diviners were often linked with prophets as a part of the cultural context of the day as in Jeremiah 27:9" but in verses 15–22 when talking about God's prophet specifically there is no such link.

I think part of the reason for the disconnect in these verses is that "prediction" was the trademark of the most famous and powerful of God's prophets so prediction is at issue here. When God's men said, "Thus saith the Lord," whatever followed you could take to the bank! Because of this these men were revered and feared but also honored, all things to be relished in the eyes of the average human being. So much insight is lost when we fail to read contextually but in this case he may be overthinking it, or perhaps, not recognizing the emphasis placed on God's prophet in verses 15–22. In Deuteronomy the diviners were using magic to convince people of their authenticity. That perceived authenticity was then used to convince the people that their words were also authentic. Today most of the prophets I'm referring to are not intentionally trying to turn people away from God's word. They use God's word as a platform then they use predicting as a hook to get people to give "seed." So the problem with today's prophets is not syncretism but materialism. If this scripture is not to be used in validating prophets, why aren't those mentioned in Jeremiah 27:9 also mentioned in Deuteronomy 18:15–22? Since predictions are such a large part of the illegitimate practices of many prophets today, modern Christians would do well to recognize, understand, and embrace this measure God has given us for protection against false prophets. With all due respect to Mr. Bratcher I think he makes a mistake that is very common when talking about God's word, over analysis. The Deuteronomy scripture makes what sounds like a very matter of fact statement that does not seem to suggest an alternative meaning. Yet as well- meaning as he may be his opinion seems to dilute the intent and importance of the verse in question. It's almost like Satan saying "You will not surely die." While I am certainly not trying to cast Mr. Bratcher in the role of Satan the result is the same if indeed this scripture should be taken literally. With this book focusing on mistakes that are made because of inadequate analysis, here we see an example of the opposite.

So what are the qualifications for the true prophet of God? Well as was just said his predictions will always come true, no misses! No 99 and 44/100th%, 99 and ½ won't do (Deut. 18:22).

A true prophet is called into service by God himself, not by the prophet, not by the pastor, or momma or daddy, by God! "Before I formed thee in the belly I knew thee; and before thou camest forth out of the womb I sanctified thee, and I ordained thee a prophet unto the nations" (Jeremiah 1:5–10, Amos 7:14–15, Isaiah 6:1–10).

A true prophet must be obedient and therefore living a life that reflects God's righteousness. "Beware of false prophets, which come to you in sheep's clothing but inwardly they are ravening wolves" (Matt. 7:15–20).

A true prophet will speak God's truth and only God's truth. "To the law and to the testimony: if they speak not according to this word, it is because there is no light in them" (Isaiah 8:19–20).

A true prophet will have visions or dreams. "And He said, hear now my words: if there be a prophet among you, I the Lord will make Myself known unto him in a vision, and will speak unto him in a dream" (Num. 12:6).

If we go back to Deuteronomy 18:15, we find what seems to be a qualification that blatantly disqualifies a great many people; in fact, most of the world from the office of a prophet. Verse 15 says, "The Lord God will raise up unto thee (speaking of Israel) a prophet from the midst of thee, (again speaking of Israel) of thy bretheren,

(Israel) like unto me (Moses whose speaking), unto him (prophet) ye shall hearken." I'm sure there are many who will disagree, but I don't see any other way to interpret this, but it seems to be saying that God in selecting, choosing, using prophets will select them from the tribes of Israel! That coupled with verse 22, which we've already covered, seems to be saying that God's choice for "true" prophets is from the children of Israel. That is, when God really chooses a prophet that prophet will be Hebrew or more recognizably Jewish. I know, some will say that I don't know what I'm talking about or this is my own opinion or interpretation. The fact is I did not write this! It is found in every Bible regardless of the version being used and the same meaning will surface if the Bible is allowed to speak for itself. Let's take it a little further.

Depending upon the reference you use the list of prophets/ prophetess in the Bible is about seventy-four including both Old and New Testaments. Other than the major and minor classification of the OT prophets are also classified as primary or secondary. Primaries had a history of functioning in the prophetic office on a regular basis. Secondary prophets may have had only one experience. In all the different situations that God had to chastise the Israelites for all their sinning and continuing to turn away from him he never chose a Gentile as a prophet. And if you are thinking, "Wait a minute, he used Balaam (Numbers 22) and he was not Hebrew." That's right but he also used Balaam's ass, and it was not Hebrew either. The point here being God did not choose Balaam, but he did use him simply because of the position this false prophet had gotten himself into against Israel. God can use anyone even anything (Balaam's donkey talked) but this scripture says that he chooses to use Israelites for prophets. So, all of the true prophets in the OT were from the tribes of Israel. So now you might be thinking, "But in the NT, God is now dealing with Gentiles as well as Jews so now it's a different story." Yes, that is true the NT is a different story. The prophets are still all Jews, but it is a different story. If this verse were in place and then God used a Gentile as a prophet anywhere especially in the NT, there would be reason to dispute the Jews only conclusion. There might be cause for discussion about God using Gentiles as prophets now. But as it stands by the words of a proven prophet in Moses, God has stated that his choice for prophets is in Israel and in the Bible it seems he has only chosen from Israel. Another interesting point is that God's use of prophecy seems to end in the Bible in the book of Acts. "God is not the author of confusion" (1 Cor. 14:33)," we are. If he instituted prophecy with his own words, carried it out with his own guidelines, and then stopped using it for a time, the logical way to resume use in my limited mind would be to continue using the previous guidelines. To do anything else only invites the question, "Is this of God?" But then part of the problem is that we don't ask enough questions, which is also why Pentecostals have so few answers.

As I said earlier, the biblical prophets spoke very specific words about very specific situations and the situations usually had to do with sin and repentance. Little if any of the prophecy that occurs today has to do with repentance. In fact, I have never been in the presence of a prophet whose predictions dealt primarily with sin and repentance. What most of these people seem to do is more like "fortune-telling" or "soothsaying" like the psychics that were so popular on TV a while back. These practices were condemned in Deuteronomy 18:9–13. How can a prophet of God be engrossed in a practice that God has called an abomination? Some of the things God's prophets actually did:

- Revealed the nature and attributes of God to men (Deuteronomy 5:4–10)
- Made known to men the laws of God (Exodus 20:1–17)
- Called people back to obedience to God's law (2 Chronicles 24:19)
- Exhort people to sincerity in worship (Jeremiah 7:1–11)
- To warn of divine judgment for personal or national sin (Jeremiah 36:30–31)
- Foretell future events which God willed (Jeremiah 30:1–3)
- Foretell the coming Messiah (Isaiah 9:6)
- Record the history of God's dealings with men (Deuteronomy 31:9–13)

- Record the word of God in his Holy Scriptures (Exodus 17:14, 34:27)

Many of today's so-called prophets imply or even advertise miracles as a part of their "ministry" and of course there were miracles performed by some of God's prophets but not all. In fact more of God's prophets did not perform miracles than those who did. Most of the time, the presentation of a miracle was to verify God's authority and or the authority of the prophet being used (Moses with Pharaoh in Egypt, Elijah at Mt. Carmel, 1 Kings 18, Jesus turns water to wine). On very rare occasions, however, there were miracles performed for individuals (Elijah provides endless grain for a poor woman [1 Kings 17] and Elisha provided endless oil for another woman [2 Kings 4]). So again a question, why are purported miracles such a staple of today's prophet when they were such a rarity for God's true prophets?

Christ warns us against false prophets in Matthew 7:15 saying, "They come to you in sheep's clothing but inwardly they are ravening wolves." In Matthew 24:11, he speaks of false prophets in the last days, likely our days. False prophets existed in the time of Christ and in his future, our present. But they existed long before Christ as well, remember Balaam? He lived as a contemporary of Moses. Let's take a look to see what made him a false prophet. The story of Balaam is found in Numbers 22–24. It takes place around the time just before the Israelites crossing of the Jordan River. The Israelites had already defeated the King of the Amorites and the King of Bashan. Balak the King of Moab was worried that he would be next and sent for Balaam seeking that a curse be brought upon Israel and prevent the Moabites being defeated like the others. We know that Balaam was not Hebrew because Balak sent to a place called Pethor, which was "by the river of the land of his (Balaam's) people." We know from Numbers 22:7 that Balaam was a "diviner" or fortune-teller and that he was accustomed to being paid for his services. "And the elders of Moab and the elders of Midian departed with the rewards of divination in their hand; and they came unto Balaam and they spoke unto him the words of Balak." So Balaam was not a prophet who was mainly concerned about people he was concerned about his pocket. This shows the lack of integrity in this man and is very similar to many of the prophets of our day. To prey on the desperation and needs of others instead of getting a job like everyone else is no better than a drug dealer. Even worse, at least a drug dealer is not taking advantage of God's word. I guess Solomon was right. "There's nothing new under the sun." Balaam also evidently had a reputation with some success. In verse 6, Balak says, "I wot (know) that he whom thou blessest is blessed, and he whom thou cursest is cursed." One has to question Balaam's power source since we know it is not from God (he is a diviner, takes money or payment, is not an Israelite). Another source could be that of suggestion. Magic is also not a new commodity and has been around for thousands of years. Wherever there have been men with possessions there have always been men (and women) who try to get those possessions unlawfully and through trickery. Just look at the number of people who spend their days now figuring out ways to get our possessions online. The fact that he has been successful at some point by whatever means leaves the impression that he can be successful again. If he wasn't right for you, maybe he'll be right for me, maybe your faith just wasn't strong enough. The magic could be in the slide of hand or in the "slide of mind."

There is also the possibility that his power was demonic. He may have performed miracles by the power of Satan. This would mean that a great many things were possible and remember, Satan is always happy to make something appear to be from God when he knows that it is from him. That also has to be considered today when talking about prophets. It is possible that people who we think are serving God and appear to be one thing are many times some-thing else. They may not even know they are powered by demonic forces. And if a person realizes they have this capability, it would take someone sincerely dedicated to God and not him or herself to sincerely seek God for guidance, approval, and perfection of such a gift. What if God denounced it, the use of it would be forbidden. Most people would rationalize the use of this power in some way without seeking God's guidance. Another source, which is probably very often overlooked, is that of a natural gift. I play keyboards by ear. I've never had any formal training but have picked up tips from place to place over the years. I'm not great, but I am able to play most things that I attempt so that the piece is recognized by anyone who knows it. Just as I was born with this musical gift, I believe people are born with gifts that we might call, mental spiritual gifts. Things like ESP, and an ability to sense some part of the future, have been well documented scientifically. Michele de Nostradamus is a famous French seer whose predictions starting in 1555 seems to have predicted historical events involving people from Napoleon to Hitler and even John F. Kennedy. When I was in a sinful state during my life, God did not take away a gift that I was born with. Many great musicians have natural gifts that started out being used for God but then for Satan and God didn't take the gift away. I think this is true of these mental gifts as well. When a person is born with one of these gifts, they can use it for God or for gain. So just because someone has a gift to see into the future does not mean they are sent or sanctioned by God. And if that person chooses to exploit that gift in the pulpit instead of asking God to refine and purify the gift and the one gifted they will someday answer directly to God for this egregious way of life. Balaam paid, with his life. But what was his crime?

Balak wanted Balaam to curse the Israelites. Balaam's response was that he could only say what God put into his mouth. This sounds strange at first because we have said that Balaam was not a prophet of God yet he sounds as if God speaks to him. After building three sets of seven altars at three different locations, instead of curses Balaam proclaimed blessings over the Israelites three different times, blessings that came directly from God. God speaking through Balaam a false prophet seems odd but is totally understandable since this false prophet is pitted against his chosen people. I think it is more curious that Balaam so easily recognizes God and the control God has over him. This could be because of divine recognition imparted by God or Balaam's recognizing that this was not the demonic force that he normally dealt with. Whatever the reason there was absolutely no question in Balaam's mind that this was God, the one and only true living God and that he had no control in this matter of pronouncing curses on the chosen Israelites. So again, God did not choose him but he did use him. He used Balaam's ass to show how asinine it was to try manipulating God. God spoke through one ass to another, but it seems the second wasn't as smart as the first. When Balaam's ass saw the light, he stopped in the middle of the road and would go no farther. When Balaam saw the light, he could have done the same, acknowledged God as the Almighty and started a new way of life. Instead he regrouped and went back to Balak telling him to entice the Israelites with prostitutes and food sacrificed to idols and in this way they would curse themselves. After direct communication with the one and only true living God, Balaam missed the opportunity to continue the relationship on a positive note and at least be in the Lord's camp and possibly used as a prophet. Unfortunately there are many people today who have the opportunity to get themselves right and start doing God's work in the way the Bible teaches and not leaning to their own understanding. Matthew 7:21–23, "Not every-one that saith unto me, Lord, Lord, shall enter into the kingdom of heaven; but he that doeth the will of my Father which is in heaven. Many will say to me in that day, Lord, Lord, have we not prophesied in thy name and in thy name have cast out devils? And in thy name done many wonderful works? And then will I profess unto them, I never knew you: depart from me ye that work iniquity."

In the evaluation of modern practices in the discipline of proph-ecy the gauge has to be the way prophecy operated in the Bible. Like all other miracles, healings, tongues, or other extraordinary or super-natural phenomenon it is illogical to think that God would change his methods without some sort of indication in the holy word that this change would occur. Again, God is not the author of confusion. Why would he do something in the same way for thousands of years and then change suddenly without warning in the twentieth cen-tury? It just doesn't make sense! Today prophets do all sorts of things to "catch" us. They say things with great authority and power, they exude confidence and assurance. They are great salesmen, and we buy everything they sell. They say things that seem very profound and mystic but many times these are things that cannot be verified either because they are so far in the future or so vague that you forget them. In 2014, I heard a prophet Karn in a prophetic rant speak about the strange weather approaching as if it were something God was showing him. But the things he spoke of could be found in the ten day forecast on the Internet weather site. He also stated with emphatic certainty that Malaysian flight 370 would never be found. To this date what happened to that flight remains a mystery, but they have found a wing and personal items that have been verified as "likely" coming from that plane. If he was speaking words from God, you would think that at least the wing (which was authenticated) would have been mentioned. When that plane is found most people won't even remember what he said. These type statements sound prophetic but many of them have at least a fifty-fifty chance of coming true and that's not bad if you are not looking for 100 percent accuracy. Prophets speak of politics, international affairs, and societal issues and changes with such authority that it sounds like God is speaking directly into his ear. But many of these are things that the Bible has already written prophecy about. We are duped so much because we fail to follow God's instruction. We don't study enough, and we don't ask enough questions. How does a child learn? They learn by asking questions. Between the ages of three and four, children reach several developmental milestones, and they reach them by asking why! Why? Why? If they fail to reach these milestones continued normal development is in jeopardy. Some of those milestones are as follows:

1— Say his or her name and age.
2— Speak 250–500 words
3— Answer simple questions
4— Use sentences of five to six words and complete sentences by age four
5— Speak clearly
6— Tell stories

When we fail to ask enough scriptural questions, our spiritual development can also be delayed.

1— (His/her name), many Pentecostals are not sure of who they are in Christ, is my salvation secure, am I sure I'm going to heaven, can I lose my salvation?

2— (250-500 words), how many scriptures do you have committed to memory?

3— (Answer simple questions), when asked questions by non-believers many Pentecostals answer with "I just have faith, I just believe."

4— (Use sentences), many Pentecostals have no idea about defending the faith

5— (Speak clearly), many Pentecostals are not clear in their minds about important basic biblical truths/principles.

6— (Tell story), many Pentecostals could not tell a condensed story of either the Old or New Testament.

One of the most contradictory practices of modern prophets is the fact that they are always "on" or at least whenever they want to be. Today when they come to a city for a two- or three-week revival or just a couple of nights the prophecies are always rolling. Have you ever heard a prophet get up to do his thing and say, "I'm sorry, but God has not given me anything tonight." Maybe it has happened somewhere, but I've never heard of it. It's all twisted around. In the Bible, the prophet waited to hear God call, tell him where to go and of course what to say. Now days the prophet sets up the itinerary and God falls in line with him! In the Bible, the prophets could not turn the prophetic word on and off at will. They couldn't turn it on and off if it were God. If they can turn it on and off now, it probably isn't God.

First Thessalonians 5:20 says, "Despise not prophesying." I'm sure it sounds like that is my position, and I want to make it clear that is not the case. False prophets are a menace to all mankind, not just God's people. Of course they steal and rob God's children not only of financial but more importantly spiritual wealth. They keep the sheep from growing and developing into shepherds themselves and this is the greatest victory for Satan. But these prophets give God a bad name and they make God seem fake when they fail. The secular world has no reason to give the benefit of a doubt or say two out of three ain't bad. When a fake is uncovered, the world has all the more reason to avoid churches after all they try to avoid con men in the street, why should they go to church to see one? When that scripture says, "Despise not prophesying," it is talking about true prophesying, real prophesying, God-sent prophesying. I despise all that is not real.

In 2 Kings 5, there is the story of Naaman the leper who was cured of his ailment by Elisha. Most who know this story know that Naaman was a captain of the Syrian army of King Ben-hadad. The familiar part of the story is Naaman being directed by Elisha to wash seven times in the dirty Jordan River. If you read further, you find that once healed he offered Elisha payment for the miracle that had been wrought in his life. Elisha declined being paid for a blessing from God and told Naaman to "go in peace." Behind Elisha's back, however, his servant Gehazi convinced Naaman that he was authorized to take the blessings offered to Elisha making it sound as if God was now in on it. When Naaman found out what his servant had done, not only did he rebuke him but he cursed Gehazi with leprosy. Obviously, God was not pleased with the action of Gehazi and directed Elisha to dole out this punishment for misrepresenting the will of God. When God blesses it is a gift and no price on earth is enough. According to the story of Elisha, Naaman and Gehazi, taking payment for a blessing from God is a punishable offence. I wonder what will happen to a person who takes payment based on a lie about God providing a blessing? Perhaps modern prophets have never read this part of the story or maybe they just don't believe it. Maybe they just don't care!

Tongues:
A Small Part of a Big Problem

"BUT THE TONGUE CAN no man tame; it is an unruly evil, full of deadly poison" (James 3:8). In verses 1–12 of this chapter, James exhorts in the importance of controlling the human tongue. It is ironic that the tongue is such a small organ of human anatomy but capable of so much damage. The 2016 presidential campaign was a clear example of this especially concerning one particular candidate. James points out that it is easier to control a horse with a bridle or a ship with a rudder than it is to control the tongue. He calls it boastful, offensive, and a world of iniquity. He refers to the tongue as a fire that is capable of defiling the whole body, and when the Bible speaks of fire, it is usually speaking of destruction. He is referring to the lies the deceit and the treachery that can come by the tongue, the pain, devastation, and ruination that this small member is capable of staging. Speaking in tongues was mentioned earlier. It is a defining characteristic, a cornerstone of the Pentecostal church, and it is based on the events that occurred in Acts 2 on the day of Pentecost. But as mentioned earlier, the tongues we hear today (for the most part) are not the type of tongues heard in the Upper Room. So what makes them different, where do they come from, and why were/are they spoken?

What makes them different is that the tongues spoken on the Day of Pentecost were "real" languages. They were languages that were spoken by people who lived in the region, and they could be interpreted by someone who was a natural or learned speaker of the language. Those words could be written down in sentences and shared with people who were not present. As in Matthew 26:73 where Peter was recognized as one that was with Jesus because "thy speech betrayeth thee," the sounds (accent, dialect) of the languages were distinct and recognizable. In the way we would recognize that someone is speaking an Oriental language or French or Spanish those "tongues" were real everyday use recognizable languages. Verses 9–11 of Acts lists the different languages that were spoken at this event. The miracle that took place in Acts 2 is called xenoglossy or xenolalia. That is not what we normally hear spoken as tongues today. As stated earlier, what we hear today is called glossolalia and refers to speech patterns that resemble words and sentences but have no comprehensible meaning. Today's tongues can best be described as gibberish. Again, this is not meant to be disrespectful, insulting, or disparaging in any way just a clear honest look at the facts. Remember, I am from a Pentecostal church as well.

So where do tongues come from? Acts 2:4 says, "They began to speak with other tongues as the Spirit gave them utterance," so the xenolalia of Acts came by way of the Holy Spirit. The million dollar question is where does today's glossolalia come from? If it is indeed from the Holy Spirit, why is it not the same presentation as in Acts that is a recognizable language instead of gibberish? First Corinthians 14:33, "For God is not the author of confusion, but of peace, as in all churches of the saints." Why would God usher in the presence of the HS with one kind of tongues, allow those tongues to disappear after the book of Acts, and then reappear in the 1800s as a different kind of tongues if he wanted to avoid confusion? Supporters of today's tongues would describe glossolalia as "unknown tongues." These are said to be "heavenly tongues," a heavenly language spoken directly to God, a language that he understands even if we don't. This unknown language is said to be used in prayer as well as worship. Unknown tongues are mentioned by Paul in 1 Corinthian 14:2, 4, 13, 19, 27 and nowhere else, why? Of all the twelve apostles, Paul is the only one to mention unknown tongues and he only mentions them in this fourteenth chapter, why? He doesn't talk about them anywhere else and no one else even mentions them, why? Asking questions does not show a lack of faith, it does not mean a lack of spirit, and it does not indicate a carnal mind. It means paying attention to God's word and trying to understand what the word is really saying, not what we believe or what someone has told us. Answering these questions will begin to shed light on what was going on in this chapter and Corinthians in general and reading this book contextually answers these questions.

Both Corinthian books were letters written by Paul to the Corinthian church while he was at Ephesus. Reports had been sent to Paul concerning problems in the Corinthian congregation. Paul was the founder of that church along with people like Priscilla and Aquilla but left it to continue his missionary journey. Though there were some Jews in this congregation, it was largely made up of Gentile converts to Christianity whose religious backgrounds were in pagan idol worship that focused on the many different gods for many different purposes. Some of the most well known from Greek mythology are Zeus (sky god and ruler of the gods), Hera (goddess of mothers and family), Poseidon (god of the sea), Athena (goddess of wisdom and war), Apollo (god of archery, music, poetry, prophecy, medicine, and the sun) Aphrodite (goddess of love and beauty). A couple of lesser known gods are Dionysius (god of wine and theater) and Nike (goddess of victory), she sounds familiar. With the many different gods came many different temples, worship practices, and rituals. Sacrifice to the gods was an integral part of worship and particular items were offered to particular figures. For example to Zeus, the ox and the oak tree were the designated sacrifice and for Athena it was the owl and the olive tree. Sexual activity was also a part of the pagan worship rituals in many of the temples. Hierogamy or Hieros gamos was a ritual that acted out or simulated the marriage between a goddess and a god, especially when enacted in a symbolic rite where human participants assume the identity of the deities. The "sacred prostitute" was associated with the worship of the great mother goddesses such as Hera. In Hierogamy temple, priestesses would play the part of the goddess and performed sexual rituals with male worshippers. Some of the problems Paul responded to in Corinth were immature, carnal Christians (1 Cor. 3:1–3), failure to separate from pagan surrounding (2 Cor. 6:17), divisiveness (2 Cor. 1:10–13, 11:17–22), secular lawsuits between Christians (1 Cor. 6:1–11), conflicts over Christian liberty (chapters 8, 10), celibacy and marriage (chapter 7). From the above references, we can see that the Gentile converts had a lot of adjusting to do related to sexuality and worship, and Paul dealt with this as well (1 Cor. 6:12–20).

There were also problems that were directly related to worship. One of these had to do with the Greek god Dionysius. Being the god of wine, you might guess that drinking wine would be a part of the worship ritual of his followers and that is indeed the case. Worshippers would drink to a state of drunkenness with the idea that this would bring them into a closer more intimate connection with the deity. When they realized the Christians were drinking wine during communion, this was likely thought to be the same or similar to the drinking during Dionysius worship, and they would overindulge during communion. This is what prompted his words in 1 Cor. 10:21, "Ye cannot drink the cup of the Lord and the cup of devils: ye cannot be partakers of the Lord's table, and the table of devils." Paul makes it very clear that there is always a distinction between the things of God and the things of Satan. You may be able to point out similarities, but that is because Satan is always trying to copy the things of God. I think it is an insult to God's very nature when we, even mistakenly, associate something Satanic with his righteous being. It's like having your own child curse at you or spit on you. It is likely that Paul is thinking along the same lines for in verse 22 he says, "Do we provoke the Lord to jealousy? Are we stronger than He?" That sentiment is still true today. Hebrews 10:31 says, "It is a fearful thing to fall into the hands of the living God." Falling into the hands of God refers to being subject to his wrath because of persistent sin (Heb. 10:26–31). When we have been given the written word but have failed to understand it the result is disobedience. God will know that it was in ignorance, but it was still disobedience. Will we get a pass in this case or will the sin be counted against us? When we are not sure about God's word, but we fail to get clarity because of tradition or laziness will God say, "That's okay"? The word *provoke* means to arouse a negative reaction from someone. Sounds like he's saying, "Don't poke the bear." Does it matter that the converts may have done these things in ignorance? It doesn't seem that Paul is suggesting that. Will God cut us some slack or grade on a curve because we just didn't get it right, or we got a little confused? Maybe, maybe not! The bottom line here was that Holy Communion was done in a certain way with a certain attitude and certain reverence. If any of these components were missing, it detracted from the sacred meaning of this very special commemoration that was instituted by Christ himself. Because the worship of Dionysius was idolatry, it was considered of demonic origin and any practices coming out of that idol worship would be considered demonic. That is what led to Paul's phrase "cup of devils." Communion practiced in any manor other than that prescribed by Christ was of the devil!

Another problem related to worship was the emphasis that was being place on spiritual gifts. As is the case in many churches today and as I have personally witnessed some people get preferential treatment. It's a fact! Pastors and other church leaders can deny it all they want, but in many cases, certain people have clout and others have none. The leader always seems to have a reason for the relationship as well as an explanation that casts our perception into the pits of hell, but there are usually other witnesses who can support the issue. This respect of persons is brought about by many things but the appearance or perception of deep spirituality can increase and sometimes decrease the influence that a person enjoys. Not only are leaders influenced but members of the congregation also fall into this trap. Because it is human nature to be captivated by the supernatural, spiritual gifts become an area of susceptibility that Satan targets often and with great intensity. When we are not discerning and equipped with accurate information we can become victims of Satan's attacks by these methods. This was a problem in the Corinthian church as evidenced by Paul's reference in 1 Corinthian 12:25 to preventing schisms in the church and in the very first chapter verse 11 he states that there are contentions among the members. Much like the focus of the Pentecostal church today the climate surrounding spiritual gifts in Corinth was distorted, misunderstood, and misinterpreted. It is easy to grasp what may have happened in Corinth if we recall our earlier discussion about today's prophets, their treatment of the people, and the people's reaction to them. The Corinthian members had allowed themselves to be distracted by and focus on the supernatural events that were associated with the Holy Spirit instead of understanding why they occurred. When this happened, it was easy to mistakenly correlate the drinking of Dionysius worship with the drinking of Communion.

In chapter 14, Paul sets about the task of clarifying the situation. He makes the point that the spiritual gifts have a purpose. They were not present for sensationalism or to make one person in the body more or less important than another. Their purpose was to edify the body (verse 3). He makes the point that more important than every spiritual gift is love (charity). It is when we allow ourselves to be distracted from this fact that Satan most easily weaves his web of confusion. When we understand that all is done for the benefit of everyone, our focus will be what is good and righteous and beneficial instead of what is spectacular and draws the most attention. Speaking in tongues was a gift that was very spectacular but not limited or assigned to a particular position or person. Not only did the Apostles speak as in Acts 2, but Gentiles as well (Acts 10:45–46, Cornelius and household). So this was an area that anyone could aspire to. But again focusing on the event more than the purpose people headed down the wrong road. In chapter 12:27–29, Paul delineates a list of ministry gifts in order of importance. At the very bottom of the list, he places tongues. In verses 7–10 the spiritual gifts are first mentioned and again tongues land at the bottom of the list. I don't think this is merely a coincidence. Throughout his discussion of tongues, Paul never seems to come right out and say, "Come on, everybody, seek to speak or tongues is a good thing or everybody should be doing it." At best he always seems to downplay the activity. Below is a list of the scriptures where he deals with this issue along with what it seems he is intending to convey:

- 1 Corinthian 12:30, "Do all speak with tongues?" (A rhetorical question whose answer is no. This refutes the idea that speaking in tongues is a sign of the presence of the HS. If it were a sign, all would speak with tongues.)

- 1 Corinthian 13:1, "Though I speak with the tongues of men and angels" (I think the first mistake made reading this is to take it as an admission of Paul speaking in tongues. He does that in 14:18 and says, "I speak," here he says, "Though I speak." Though suggests a supposition, a possibility as in if I speak or even if I speak or suppose I speak. This supposition is also meant to include the reader in the outcome of this verse. This could be better understood as "If we speak" because Paul clearly intends for the reader to include him/herself as possibly becoming as sounding brass or tinkling cymbals. If we make the first mistake, it leads to the next that Paul is saying he speaks in the tongue of angels. This idea may seem to be supported by 2 Corinthian 12 where Paul talks of being "caught up into the third heaven and hearing unspeakable words." Many take this to be the heavenly language of "unknown tongues" and the tongues used today for prayer and praise and what I refer to as glossolalia. But that can't be because in 2 Corinthian 12:4, not only did Paul say the words he heard were "unspeakable" but they were also "unlawful for a man to utter," which is likely what the unspeakable meant, not that Paul couldn't pronounce them. So are we to understand that Paul went to heaven heard these words, was told not to speak them but decided to speak them anyway? So I don't think Paul is saying that he spoke in unknown tongues.
- 1 Corinthian 13:8, "Tongues fail" (Tongues will fail like all other imperfect commodities, only charity has true lasting value. Tongues are of little value in and of themselves.)
- 1 Corinthian 14:2, "For he that speaketh in an unknown tongue speaketh not unto men but unto God: for no man understandeth him" (With edification of the church body being the top priority it is useless to the church to speak in an unknown tongue if the words remain a mystery.)

- 1 Corinthian 14:4, "He that speaketh in an unknown tongue edifieth himself; but he that prophesieth edifieth the church." (Words that are spoken with no understanding are useless to the body of Christ.)

- 1 Corinthian 14:6, "Now, bretheren, if I come unto you speaking with tongues, what shall I profit you, except I speak to you either by revelation, or by knowledge, or by prophesying, or by doctrine." (Tongues are not beneficial on their own merit.)

- 1 Corinthian 14:9, "So likewise ye, except ye utter by the tongue words easy to be understood, how shall it be known what is spoken? For ye shall speak into the air." (If what you are saying cannot be easily understood it's like talking to the wind.)

- 1 Corinthian 14:11, "Therefore if I know not the meaning of the voice, I shall be unto him that speaketh a barbarian, and he that speaketh shall be a barbarian unto me." (If I don't understand your words, we are like two people who speak different languages.)

- 1 Corinthian 14:12, "Even so ye, for as much as ye are zealous of spiritual gifts, seek that ye may excel to the edifying of the church." (For all the great energy and enthusiasm that you put forth in pursuing spiritual gifts, see that you put as much energy into what is truly beneficial to the church.)

- 1 Corinthian 14:15, "What is it then? I will pray with the spirit, and I will pray with the understanding also; I will sing with the spirit, and I will sing with the understanding also." (When praying and singing in the spirit everything is fully understood. All things done in the spirit should be fully understood.)

- 1 Corinthian 14:18–19, "I thank God I speak with tongues more than ye all. Yet in church I had rather speak five words with my understanding, that by my voice I might teach others also, than ten thousand words in an unknown tongue." (Ten thousand words that no one understands mean nothing compared to five words filled with clarity and wisdom.)

- 1 Corinthian 14:22, "Wherefore tongues are a sign, not to them that believe, but to them that believe not..." (The presentation of the miracle of tongues on the Day of Pentecost was not for the benefit of the Apostles. It was not meant as an indicator to the Apostles to let them know that they now had the Holy Spirit. It was not to establish a pattern for all future recipients of the Holy Spirit to let them know when the Spirit comes into them. It was meant to announce to the world that *this is the day*! The day prophesied by Joel when God would pour out his spirit upon all flesh. It was meant to say these are the men I have chosen to spread the word and lead the entire world out of bondage! It was meant for unbelievers to witness the great miracle of tongues and become believers and witnesses themselves of the great miracle that signaled the beginning of a new era in the history of mankind. For this reason, there is no great need for tongues to be spoken in the church which is primarily a place filled with believers.)

- 1 Corinthian 14:23, "If therefore the whole church become in one place, and all speak with tongues, and there come in those that are unlearned, or unbelievers, will they not say that ye are mad? (If tongues are demonstrated in a haphazard, willy-nilly fashion [as in most modern churches] visitors who witness the spectacle will think the speakers or the whole church are crazy.)

- 1 Corinthian 14:27–28, "If any man speak in an unknown tongue, let it be by two or at most by three, and that by course; and let one interpret. But if there be no interpreter, let him keep silent in the church; and let him speak to himself and to God." (Paul is presenting the order and manor in which the Holy Spirit would administer the gift of tongues. The HS would never initiate speaking in tongues and break its own rules in the process.)

- 1 Corinthian 14:33, "For God is not the author of confusion, but of peace as in all churches of the saints." (The methods, patterns, and practices of modern tongues [glossolalia] do not line up with what the scriptures say about tongues or how they should be presented in church. If the Holy Spirit is the author of tongues it will surely follow its own guidelines.)

I think it is plain from examining the above scriptures all together that Paul was not advocating tongues as important in the scheme of Christian worship practices. It is not so plain why he speaks as if "tongues" and "unknown tongues" are different. When he refers to himself speaking, he uses tongues. In only three of the previous scriptures do we see "unknown," why? Well that's the million dollar question. Where we see unknown tongues, the unknown is always "italicized," slanted to the side so that it looks different from the rest of the words. Greek scholars tell us that this is because the word *unknown* does not appear in that scripture in the original Greek text. It seems the translators added the unknown, but no one is really sure why. It is assumed that it helps the understanding of the translation in some way but how? One writer who supports the idea that unknown meant a legitimate heavenly language states, "The unknown tongue was not ecstatic babbling. It was a language that nobody in the assembly understood (verse 2)." How does he know that? Verse 2 never said it was not babbling, that is what the unknown leaves unclear. He further states, "Those words are there simply because it takes more than one English word to convey the sense of the original Greek word or concept." So why not just use more than one English word, we have the whole Bible? I think it's clear that the translators had a reason for adding it, but I think it's grabbing at straws to assume this was a heavenly language when there is no reasonable evidence to support that. Another way to attack the problem is by looking at the context of the chapter.

We know that Paul was dealing with many issues that new Gentile converts were having with bringing pagan practices into the church of Christ. Glossolalia was another one of these practices. The incoherent speech we hear in many Pentecostal churches today is not new. This practice has been around for centuries even before the time of Christ. Almost one hundred years before David became King of Israel, the Egyptians were speaking "unknown tongues" in the worship of their famous sun god Amon Ra (1100 BC) Plato reported as early as the fifth century BC religious ecstatic speech where the speaker had no control of his mental faculties, did not know what he was saying and needed to have an interpreter (a diviner) tell what was being said because the speaker was under the control of the god.

Virgil writing in about 17–19 BC a priestess of the temple of Apollo who would go into and ecstatic state where she was unified with the spirit of Apollo, and she would begin to speak in tongues in ecstatic utterances.

John Chrysostum, Archbishop of Constantinople writing of Pythia (who was another priestess serving in the temple of Apollo part of the year and the temple of Dionysius the other part of the year) "This same Pythoness is said, being a female to sit at times upon the tripod of Apollo astride, and thus the evil spirit ascending from beneath and entering the lower part of her body fills the woman with madness. And she with disheveled hair begins to foam at the mouth (sounds familiar to me) and thus being in a frenzy, to utter words of her madness." Also around this time in Greece there was the rise of the mystery religions. They were all mystical and emotional in orientation not very different from a lot of new age religions, and not too different from the charismatics and Pentecostals as well. Ecstatic utterances were associated with numerous other groups as well. Hindus, Moslems, Chinese the Mirtha cult of Persia, Osiris of Egypt, Eleusians of Greece, Orphic of Greece and Macedonia, Shamanism in Africa, and voodoo religions of Haiti, cannibals from Borneo, and even Eskimos practice glossolalia.

We see from the above examples that over a thousand years before Christ was even born, people were speaking "unknown tongues." These were not tongues prompted by the Holy Spirit because first the Holy Spirit was not dwelling in mankind as yet and second these earlier tongues were associated with pagan gods. Growing up in the Pentecostal church, I have witnessed some of the same scenes described in the above paragraphs including the "foaming at the mouth." What I have just written about is ancient history but these scenes played out before my eyes. I have seen the ecstatic frenzy, uncontrolled writhing, rolling all over the floor, nasal mucous, and foaming at the mouth. I have seen people hurt during these frenzies from minor scrapes to fractured bones. But nowhere in the Bible do we see any behavior that even remotely resembles these uncontrolled outbursts that are associated with the glossolalia. So back to the million dollar question, what was Paul talking about when he referred to "unknown tongues"? It sounds like he was talking about the tongues that the Gentile converts were bringing into the worship, which were tongues spoken to their pagan idols and not the tongues prompted by the Holy Spirit. This would explain his delineating the order that should be observed when tongues are spoken (1 Cor. 14:27–28). If you notice this is the only place where there is the need for an interpreter. In all other instances there seems to be no question as to what is said because true holy tongues were languages that people could understand so there was likely always someone who spoke the language who interpreted automatically. Also as is the case in many of our larger cities, many different languages are spoken and are familiar to much of the population as was the case in the Upper Room at Pentecost. It seems more likely that Paul was giving a measuring device so it would be known that these were not the tongues from the Holy Spirit if the rules were not followed.

Another question is why are there so many different religions that practice glossolalia? In the secular world, a person who regularly spoke in an unintelligible language would be considered mentally defective in some way. Why is it that religions seem to gravitate to this practice? Paul mentioned hearing "unspeakable words" in 2 Corinthian 12:4 when he was "caught up into paradise." Many take this as evidence of a heavenly language spoken by angels and thus Paul's remarks of "though I speak with the tongues of men and angels." If there is a heavenly language and if that is what he was referring to Paul also said the words he heard were "unlawful for man to utter." But someone else knows about these heavenly words or this heavenly language, Satan. Remember, Satan is the "ape" of God.

With this information, it would make total sense for him to inspire religions all around the world to practice something that is a cheap copy of something in heaven, especially something that Paul tells us is unlawful. So it is possible that for centuries Satan has tricked worshippers into mimicking heavenly words or language, words that are not even lawful for men to speak. So for hundreds perhaps thousands of years, people have been duped into speaking a gibberish that is thought to make them closer and more intimately involved with fake gods and perhaps now he has done it again with the church of Christ even though Paul gave us a set of rules to prevent such a mistake. I know there are those who will say that my view on this is because I have not had the Holy Ghost experience, or everyone doesn't have the same experience or I think that I know more than the many great Pentecostal leaders. But the question I raise here cannot just be cast aside if we are to get a clear understanding of this pervasive phenomenon.

Scientists have also tried to get a clear understanding about glossolalia and what is really going on during this activity. The faithful will say that this is a spiritual thing and since science has no place in it science can't be used to understand it. They may even quote 1 Corinthian 1:27, which they think supports that attitude. But being spiritual does not preclude us from being scientific. Remember, God is not the author of confusion (1 Cor. 14:33). There would be a lot more understanding of God's word if we were more logical. Good research with proper technique and unbiased scientists are no match for God. His creation is full of scientific laws that the creation was established upon, laws that God created. So in essence, good scientific practices are seeking the truth and will ultimately serve to support the Bible which is true. In fact, there are scientists who are now using unbiased techniques and reaching unbiased results that show the earth is not billions of years old but only a few thousand years old, which supports the biblical account of creation. There have been a number of scientific studies that have attempted to authenticate this speech as an actual language. In 1972, Dr. William J. Samarin in one such study evaluated tape recordings of people from all around the world supposedly speaking in tongues. Over a five-year period the information was compiled and analyzed looking for factors and characteristics that are found common to all human languages. In short, his conclusions are the following:

- While speaking in tongues does appear at first to resemble human language, that was only on the surface.
- The actual stream of speech was not organized and there was no existing relationship between units of speech and concepts.
- The speakers might believe it to be a real language but it was totally meaningless.

Note that when he used speaking in tongues, he was referring to glossolalia and not to the tongues in Acts.

Linguists are not the only scientists interested in this subject. Psychiatrist Andrew Newberg at the University of Pennsylvania studied brain activity of people speaking in tongues. An immediate problem exists in this study not with the researcher but with the subjects. These participants were connected to an EEG machine, which monitors brain waves. This was not done in the middle of a church service but in the doctor's office or laboratory. That means these subjects were basically able to speak in tongues at will! That should give pause to anyone who can read the Bible and understands that the Holy Spirit is the initiator and controller of "tongues" and it is not something that an individual can call up anytime night or day at least not if you follow the pattern seen in the Bible. I know there are those who claim to teach individuals to speak in tongues but that is also something that is not seen anywhere in the Bible. What Dr. Newberg found was that frontal lobe activity decreased in people speaking in tongues. The frontal lobe is the area of the brain that allows for reasoning or conscious thought and self-control. In other words when those subjects were speaking in tongues, there was a measureable loss of self-control. Something else was trying to control them. He found that brain responses during glossolalia were different from responses of people who were meditating. Unlike glossolalia when people were meditating, their frontal lobe activity increased while parietal lobe activity decreased. The parietal lobe basically controls the senses. So during meditation, people were consciously tuning the senses out and controlling and focusing their thoughts while in glossolalia they were losing reason and control.

So when through science we observe the brain during glossolalia we see a picture of someone "losing" control of self. Amazingly, this is to be expected and actually to be desired from the Pentecostal point of view. "Let go and let God," "Let Him have His way with you," "Give up to Jesus." Though these phrases may not be as common as they once were they exemplify the mental state that leads to glossolalia. The great desire of the Pentecostal believer is to experience the presence of God in such a way that he overshadows and takes control of the individual. This is what is thought to happen when the presence of the Holy Spirit is felt and this is what happens when glossolalia occurs. So science confirms that at least in the people who participated in the study subjects were losing control. That also means they were either relinquishing their self-control or it was being taken from them. Again this raises a question between what is believed and taught and what the Bible actually says.

All through the Bible we see the importance of the principal of self-control stressed over and over again in both the Old and New Testaments. Whether talking about drinking too much wine Proverbs 20:1, Leviticus 10:9, or saying too much Proverbs 29:11, 16:23 the principal is there. In an area given and designed by God himself for human enjoyment and pleasure, 1 Corinthian 6:18 says, "Flee fornication." In Matthew 5:39 we are told, "Turn the other cheek" when someone strikes us. In Galatians 5:22–23, we see longsuffering and temperance mentioned in the cluster of fruit that should develop in our lives as a result of the baptism with the Holy Spirit. Ephesians 4:26 tells us it's okay to get angry but the anger should be controlled so that it does not cause us to sin. In 1 Corinthian 9:25, Paul teaches us to be moderate (or controlled) in all things. From all these verses, it seems that in every area of human experience we are admonished to remain in control at all times even when we are in danger of physical harm, control. Yet the doctrine of a "Holy Ghost Experience" in the Pentecostal church teaches, even encourages the total loss of control to experience a sign of the presence of the Spirit. This allows "speaking in tongues" as well as all the other physical behaviors that resulted in the name "holy rollers." Supporters of this doctrine might say something like, "You are mixing apples and oranges, these are two different things. The verses mentioned were talking about things that are experienced in the human realm and speaking in tongues is in the spiritual realm. Furthermore, there can be no excess when it comes to worshipping and praising God so moderation does not apply here." Well they may be apples and oranges but the common denominator is humans and you don't get to apply a different set of rules when it is convenient, God's principles are universal and timeless. Consistent application is important for clear understanding. The loss of control demonstrated when "speaking in tongues" or "shouting (the holy dance)" is not consistent with the biblical principle of control. This loss of control was also not apparent in descriptions of events at Pentecost. There was no rolling around on the floor or foaming at the mouth. No thrashing about with ladies' undergarments being exposed, no screaming or yelling in scenes resembling a ward in a mental institution. In fact, remember that Paul warned of people thinking we are "mad" in 1 Corinthian 14:23 if tongues were not spoken under control of the rules he laid out. There was never a spectacle associated with speaking in tongues in the Bible. It was amazing but not maniacal, it was miraculous but dignified. It honored God and did not draw so much attention to the person's activity that the miracle was overshadowed and the message missed.

So, if we are completely honest, we have to at least admit there is no similarity between the tongues spoken at Pentecost and what we hear most commonly today. There is no biblical scene related to the Holy Spirit where anyone falls out into an uncontrolled frenzy with bodies flailing or jumping about or foaming at the mouth. There are scenes in the Bible that portray these behaviors (Mark 5:1–20 and 9:14–32) unfortunately both of these are examples of demon possession. If we are dedicated with a heart full of sincerity to follow Christ and his example and his teachings and his teachers, then we cannot allow ourselves to deviate from anything that is taught in the Bible. Conversely, we should not make worship or devotional practices of things that are not clearly present in the Bible. If it is not done in the Bible specifically in the New Testament it should not be done by those calling themselves followers of Christ.

The possibility that I am on the right track about glossolalia paints a glaring picture of what can happen when scripture is misunderstood and when things that are not scriptural are treated as doctrine. Unfortunately, glossolalia may be just the tip of the iceberg when it comes to misunderstanding the Holy Spirit. The book of Acts introduces us to a new era in human history. Much like the birth of Christ this monumental event warranted a heralding like that of the heavenly messenger and host that appeared to shepherds. But unlike Jesus whose work would not begin for thirty years the Holy Spirit would begin work immediately. It is totally logical that the announcement be made in a miraculous way but with totally functional methods. It is quite possible that the main purpose of this amazing book has escaped the Pentecostal church because of the focus on the amazing "Acts" that appear instead of why they appear. Let me reiterate until the book of Acts the Holy Spirit did not take up residence and live within any individual human being. In the OT, the Spirit came upon God's servant or whom (or what) he chose to use and when the job was done the Spirit was gone. For the two-thousand-plus years before Christ in general most men had to rely on other men to seek God's forgiveness. But the prophet Joel (2:28) told of a wonderful day when that would no longer be the case. A day when there would no longer be the need for a dove or a goat, when it would no longer be necessary for a priest to be reached to ask forgiveness. A time when it wouldn't matter if you were dying and couldn't get to a priest when the Spirit would walk with you daily guiding your every step and fighting in your every battle, when the security of our salvation was no longer in question but verified by the very presence of the Spirit. Even when Christ was here with them the disciples did not have the HS in them. But then one day after the master was gone and the disciples thought with him all hope gone as well, they gathered in the Upper Room waiting! But waiting for what?

They gathered because of the Passover, they gathered because of fear, they waited out of obedience, but they probably didn't know for what. They were expecting the Holy Spirit but probably not then, and they surely didn't know how. The Holy Spirit arrived using three distinct signs that what was about to happen was in fact supernatural in origin. Signs and symbolism are found throughout scripture and in many cases serve as connections between the Old and New Testaments. It is no coincidence that Jesus's choice in disciples was the same number as the tribes of Israel, 12. When Daniel interpreted the dream of Nebuchadnezzar in chapter 2 he was giving a synopsis of world history using symbolism for major powers that would exist over time. If we fail to recognize that a sign or symbol is being used or the meaning in a particular situation we will likely misunderstand what we are reading. "And suddenly there came a sound from heaven as of a rushing mighty wind and it filled the house where they were sitting" (Acts 2:2). Most of us today recognize the sound when wind stirs up outside our homes and begins to affect anything that is not heavy or fastened down. If there was a sound like wind perhaps there were also the reactions expected in the presence of wind. The food from the Passover meal all over the floor, perhaps some small children having to be held down. The wind has a distinct character and when heard it is a sound that is recognized as belonging outside. There are few sounds that would be mistaken for the wind and if that sound is heard inside a building something is very, very wrong. There may also have been the expected chill associated with wind blowing. So the wind in scripture as in nature is associated with great power. In Genesis 8:1, it was the wind that caused the waters of the great flood to recede. It was also the wind that caused the parting of the Red Sea in Exodus 14:21. The wind brought and removed the plague of locusts in Exodus 10:13–19. But in Hebrew and Greek, the word for wind is also associated with spirit and breath (Hebrew: *n'shamah*— wind or vital breath; Greek: *pneuma*—current of air, breeze, figuratively spirit). So we see a double meaning possible in the use of the wind.

Next, "And there appeared unto them cloven tongues as of fire, and it rested on each of them" (Acts 2:3). Fire as a natural occurring element is amazing in its own right and this may be the most amazing of the events that took place in the Upper Room. As distinctive as sounds of the wind are, fire is even more so due to the visual aspect of its character. There is just no mistaking fire yet as surely as this was fire it was surely not acting like fire, but this is also the case in many appearances of fire in scripture (Daniel 3:19–25). The power to be so beneficial and so destructive places it near the top of the list of most important forces of nature that man has learned to harness. But to have fire just come into being on its own, to appear out of nowhere, rest upon human beings without causing any pain or damage had to blow the minds of everyone there. If the indoor wind made them wonder this spontaneous human combustion had to worry even frighten them. How much fire would appear, would it engulf the individuals completely? Would they be able to control it, is it going to burn them? They had to be totally aware of the danger this event posed, and they should have been breaking for the exit, but Paul gives no indication that anyone was trying to leave. Again as with the wind fire in scripture is associated with great power and is often seen as a destructive force related to God's wrath, anger and judgment (Genesis 19:24, Sodom and Gomorrah; Revelation 20:14). But in Zechariah 13:9, Malachi 3:3, 1 Peter 1:7, 4:12, it is seen as a means of purification. The most important use of fire, however, is to indicate the presence of God (Ex. 3:2–6, burning bush; 13:21, pillar of fire; 1 Kings 18:38, Elijah at Mt. Carmel). Thus, we see that fire can have three symbolic meanings when used in a scriptural reference.

Finally, "And they were all filled with the Holy Ghost, and began to speak with other tongues, as the Spirit gave them utterance." As noted earlier, these tongues were the languages of the region and are listed in Acts 2:9–11. What was being said was likely occurring simultaneously in fifteen different languages, words that could be repeated, shared, and written down and not some language-like gibberish that had no meaning to anyone within hearing. So the Holy Spirit is ushered in by three miraculous phenomena. But why three and why these three? Why three should be obvious, the trinity. The third person was being introduced, the trinity was being represented, trinity, third person, three miracles. With what has just been stated about wind and fire as signs, we can see that the wind may have been meant to represent the "power" of the Holy Spirit in our lives as well as the idea of new life being breathed into an individual (being born again) as life was breathed into Adam. Fire likely represents the purifying and cleansing that will take place by the work of the Holy Spirit (burning up the old sinful nature), as well as the very presence of God by the presence of the Holy Spirit now in each person individually.

Pentecostal churches have taken speaking in tongues as a sign of the presence of the Holy Spirit in a person to the extent in some cases that if you have not spoken you don't have the Spirit. At first glance this may seem logical. But if that is true why stop with tongues? If God intended the language as an indicator of the Spirit's presence because of the speaking when it first appeared, shouldn't wind and fire also occur as they did at Pentecost? Why don't we hear a sound as a rushing mighty wind today? Why don't we see cloven tongues of fire resting on recipients of the Holy Spirit today? In fact the wind and fire only happened once and that was at Pentecost, only in the book of Acts. Why should tongues be separated from the wind and fire when they occurred together? Is it because tongues are the only one of those that we can duplicate on our own? The tongues continued after Pentecost but again, only in the book of Acts. There are no scriptures noting anyone speaking in tongues not even the Apostles after the book of Acts. The only Apostle to even speak of tongues after Acts is Paul and as stated earlier it was in the context of clarifying and regulating their use. Maybe tongues have been taken out of context and out of place. If we let the Bible speak for itself and try listening to what is being said rather than finding a scripture that supports what we think or believe there would be less confusion and more clarity in our understanding. Maybe the reason tongues are only found in Acts is because that's the only place they were meant to be. The angels announced the birth of Christ just once we don't find continued announcements all through the New Testament. Similarly if tongues were meant to be an ongoing operation throughout human history you would think it would show up again somewhere in the New Testament. So after Pentecost there was no sound of wind and no fire resting on recipients who received the Holy Spirit. Yet the miracle of tongues did continue. But this is totally logical when we think about what happened in the Upper Room or more precisely who was there.

As was said fifteen different languages were represented in the people who were there. In just a few seconds what the Holy Spirit had to say was delivered to fifteen different groups of people because those attending would be able to share what they heard and witnessed in their own language to others who spoke that language. In the very beginning of the Holy Spirit's ministry this use of language was then as something going viral on the internet now. Whenever people are mentioned speaking in tongues it is associated with a group and this "ancient Internet" or "languagenet" was put into play. So the use of tongues (real tongues) had a very distinct purpose in the ancient world and even so we still don't see any indication of their use after Acts.

Tongues are not the only thing that suddenly disappeared after Acts. Healing and miracles in general are strangely absent as well. The last of these occurs in Acts 28:3-9 when Paul was shipwrecked on the island of Melita (modern Malta) which is about sixty miles south of Cape Passaro in Sicily. Chapters 23–28 involve a plot by the Jewish leaders to get Paul to Jerusalem in a plot to kill him but he ends up being sent to Rome. However, on the trip to Rome he is shipwrecked and the "barbarians" who rescue him are warm and kind to the castaways. It is very interesting that the book of Acts begins with three miracles (wind, fire, tongues) and ends with three miracles. (1) In chapter 27 an angel appears to Paul while the ship is in danger and lets him know that the ship will be lost but no one will die. In chapter 28 after landing on Melita a fire is built by the inhabitants and as Paul was placing sticks on the fire, a viper latched onto his hand. (2) When Paul did not drop dead as they expected in just a few minutes they thought he was a god. (3) Paul healed the father of the island's chief and many others while there. No more miracles after that at least no more healings. Oddly enough to emphasize this point, there are instances where healing is needed but none is attempted. In 1 Timothy 5:23, Paul instructed Timothy, "Use a little wine for thy stomach's sake and thine often infirmities." Some scholars suggest that the stomach issue suffered by Timothy had to do with the high alkaline water at Ephesus. Why not just heal him? We have Timothy a servant of God stationed in a place that was causing physical distress which had to hamper his effectiveness at times. We have the Apostle Paul who had at time laid healing hands on multiple sufferers at once, why didn't he just heal Timothy of his infirmity? Though this writing was a letter to Timothy surely Paul could have prayed for healing from a distance. Some may say, "Paul could not heal him without being near him, to touch him." In 2 Timothy 4:20, Paul states, "Trophimus have I left at Miletum, sick." This statement insinuates that he was with Trophimus which insinuates he was close enough to touch but he left him sick, why didn't he heal him? Again in Philippians 2:25–30, Paul is aware of the near death illness of Epaphroditus but does not seem to have acted in attempting healing by prayer since he was still in prison.

Healing is another spiritual barometer held in high regard by Pentecostals. We are taught to expect healing that it is our God-given right as his children to expect healing. There is often the impression given that if you are sick and are not healed, there is something wrong with you spiritually. I have seen sincere God loving and fearing leaders confused and dejected because they prayed for someone's healing and the person died. Conversely, I've seen leaders blame sufferers for having too little faith when healing does not come. Some leaders go so far as to say that sickness does not belong among God's people. Comments like this can cause disillusion in the hearts and minds of sincere Christians who are ill and confusion or distrust in people who are logical thinkers and can see past the smoke. Should we as Christians today be expected to lay hands of the sick and affect a cure when it seems that God's chosen few stopped? At issue also is the fact that not all the Apostles are recorded as having performed miracles of healing or any other kind. So why did it all seem to come to a halt after the book of Acts?

It could be that the book of Acts and the miracles that occurred therein were meant to be indicators of the presence of God's Holy Spirit now dwelling in mankind and that these chosen few were chosen by God to minister to mankind on this most important mission. It could be that the events in Acts were meant to get the attention of the world then and to keep it even now. The purpose of those miracles may have been to verify the authority of those performing them much as the miracles performed by Jesus demonstrated that this was no ordinary man, but one powered by a very special supernatural power. Once their credentials had been established before the world, then their words would be taken more seriously. After all, the most important part of the Day of Pentecost was what was said not what was seen.

When I came to Christ as a teen, I was told I had to "tarry" for the Holy Ghost. This involved a cleaning out of my life any known sin because "the Holy Spirit would not dwell in an unclean temple." Once I completed the process the Spirit would come into me and I would speak in tongues. Initially I was okay with not speaking because I knew that I was not sinless so the spirit couldn't come to me. But as I became more dedicated to righteous living, I became more frustrated that I had not spoken.

I understand now that my frustration was really unwarranted. I found out on my own through diligent study of the subject that there was nothing wrong with me, but there was something wrong with what I'd been taught. My heart aches for the countless thousands who find themselves in the same situation. Being told "you oughta show some sign," but the sign has been misread. Looking for an indicator that doesn't exist! Waiting and hoping for something that is never going to materialize. Wanting something so bad that you start trying to make it happen! There had to be an answer to all this. But the answer was not found in giving up or trusting in tradition. It was not found in just having faith or hanging onto what I was taught and what I believed. The answer came because I continued to ask the questions. Why hasn't it happened for me? What do the scriptures say about it? What am I doing wrong? Ultimately, these prayers led to clarity and a new understanding in the matter of tongues and many other subjects.

For God's Sake Get Understanding

So FAR WE HAVE seen examples of the problems that result from a lack of clarity when dealing with scripture. Most of these problems can be traced to shortcomings of clergy and leadership in the area of formal biblical training. Because most Pentecostal denominations don't require credentials in the form of college or seminary there are many untrained, uneducated, unqualified people misinterpreting the teachings of the Bible, failing to convey the rich essence of the word and leaving God's people with a plethora of misconceptions. James 3:1 reminds us of the responsibility that exists for teachers of God's word but perhaps because of a lack of training this information has escaped many of them. Or maybe this indicates that their reason for being in ministry is not as much to serve God as it is to serve themselves. Sadly many if not most Pentecostal sermons fall somewhere between a greeting card and a stand-up comedy routine. You will likely be encouraged in some area and you might get a laugh or two, but you are not likely to come away with knowledge that you did not have, nor increased understanding of an area you are already familiar with. This is not meant to be cruel it is simply the truth. On one level those who are preaching this way are not to blame because they are only doing what they see being done. They gauge success on the amount of feedback they get from the listeners during presentation. On the other hand, sincere dedication to serving God from the pulpit should inspire each and everyone who functions in this capacity to strive toward improving what they do and to give God's people the best. Because entry level educational requirements are minimal does not mean these clergymen have to remain "minimalists." There are too many resources available for those in ministry to remain at the same level of biblical knowledge year after year after year. Preachers who have failed God's people will surely be held responsible as James says, but what about us as laymen? If the leaders are falling short of their responsibility does that mean that we are off the hook because they didn't give us what they should have? Seems we should get an automatic pass in these cases, unfortunately that's not how it works.

The Bible is very clear about our responsibility in this matter. Philippians 2:12 tells us to "work out our own salvation." Our own! Each of us is ultimately responsible for what happens to us in our walk with God. If we sit under leaders year after year without growing spiritually or without changes in our habits, attitudes, or character we will be the one who's questioned at the judgment seat not the pastor. We will be held accountable for us not the pastor. We will be in danger of losing rewards not the pastor. His will be a greater penalty but his shortcomings will not let us off the hook. Work out your own salvation, what does that mean? One thing it means is to fulfill Galatians 5:22–23, which lists "the fruit of the Spirit." That scripture lists nine qualities that should become apparent in us as a result of the presence of the Holy Spirit in our lives. Notice the word *fruit* is used without an *s*, suggesting that the nine things listed are considered one group of things that should all be present together like a cluster of grapes. Many times I have heard people teach this scripture as if these are gifts that some have and others don't. It is certainly possible that some people have some of these qualities before the Spirit enters their lives but with time everyone should expect to develop the ones they don't have. But if no one has told you this how do you know it, how do you understand this concept? We understand it by studying!

Having completed a bachelor's degree, as well as six years of medical training, I feel confident saying I know what it means to study. But let us start with Webster's definition.

Study: the devotion of time and attention to acquiring knowledge on a subject, especially by books, or detailed investigation and analysis of a subject or a situation.

Chapter 17 of Acts talks about Paul traveling to Berea and speaking in the synagogue there. Verse 11 says the Bereans searched the scriptures daily in an effort to verify what Paul was saying. They didn't just blindly accept what he was teaching after all this was their heritage and their destiny he was talking about. They needed to be sure he knew what he was talking about. In much the same way, we need to be sure that what preachers are saying over the pulpit corresponds to what God's word really says and means and not someone's interpretation. In most Pentecostal services the scene is that the speaker is up talking to a group that seems more poised for a show than anything else. No pads no pens and no questions. You can't devote time and attention to acquire knowledge about a subject if you haven't written the subject down. So studying is essential if we are to understand what the scriptures say. Proverbs 4:1–7 speaks about the importance of getting understanding. Again Mr. Webster,

Understanding: to perceive the intended meaning of words, language or a speaker.

The most important part of that definition is "intended meaning." Many of the problems discussed earlier mask the intended meaning of scriptures. Only through diligent effort and time spent in the word will we be able to verify that we have it right or get clarity when we have it wrong. The important thing is the desire to get it right. Many people for whatever reasons will argue to support a conclusion that is invalid just for the sake of "winning" the argument. They may sound eloquent in presenting misinformation that leaves listeners awe struck. There may be a cockiness of attitude suggesting these errant words must be true and anyone who doesn't agree with them is really stupid. They may actually laugh at anyone who does not understand or agree with what they are saying but none of the posturing matters, if they are wrong they are wrong. All the examples discussed earlier involve missing the intended meaning of God's word. Whether by accident or design, ignorance or laziness the result is the same. False information is delivered as truth and those who receive it are in jeopardy of at least stunted spiritual growth.

As I stated earlier, I feel very confident talking about studying. Whenever I speak to young students about study habits invariably they say they have finished studying when they have completed their homework. Actually, homework is just the beginning of the study period. Homework basically lets you know in general terms what you should understand. Exams let you and your teacher know what you truly understand. Between homework and exams is studying, and exam results usually indicate the efficiency of your study habits. If you don't spend enough time, you probably won't do well. If you spend ample time but fail to get the "intended meaning" you probably won't do well. Therefore both ample time and clear, accurate information is integral in the process of understanding something. One without the other will not suffice and this is exactly where most Pentecostal believers find themselves. Unfortunately in most cases, both these commodities fall well short of the levels required for growth and progress. I finally realized after many Cs that I didn't really understand a subject until I could explain it to someone else, until I could guide or tutor another student. Again this is an area where most Pentecostal believers fall short. It is not that they fail to share the Gospel message but most of the time it is from a spiritual rather than a factual frame of reference. For example, earlier I shared the idea of someone speaking to a friend after Sunday morning service saying "Chall, we sure had a good time in church today." The friend responds "Yeah? What did he preach about?" Answer, "I don't know, but we sure had a good time." The good time spoken of by the first person reflects the joy and jubilation of the Pentecostal services. The praise, the holy dance (shouting), the singing, the unbridled expression that exist in this style of worship. I am not saying these are bad things of course not. But the most important thing in any worship service is what we get from God and that comes from his word. In the beginning was the Word! God created the heavens and the earth with his Words! He is the alpha and the omega, which are the first and last letters of the Greek alphabet and all the letters between them are used to make Words! Words give us all the knowledge of God, his as well as our beginning and ending and everything in between but to understand what he is saying to us we must study.

There are several reasons that studying is so important, and I don't claim to know all of them but here are a few that I think stand out in the crowd. Truth! The only way to really know the truth is to study. Many of us as I did for years relied on leaders and trusted that they knew what they were talking about and therefore there was no reason to look into it any further. Again, this is not meant as an indictment against any of our forefathers, but many times they just didn't know what they were talking about! So we need the truth and we need to be willing to search until we find it and search until we are confident that we have "God's" truth and not our own or that of someone else. St. John 8:31–32 Christ says, "If ye continue in my word, then are ye my disciples indeed: And ye shall know the truth and the truth shall make you free." The Greek word translated continue in that passage is *meno* and means to stay, remain, or abide. The idea here seems to be twofold. We can abide in God's word in the sense that we consistently function in accordance to the precepts, commandments and ideals set forth in the scriptures. When we allow our lives to be a mirror that reflects the teachings of the Bible, we are "continuing" in his word. But to do that successfully we have to spend sufficient time "in" the word that is digging into the word. Becoming intimately acquainted with what scriptures actually say as well as what they actually mean. In this sense we are literally continuing in the word when we return to study it over and over and over again. Ephesians 1:13 says, "Ye are sealed with the Holy Spirit of promise." This means the Holy Spirit is like God's stamp of ownership and not only serves to identify us but also to protect us. But the scripture also states that we receive this seal after hearing and believing "the word of truth." Ephesians 6:10–17 talks about "The Armor of God" listing six items that are essential for the battle against Satan and the very first item is truth and that refers primarily to the truth of God's word. We are warned of false prophets in Matthew 7:15, 24:24, and 2 Peter 2:1–3 and obviously we need to know the truth if we are to recognize the false. Several scriptures adjure us strongly or pronounce curses on anyone who adds to or takes away from the words of the Bible or the Gospel message (Deut. 4:2, 12:32; Prov. 30:6; 2 Cor. 11:4; Gal. 1:8; Rev. 22:18). There is a high price to pay for those who altar God's word and none of those scriptures gave a pass to those who act out of ignorance.

In St. John 18:38, Pilate asked Jesus, "What is truth?" Today it is likely that many people are asking themselves this question because so many things are being challenged that were taken for granted in the past. Is there a God? Is there only one God? Did God create the universe? Did God create man? If you have a biblical worldview you probably answered yes to all those questions. If not then you probably answered no to all of them. The natural sciences have spent so much time and attention explaining the origin of the universe and the theory of evolution that many Christians are wondering, big bang or Genesis, Darwin or creation. The "truth" of the matter is that the big bang theory as well as the theory of evolution is just that, theory. Neither has been proven (nor can they be) but both are presented by the scientific community as fact and that is what children are taught in most if not all public schools. That the two seem to support each other gives even more validity to each idea separately. For example science teaches that the earth is millions and millions of years old and this is supported by carbon-12 dating methods applied to fossils found all over the world. The Theory of Evolution would have us believe that all life evolved from a very "spontaneous" coming together of very "specific" proteins and polypeptides, which created the first single cell organism that then evolved into every other form of life on the planet. It would of course take millions and millions of years for this process to occur so the old earth fits nicely with the evolution process. The problem is that there are flaws in the carbon dating system that render the million-year-aged earth inaccurate and actually substantiate a much younger earth. In fact, there are now Christian scientists who are dating the earth closer to ten thousand years old, which would fit the Genesis record and earth age related to the creation. Can you imagine how difficult it must be for children who are inundated with these secular ideas, have little or no training to the contrary either at home or church but are expected to remain practicing Christians as adults? If we are not seeking the truth, if we are not asking questions, if we are not looking for clarity in the study of God's word, how can we effectively serve as a guide to a child or anyone else?

According to Timothy, we are to study in order to receive the approval of God (2 Tim. 2:15). He doesn't say how this approval is manifested, but it is likely in the fulfillment of the promises to the righteous that are found throughout scripture (Deut. 31:6; Ps. 34:7, 17; Isa. 58:6; Matt. 17:18–21; 2 Cor. 1:2–4) to name just a few. In contrast it seems we must be a disappointment to God when we fail to study his word regularly and efficiently with the intent of gaining clarity and accuracy. So God is pleased with us when we study his word, and it makes sense that the more we study the more pleased he is. Unfortunately, this fact gets lost in the forest of misinformation that is so pervasive from many pulpits today. If there is a way to increase the amount of pleasure God gets from us I for one would be most interested in mastering the methodology.

Let's take this a step further. Not only is God pleased when we study, it may be that we are commanded to study. There are several passages of the New Testament where different writers seem to assume that we are studying. The apparent intent is to portray a picture of our mind and that of Christ somehow becoming one:

- 1 Corinthian 2:16, "For who hath known the mind of the Lord, that he may instruct him? But we have the mind of Christ."
- Philippians 2:5, "Let this mind be in you, which was also in Christ Jesus."

Obviously these scriptures are not talking about a brain transplant, and if they were, then only one person could get it. We are not talking about some sort of telepathy because that would also require that the physical brain of Christ be available. How can you and I in 2017 possibly have the mind of Christ? How can his mind be in you and me? Webster defines the *mind* as "the element of a person that enables them to be aware of the world and their experiences, to think and to feel, the faculty of consciousness and thought." The Greek word used for mind in the 1 Corinthian scripture is *nous* and refers to "thought processes, feelings, will, knowing and understanding." The word for mind in Philippians is *phroneo* and means to entertain or to have a certain opinion or sentiment, to be mentally predisposed in a certain direction, to think a certain way. All three of these definitions point in the same direction. They are not speaking about the physical brain but the aspect of the brain that makes humans different from other life forms, that is the ability to reason, draw conclusions, and develop attitudes about moral (and other) ideas and issues. These scriptures assume and encourage that our conclusions, attitudes, and moral ideas be the same as those of Christ; and we find these ideas nowhere else but in his word. This does not seem to be a suggestion, it does not seem to be something that is optional or that we have any choice in. It seems to be something that is expected that all followers of Christ will develop at some point in their walk. Another example: Romans 12:2, "But be ye transformed by the renewing of your mind…"

This scripture implies that our minds must go through a change, a process of renewal that is necessary because of the influences of the evils in the world. Verse 1 suggests that we sacrifice our bodies (which of course includes our minds) in active separation from the world (worldly attitudes, ideas, etc.) and that we would "be transformed" if our minds are renewed. In other words, our minds need to be "rebooted" from the influences of the world and given a new "hard drive" written in the "format" of Christ. Written means words, his words, his teachings, his ideas. Again a reason that many of us don't undergo substantial change (transformation) is not necessarily because we don't have salvation but there has not been enough absorption of his Word and its true meaning into our minds. The phrase "renewing of your mind" seems to also suggest an active role on the part of each individual and the "be ye transformed" sounds a lot like a command. It sounds as if we not only have an active role in the transformation but that we also have some of the tools required to affect the transformation.

- 1 Peter 1:13—Gird the loins of the mind
- Hebrew 8:10—Laws in their minds

- Acts 17:11—Received the word with readiness of mind
- Luke 10:27—Love the Lord...with the mind

All these scriptures refer to the mind and the human capacity to think reason and understand. They refer to the ideas, attitudes, conclusions, morals, and philosophies of one person (Christ) being transferred to the minds of others (believers). The transformation does not occur by feeling anything or by anyone laying hands upon us. It does not come by just believing and having faith. It comes by actively and regularly opening the Bible and trying to understand what God is saying to us collectively and individually. Colossians 3:16 says, "Let the word dwell in you richly"; 1 Peter 1:13 says, "Wherefore gird up the loins of your mind, be sober, and hope to the end for the grace that is to be brought unto you at the revelation of Jesus Christ." Dwelling in us richly has a sense of abundance, rich people have more than enough money, more than just enough to get by. If the word dwells in us richly, we certainly have more than just a general knowledge of the Bible. We should be capable of answering at least most general questions and give explanations to commonly puzzling issues. The word is not dwelling richly if you only have a bare minimum of knowledge and understanding of it. The phrase "gird up your loins" suggests being or getting prepared for action and you certainly are not ready for action if you don't have a clear understanding of the revelation of Jesus Christ.

Ephesians 6:10–17 paints a picture of us as soldiers or warriors and delineates the weapons that should be in place if we are to win this spiritual battle. This scripture describes six items that should be present in the Christian arsenal. The first item, "truth," and the last, "the sword of the spirit which is the word of God" both specifically indicate the importance of understanding God's word. So the first weapon and the last are the word of God. Truth is really self-explanatory and it is also obvious that a sword is a weapon of attack to be used against the enemy which includes false teachers and teachings as well as false prophets. But if we are not armed with enough ammunition (understanding of the word), there will be many battles that are lost because we are ill-equipped. Two of the other four weapons, righteousness, and the gospel of peace also come from the knowledge and understanding of the written word. It is imperative to understand God's standard and what he sees as righteous if we are to walk within that standard which is found in the word. We also need to clearly and accurately understand the gospel of peace so that we will be able to share it as well as being comfortable that we are at peace with God and be able to clarify any misunderstandings as we witness to those who come our way. Though it may be debatable whether the previous scripture examples are commands there is no debating Ephesians 6:11 as a command which says, "Put on the whole armor of God." We are certainly commanded in this passage, there can be no mistaking that.

An area touched on earlier warrants attention again here and that is the importance of language and translation when seeking to understand the scriptures. As has been stated before the Bible was not originally written in English and while most of us who read it at all realize this, we usually don't recognize the problems that can occur between translation and understanding. Some of the earliest writings of the Old Testament were written in Aramaic, which was an early form of Hebrew but most writings were originally in Hebrew. There is also a Greek translation of the Old Testament the Septuagint. The New Testament was first written in Greek and later translated to English. One of the problems in translating from one language to another is that sometime there is no equivalent word between the two. For example try to find another language with a word that translates "flabbergasted." In Spanish there is the word *Sobremesa* that is the moments after eating a meal, when the food is gone but the conversation is still flowing at the table. This happens quite frequently in Greek. When we see the word *love* in the KJV Bible it is used in many different situations between many different people and it is always spelled l-o-v-e. We usually get a sense of the kind of love the passage means from the setting and the context, but it is left up to us to extrapolate and make the correct interpretation. The Ancient Greek language on the other hand took all the guesswork out of the equation by using at least seven different words for love.

- Agape—selfless or unconditional, Christian, godly love
- Philia—deep friendship/brotherly love
- Eros—sexual love
- Ludus—playful/childlike/puppy love
- Pragma—love between long married couple
- Storge_parents love for children
- Philantia—self-love

So when reading the Greek language, we are very unlikely to get the wrong idea because the word was not understood. This is the case with many, many, many other Greek words with some having many more words for one concept. This leads to very precise and specific ideas being related with little chance of confusion. When there is no English equivalent for a word the translator has to come up with a word that he feels best approximates the intended meaning. When this happens at least a portion of the intended meaning is lost. When the word had a very specific meaning as in the love examples much more of the intended meaning is lost.

Another example of the translation problem can be seen in a very popular scripture from 2 Timothy where verse 15 tells us to "study to show thyself approved unto God, a workman that needeth not to be ashamed, rightly dividing the word of truth." With beginning this chapter on the importance of studying you may have wondered why this was not the first scripture referenced. It would have been except that previous examination of this scripture shed new light on its meaning. This has been one of the most quoted scriptures I've heard over the course of my lifetime. No matter who quoted it the basic meaning has always been "devoting time and attention to acquire knowledge about the Bible so as to accurately share and explain what the scriptures are saying. This is in essence the Webster definition of study. Ironically, when you "study," the Greek word for study from 2 Timothy 2:15, you get a very surprising result. The Greek word for study is "spoudazo" and it has nothing to do at all with picking up a book to understand what it is saying. The meaning is to hasten or make haste, to exert oneself, to endeavor consistently, to be diligent. In fact, an NIV text renders the verse "be diligent to present yourself," another "Do your best to present yourself." When reading through the definition of *spoudazo*, you get the sense of always being ready, always on the job, always focused on the task at hand. Be quick to do this job, always be ready to do this job consistently and persistently. What is the job we are told to be diligent in, "rightly dividing the word of truth." Rightly dividing comes from the Greek word/phrase *orthomoteo* and literally means to cut a straight line. However metaphorically it is rendered "going in or following a straight path." Taking these two definitions into account it is unlikely that Paul is speaking to Timothy about acquiring education or knowledge. If a person wants to force the argument to the contrary, we can make a case for the usual idea this scripture prompts. That is the only way to be diligent is to spend time in the word. There would have to be time devoted to studying and this is the only way that clarity or rightly "breaking down" the word can happen. But if we pay strict attention to the meaning, we get from the Greek words we get a thought more like; persevere in your daily living to walk the straight and narrow path that was given to you by the Gospel of Jesus Christ. This latter idea also seems supported by what is said in chapter 2 from verses 1–14, things like "Hang in there," "You're a soldier," "Remember what you were taught," "It's normal to suffer." Contextually this makes much more sense. Why would Paul spend 14 verses on encouragement and endurance and suddenly jump into education? When we look at these things more closely, sometimes we see them more clearly. But we sometimes have to be willing to look at things differently if we hope to get an understanding.

Let's stick with Timothy to begin the next discussion, 2 Timothy 3:16. This scripture states, "All scripture is given by inspiration of God, and is profitable for doctrine, for reproof, for correction, for instruction in righteousness." When we look at this scripture we likely think of the sovereignty and the majesty of God the holiness of scriptures and the honor and reverence due them. Of course this is all true but we also have to remember that the Bible is a book, a piece of literature, and if we fail to recognize this aspect of its character we also do it a disservice. For example the churches that took Mark 16:18 to mean that they should use deadly poisonous snakes in their worship services as a way to honor God failed to recognize that scripture was not a command. It was not meant for doctrine, reproof, correction, or instruction in righteousness and it certainly wasn't meant to expose so many innocent lives to so much mortal danger. For our study of God's word to be most efficient, we need to recognize what we are reading.

As stated before, both the Old and New Testaments are made up of a few different types of writing. The OT is made up of history, poetry, and prophecy and the NT, history, Pauline epistles, and general epistles (prophecy Revelation). In the OT, the history is from Genesis-Esther, poetry from Job-Song of Solomon and prophetic from Isaiah-Malachi. The NT history is from Matthew-Acts, Pauline epistles Romans-Philemon, and general epistles Hebrews-Revelation. When we fail to recognize what we are reading, there is a great chance that we will not interpret correctly and therefore our understanding will be greatly flawed. With flawed understanding the resultant reaction will likely also be flawed, which in many cases can be quite dangerous as we have seen with the snake handlers. Another example that is not biblical but a great illustration is a famous radio broadcast from 1938. Many of us are familiar with the 2005 movie *War of the Worlds*, starring Tom Cruz. This was a remake of a 1953 classic sci-fi thriller of the same name. Both were adapted from a novel with that title written by H. G. Welles. In 1938, the not yet famous aspiring actor Orson Welles (no relation to H. G.), adapted a play from the novel and with the help of other performers it was broadcast on the Mercury Theatre Radio show for CBS radio on October 30 as a Halloween show/prank. The plot or "context" of the story is simply that earth is being invaded by Martians. The format used however was not that of a narrator telling a story but a news reporter jumping in with what seemed to be an on the spot report of events much like we see on television now with breaking news of terror attacks. There was an announcement at the beginning of the broadcast explaining what was to be presented that night the problem is many that tuned into the program tuned in late. They tuned in to hear a reporter describing what seemed to be eyewitness events that were actually taking place rather than a fictional presentation.

The fact that it was on the radio not TV probably aided in the realism of the presentation, which many listeners bought into. There is some dispute about how many people fell for it, but it is clear that enough outrage occurred that the FCC (Federal Communications Commission) became involved. The point is that because people didn't know what they were listening to their minds took over and began to make assumptions that were based on flawed information. They jumped past rationalizing whether there was life on other planets, all the way to Martians are here and trying to take us out. This may seem like an extreme example but it is very similar to what can happen when we fail to recognize what we are reading and that all scripture is not meant to be treated or reacted to on the same level.

Mark 16:18 is likely the source of the practices of the snake-handling churches. In verses 14–20 of this chapter Christ addresses the Apostles and charges them with "The Great Commission" where he tells them to go into all the world and preach the gospel. In this ancient world, these men would travel mostly by foot on dirt roads when there were roads. The Middle East was and still is a terrain that is very rocky and warm, which is well suited for and bountifully occupied by reptiles of all sorts. In their travels through this region, it is totally logical even expected that at some time one or more of the Apostles would encounter a poisonous snake and in verse 18 Christ seems to pronounce protection for their travels stating that they would not be harmed in such a case. But maybe this is more than announcing protection. Maybe Christ is actually stating prophecy in this passage because in Acts 28:5 that is exactly what happens. While stranded on the island of Melita, Paul gathers sticks to help build a fire when a very venomous snake (viper) was apparently in the bundle he gathered and fastened onto Paul's hand. The natives of the island knowing this viper all too well basically expected Paul to drop dead before their eyes. Not only did he survive, he showed no sign of ever being bitten. Verse 18 also mentions drinking any deadly thing and while not mentioned in the Bible, other historical accounts state that Aristodemos a priest of the temple of Diana challenged St. John to drink poison, which he did with no harm. It is obvious that the snake handlers have taken what is surely a great historical and prophetic account and turned it into a command or a doctrine. But the snake handlers are not the only ones who may have fumbled this passage. Pentecostals and charismatics very commonly take this passage of scripture to indicate that Christ's followers today should expect to be "followed by these signs," specifically laying hands on the sick and having them recover. This passage is also used to support speaking in tongues and the ability to cast out demons (verse 17). It is important that we question the mental processing involved when dealing with this passage. On the one hand, we have group A, the snake handlers; and on the other group B, the healers. I have spoken to and been in discussions many times with groups who basically look at the snake handlers as ignorant uneducated people but see themselves as the righteous, enlightened, and faithful servants of God, yet they are dealing with the same passage of scripture. In fact both groups make the same mistake with this passage. Both groups fail to recognize the historical significance of the Great Commission and both groups apply spiritual significance to the wrong portion of the passage. Historically this is a major turning point. Up to now Christ has been with them and walked them hand in hand through training and preparation for the task they were chosen for. Now the Apostles were going to be on their own. They were being given their assignment, and Jesus wasn't going to be by their side to clean up any mess they made. I think where it gets confused spiritually goes back to our old friend context. We are so quick to jump on "these signs shall follow them that believe" that we misunderstand who Christ is talking to and why.

In the beginning of chapter 16, Jesus has risen. Mary the mother of Jesus, Mary Magdalene, and Salome had visited the tomb found Christ gone and were told by an angel he had risen. Later Christ appeared to Mary Magdalene after which she told a "group" of the disciples he was alive and she had seen him, and they did not believe her. Jesus also appeared to two disciples on the road to Emmaus, and they did not recognize him. All in all after being taught and told what things would happen to him the disciples failed to believe what Jesus had said or the witness of those that reported seeing him after the resurrection. Jesus was not pleased with their unbelief and when he appeared to them all together he blasted them verbally for it. He blasted that group, the group who failed to believe. He was talking just to that group, the group who failed to believe. This was not a gathering of Christian converts as in the Sermon on the Mount. It was just the chosen few who would now be sent out to spread the gospel. As Christ sent them all out to do the work he adds speaking just to those who could hear him "and these signs shall follow those who believe." To paraphrase, he was probably saying something like, you all have been trained for what I want you to do and now it's time to get to work. I'm disappointed that so few of you believed the things I told you but those of you that do believe will see great signs manifested as a part of the work you do for me. Christ was likely saying, these signs will follow those of you that I am speaking to who believe. That would explain why there is only a record of just a few of the disciples performing any miracles. Christ was talking just to the twelve and not even all of them produced the "signs that would follow those who believe." If there are members of Christ's chosen group who never laid hands on someone and healed them or who never cast out a demon why should we expect that each and every one of us should be able to? So spiritually group B rejects the snake-handling but embraces the laying on of hands, etc. Why? If both things were spoken by Christ in the same context, why accept one and not the other? Why is one logical and the other ignorant? This situation demonstrates what I will call "contextual separation." This occurs when ideas or beliefs that are related in context are separated, treated individually, and then embraced or rejected as a person or group chooses. So recognizing that we are reading history or poetry or prophecy can make a great difference in our understanding what we are reading. Even with the words that are direct quotes from Christ we need to be careful to recognize the kind of book and the context in which he is speaking.

It is also important to recognize that as a book, the Bible like any other book uses literary tools common to other literary works. Metaphor, similes, analogies among others are just some of the literary tools present in the scriptures and as with other things mentioned can be a source of confusion if not recognized and understood. Jesus used metaphors probably more than any other tool and probably more than any other writer. Euphemism is a tool used throughout the Bible especially in reference to sexual topics. It is a tool that allows description and discussion of sexual things in more palatable language. But these tools are used for specific reasons and usually not meant to be taken literally. For example all through the Bible Old and New Testaments we find the metaphor of Gods children as sheep and God as shepherd. Most of us are acquainted with the twenty-third Psalm, "The Lord is my shepherd I shall not want." The shepherd motif was one that Christ used often as in St. John where he calls himself "the Good Shepherd," distinguishing himself from all the bad shepherds mentioned in the Bible primarily in the OT. The idea of the sheep/shepherd relationship is to paint a picture of the relationship between Christ and his followers. It was used because the relationship between an actual shepherd and his flock was something that the people of Christ's day would have fully understood and made the connection to what he was saying to them. So, a metaphor was used to help bring clarity to what was being said. But suppose like so many other things, someone got the wrong idea about the sheep metaphor. Because Christ said, "I am the good shepherd" and "my sheep hear my voice," someone could get the idea that we should come to church services with little lamb skins on our heads or shoulders and the preacher or pastor should carry a staff during worship. Maybe a good name for the denomination would be "The Church of the Living Lamb." That may sound silly, but when we look factually into some of the things that have been discussed, it's no more silly than some of those.

An area that is very neglected in Pentecostal circles is eschatology (end time prophecy). This is a topic that is so very relevant today with the issues in the Middle East and radical Islamic terrorism but is seldom discussed in a concise manor. This is again I believe related to the lack of formal training and education on the part of leaders but that is still not an excuse. There are too many resources available either in terms of materials or speakers with expertise in the area for any group to be ignorant in this topic. Yet I am reasonably sure that very few pastors, not to mention parishioners could give a concise and clear description of end-time events starting with the rapture and ending with the millennium. Satan is using many tools in his war against the world and I think another of his favorites is complacency. We have been lulled into a sense of calm as if nothing is wrong and all is well with the world, when nothing is farther from the truth. The United States of America has not experienced a war on her soil since the Civil War but that all changed with the 9/11 attack and the world will never be the same again. But many Pentecostals have no idea of the significance of the struggle between the Palestinians and the Jews and the importance of the role the US should play in this struggle. These events are setting the stage for the appearance of the Antichrist if he is not already born. Having a better understanding of these events will not only strengthen the confidence of believers but will empower them for witnessing in their daily lives when these events come up at work and school as they often do.

As limited as the discussion of eschatology is among Pentecostals, the topic of apologetics does not exist at all. Apologetics is defined as reasoned arguments or writings in justification of something, typically a theory or a religious doctrine. It is derived from the Greek word apologia, meaning a speech in defense of something. Basically relative to Christianity, it means to give reasons for our belief or to defend the faith. I remember as a child Sunday school was a big deal at our church, but it wasn't until my father shared some of his memories that I realized just how big a deal it was. On Saturdays the ladies in the church would sell dinners to raise money for different church projects or needs. It was always a great atmosphere, the aromas from all the wonderful food and the laughing and playful banter that was never apparent during worship services because they were always so serious. But I also remember next to the plates of food, Bibles out on the tables with paper sticking out of them, or Sunday school-books placed in a particular portion of scripture. I never paid much attention to what was being said. When I was there I was preoccupied with getting some of that wonderful fried chicken, some sweet potato pie, or pound cake. My father recently explained that many of these sessions were warm-ups for Sunday school. The male leaders of the church after studying and searching the scriptures all week were comparing their findings for the coming lesson with the other scholars, looking for new insight or shooting someone down for weak or unfounded information. They would come to the adult session the next day with books under arm or in briefcases and anyone who presumed to shed light or new insight on a particular subject or issue had better be prepared to support it with sound explanation citing chapter and verse. Dad said that many times the discussions would get quite heated so much so that my grandmother stopped coming to Sunday school all together for a very long time because she didn't like the climate that sometime developed. Deacon Lofton was one of these men that always stood out because of his interest in books. Whenever I had occasion to visit his home, he was likely reading or there was evidence of a break from or starting because a book was open. My uncle Jay was another one that was a voracious reader and full of information that at the time seemed a bit contrary. These men these patriarchs were apologists. But at issue for apologists then and now is another "A" word, argument. This was the reason my grandmother stopped coming to Sunday school, she felt that what was going on in the Sunday school sessions was arguing and therefore at least distasteful and considered wrong.

It is very unfortunate that this word has such a bad reputation and frankly I suppose it is deserved. When we think about this word, usually the first thing that comes to mind is a fight. Most fights don't begin spontaneously. You seldom see two people make eye contact and instantly come to blows and when that does happen usually there has been some prior incident between them. Usually a fight, a physical altercation begins with a disagreement leading to a heated verbal exchange that escalates in volume and intensity leading to anger loss of control and ultimately people hitting one another. It's only a fight if both participants land blows, right? If I get hit but fail to retaliate that is not a fight (God help me to be so strong). So when we see fights they are most commonly initiated by arguments and no one wants to see a fight break out in a church. There have been instances in the news where such things occur in municipal government settings and yes in churches. It is a disgraceful scene and should of course be avoided. Pastors of all denominations would do anything to avoid such deplorable behavior in their congregations. Sadly with this being the case it may also be a weakness that Satan has been able to exploit. Again due to our lack of understanding on the one hand and the desire to preserve respectable behavior on the other we miss a very important aspect of our Christian responsibility.

We are soldiers and scripture makes this clear: Proverbs 16:7, Psalm 18:31–36, Psalm 138:7, 1 Corinthians 9:7, 2 Timothy 2:3–4. Paul paints the clearest picture of this in Ephesians 6:10–17 when he talks about the armor of God. Armor is meant for soldiers and what good would a soldier be without armor which does include a weapon of attack in the sword of the Spirit. Ah, but is not Paul just using a "metaphor" here? Does he really mean for us to see ourselves as soldiers in the sense of actual fighting? I think the answer is an unequivocal yes. Jude 3 says, "Beloved, when I gave all diligence to write unto you of the common salvation, it was needful for me to write unto you and exhort you that you should earnestly contend for the faith which was once delivered unto the saints." There is no metaphor in use here and this is in the form more of a command that a suggestion so it is absolutely meant to be taken literally. *Contend* by definition is struggle to overcome a situation, difficulty, or danger. Synonyms include compete, contest, struggle, strive, battle, and fight. The Greek word for contend (*epagonidzami*) has the same meaning. In fact *earnestly* is used in the Greek definition as in Jude's writing and is said to convey the intensity that is intended. So Jude is not only saying fight for the faith, he's saying you must reeeeeally fight for the faith, in fact using "exhort you" in the passage says; I stroooooongly urge that you must reeeeeeeally fight for the faith. As always our old friend context can bring further clarity that this is Jude's point. In the rest of the passage he is talking about and condemning false teachers who have "crept in unawares" who were undermining the truth and the righteousness of the church. Jude describes these false teachers as sexually impure, covetous, rebellious, arrogant, deceptive, sensual, and divisive. The fight is meant not only to guard the believer from the same perversities but verse 23, "And others save with fear, pulling them out of the fire," we are called on to rescue those that are in danger of being lost to their confusion or errant teaching. In essence, we are not fighting only against false teaching and misunderstanding, but we are fighting for those that are lost in the muck and mire of error and confusion. So as soldiers, we are basically called upon to be apologists or people filled with information or reasons, arguments that support the faith (the Gospel) and "attack" and bring clarity to people who are misquoting, misunderstanding, or misinterpreting the Gospel message and the words of the Bible.

But there's that word again, *argument*. But in all honesty, it is not arguing that is the problem, it is the loss of control that can accompany the process leading to a heated exchange of words. *Argue* defined is to cite evidence in support of an idea, action, or theory, typically with the aim of persuading others to share one's view. This is often seen in court as depicted in many TV law drama. But notice that in the court setting with the attorney's arguing they never seem to come to blows. They get heated and sometime there is even yelling but usually no fights. Why? It's because of the mediator. The judge with the rules of the court controls the situation and keeps things from getting out of hand. So it is not the arguing that is the problem it is the loss of control. It's not even anger that is the issue as Paul said in Ephesians 4:26, "Be angry and sin not," so it is possible to be angry without committing sin. But because argument is almost synonymous with fight to avoid the appearance of unrighteousness and confusion we avoid discussions that seem to be heading down argument lane. We avoid them like Ebola; we avoid them like we avoid drunken debauchery and sexual infidelity. Don't get me wrong, I totally understand why it is done. I've seen video of church leaders brawling or going on an obscenity tirade and of course it is disgusting, shameful, and embarrassing to Christians everywhere. If we can keep that from happening, of course we should do all that we can, everything humanly possible to keep things from getting out of hand and becoming violent. But even to the point of disobeying scripture? Remember, Jude said "contend" or fight for the faith, and he wasn't talking about a physical fight of course but a verbal fight. In 1 Peter 3:15, we are told, "And be ready always to give an answer to every man that asketh you a reason of the hope that is in you with meekness and fear." In Isaiah 1:18 the Lord admonishes, "Come now, let us reason together." Timothy uses reason as in explanation or justification. Isaiah is speaking of the capacity of the human mind to think and understand. These two scriptures use the two different meanings of the word reason but bring together the one primary thought that has driven this book, it is imperative that we clearly understand God's word in order to share it effectively. So should we disobey scripture to save the reputation of the church? Is it more important to be "doers of the word" or to appear godly to the world? Another supposed scripture I've heard most of my life that seems to apply here is "we should not argue about scripture." Now, what will happen with some who are confronted with Jude is no matter what they read in the Bible because the first statement is engrained in their hearts they will continue to hold on to it. But like so many other examples in this book, the "not arguing about scripture" is only a partial quotation. The complete verse of 2 Timothy 2:14 reads, "Of these things put them in remembrance, charging them before the Lord that they strive not about words to no profit, but to the subverting of the hearers." As you can see the scripture does indeed say, "Strive not about words," which can be understood as don't fight or argue about words. But avoiding the rest of the sentence from that point leaves the intended thought incomplete. When we add "to no profit," the thought goes from don't argue about words, to don't argue about words for nothing. Granny used to say, "Some people will argue with a stop sign." That's what this scripture is condemning, arguing for the sake of arguing, just to be different, just to keep things stirred up. Not because you are looking for answers but just because you like to argue or because you have a need to be right all the time. The next word in the verse is *but* and acts as a conjunction in this verse, introducing in the next sentence a contrast to the previous sentence. Taking this into account the thought is, don't argue about words for nothing but argue about them with a purpose and that purpose is the subverting of the hearers. *Subvert* means to undermine the power and authority of something/someone, to destabilize or overthrow, also (unnerve, upset, disturb, disquiet). Subvert gives you a feeling of shaking things up or throwing a monkey wrench into the works, getting someone out of their comfort zone, or making them think outside the box. So there is no scripture that says we should not argue about scripture but there are a couple that say we should.

Like the term used in professional boxing, we are called to be contenders, fighters or soldiers, apologists. While Jude is calling for us to fight, he is of course not talking about physically. As apologist, our tools and our weapons are words. So there is a dilemma especially in the Pentecostal church. In many cases there is a reluctance on the part of leaders to consistently provide answers to questions that surface in Bible studies and Sunday school sessions. Of course one reason is the lack of formal training and education but another is ego and a need to maintain certain perceptions among the followers. In my experience as an adult most pastors don't attend Sunday school. Some will stay in their office preparing the sermon and or praying (supposedly). That is a good excuse, but there are those that are just puttering around not doing anything in particular. Is the attitude I don't need Sunday school or I'm too busy for it? But anyone doing the same would be told how they need to be in the class. If he is not preparing or praying what could be more important than making sure the class is getting it right? But then what if someone asks a question that the pastor can't answer but someone else can, quite embarrassing. It is a common problem. I know a young lady who discusses issues with my wife and I because her church leaders say they will get back to her about her questions but they never do. She loves the church and wants to stay there because that's where she found the Lord and feels that is her home, but she is very frustrated and does not feel they are helping her to grow. When people leave churches in situations like this, then pastors usually find other reasons for the exit. Failure to get answers not only stunts growth but fosters a lack of confidence for witnessing. If we are to be contenders, if we are to be soldiers we need to have information and we need to have questions answered. I have been in many discussions where disagreement about the meaning of scripture comes to a stalemate. I have been the reason for many of these discussions as you might guess. Over the years, this has happened over and over and usually what happens is the pastor will bring the discussion to an end with the promise that it will be revisited at a later date. The later date never comes. When confronted about returning to the subject that was avoided it usually becomes clear that the concern was to avoid confusion. But in essence by leaving the subject open, neither side of the discussion is brought into clarity and the other participants are left further in the dark. So there is actually more confusion produced by avoiding the topic than by trying to get an understanding. It is quite comical to me that there is so much noise in our churches with the music, the holy dance, several people speaking in tongues at one time, sometime uncontrolled screaming and yelling, but when a discussion starts to get the least bit loud everyone freaks out.

Questions are not the enemy. Information is not the enemy. Satan is the enemy, and he is using this scenario against the Pentecostal church. There is nothing wrong with asking questions and people should not feel hesitant about doing so. In fact in my opinion, we don't ask enough questions. What if Eve had asked the Serpent, "What did God really mean?" or "Then why did he say it that way?" Sometimes we don't ask more questions because we are happy with what we are doing and don't want to know the truth because that would change what we are doing. Sometimes asking questions brings to the surface things that have been kept in the dark for years in many cases for a lifetime. What's wrong with questions is when we don't get answers. Christ answered every question asked of him even from the scribes and Pharisees who were only trying to discredit and trap him. He never avoided their queries, and we should try to be as well equipped with answers as we can be and it is up to the leaders of our churches to provide the weaponry. But when they fail to do so because of poor training, ego, or control issues God is not giving us a pass because of the leader's negligence. Serving God is not just about faith it's also about facts. If we don't have all the facts we can't understand what the word is really saying. If we don't understand what the word is saying we can't really do what it is saying. I believe this is primarily a trick of Satan. When we focus more on the feelings and emotions as we do in the Pentecostal church, we will miss much of the important information in the word needed for growth. If we don't grow, maybe he will be able to knock us down and finally out. If we don't grow, we never find the "peace that passes all understanding" or "the Lord as the strength of my life." When we fail to grow as problems occur, we "try everything and when everything has failed we try Jesus." Actually when problems occur, Jesus should be the first place we turn to. Satan has tricked us into thinking that arguments are always bad, but it is also very bad when we are kept from clarity and the truth. When we are kept from truth, we are kept from freedom and victory. I am in no way suggesting that Bible study be commonly visited by arguments but when they do happen the most important thing is getting an understanding and the truth of the word. Scientific thought and logic are not enemies of the Bible; they are enemies of Satan. Satan has tricked the Pentecostal church into the mind-set that the more you are thinking the less faith you have and the farther away from God you are. Nothing could be further from the truth but that is exactly where Satan wants us all to be, as far from the truth as possible and he will even get into doctrine to keep us there. Jesus said, "I am the way, the truth, and the life." If we are to truly walk in his "way," we must know his "truth," not man's truth, his truth. Without his truth, we will never attain the "life" he means for us to experience here on earth. It's all about truth. Truth comes by understanding and understanding by words. God said, "I am the Alpha and the Omega." These are the first and last letters of the Greek alphabet. All the letters that are needed to make all the words that God wants to share with us. He is everything, and everything he wants us to know comes from words made with letters. He tells us about the beginning with words, he tells us about the end with words and everything in between that he wants us to know is found in words. Maybe we should be paying a little more attention to the Word.

So studying the written words of the Bible is the way to understanding it. So here are a few things that have helped my study habits and increased my understanding.

- Context is king: Remember that context is what the passage is talking about. It's like the plot of a movie and tells you what's going on. Unless you are trying to memorize a particular verse, you really should never read just one or two verses of scripture and think you are studying. You have to understand the context of what you are reading and in most cases that will take reading at least a few verses above and below the verse you are focused on. In many cases, especially with the Old Testament, it may take reading not only the entire chapter but the one or two before the one you are interested in.

- Tools: The material you use is very important. A good study Bible is essential because it will have notes in the margins that give insight into specific verses and important concepts that may not be obvious. A Bible dictionary is also very important because some words will not be found in standard dictionaries. A Hebrew/Greek concordance will really enlighten many scriptures and is absolutely essential for clergy. There are many great Bible teachers on the radio and television who have spent years in formal study with doctoral degrees in theology, Greek and Hebrew who have already done the work for you. Be mindful that anyone can buy TV or radio time. The networks don't care if you are sincere or accurate as long as you can pay so it's important to find out about a person's credential (if they have any) before you trust what they are teaching and invest your time in them on a regular basis. The Internet can be extremely helpful but there you will really need to be diligent about researching the contributors because there are many people who are just passing their opinions and are not really interested in being helpful. Speaking of the Internet, what about a study app?

- APP (always presume problems): In studying, especially with a subject for the first time, assume you are missing something. Sometime this will be obvious and will lead to obvious questions. But in some cases, you will simply have to play detective and ask who, what, where, when, why? Does this mean what I think it means or what I've been told it means? It doesn't matter what you or anyone else believes what matters is what the Bible says. Our belief should come from what the Bible says. We should not make the Bible say what we believe. It can be very hard to do this when you have held on to something for many, many years and find that you could be wrong. But remember, God is not the author of confusion. If what you believe with all your heart does not mesh with what the Bible says, either your heart or the Bible is wrong, both can't be right. It is not a sin to ask questions and it doesn't mean you are "questioning God" you are looking for answers and we have been commanded to do that.

- Time: As in the definition given for study, it takes time. Not the time you read a scripture before bed or first thing in the morning. You need a special block of time devoted each week for digging into whatever topic you are focused on. This could start with Sunday school or Bible study topics or it could come from seeking answers to personal spiritual problems like what do I keep falling to the same sin. Again you should be studying so that eventually you will be able to explain the topic to someone else. There is no substitute for spending ample time studying.

- Clergy: It may seem that I'm contradicting myself here because the premise of this book has been the problems clergymen have caused. But you know the ones you have confidence in versus the ones who are a bit shaky. Because they have usually spent more time in the Bible most of the time they are at least a good starting point and can get you going in the right direction. Asking them questions can also serve to ignite a fire under those that are not studying as much as they should be.

- Prayer: Of course starting your study session with a prayer that the Holy Spirit guides your effort is also essential to success in this as in any endeavor.

For those who have come all this way with me, I applaud you, especially any members of the clergy. It can be very difficult to take a look at something with new eyes and from a new perspective.

Speaking of race relations in the US in his farewell address, President Barak Obama quoted Atticus Finch from *To Kill a Mockingbird*: "You never really understand a person until you consider things from his point of view, until you get into his skin and walk around in it."

The president went on to say, "We need to listen. Too many of us fail to understand the problems of race in this country because we retreat into our own little bubbles. We hear only what we want to hear, and we never allow our assumptions to be challenged. Soon we become so secure in our bubbles that we begin to accept only information that fits our opinions whether true or not rather than basing our opinions on the evidence that is there. Without a common baseline of facts or a willingness to admit new information, concede that the opponent might be making a fair point and admit that science and reason matter, we will continue talking past each other." This is a perfect description of what has happened in the Pentecostal church. As I have tried to point out we have retreated into a number of bubbles. Bubbles of inaccuracy, error and misinterpretation. If we continue to hear only what we want to hear instead of looking for God's truth Satan will continue to win the battle for the minds of many. If we don't update our arsenal with the true sword of the spirit, society will continue to treat Christians as aliens or second class citizens. The Pentecostal church will continue to see and exodus from what was one of the fastest growing denominations. The Pentecostal church will morph into a barely recognizable entity much like the Jews did under the influence of the Scribes and Pharisees. I know this personally having experienced people in bubbles. But I also know that if you really want to worship and serve God in Spirit and in truth, you must be equipped with his truth. Not the truth of mom and dad or the truth of family tradition. Not the truth that's in your heart or what you believe and feel. Not the truth of a doctrine if that doctrine even accidently or unintentionally misrepresents God's truth in any aspect. Times have changed, people have changed, Satan has changed so the Pentecostal church must change. Satan is using twenty-first century technology, entertainment, social mores, financial instability and sexual ambiguity to distract, dissuade and disconnect humanity from anything Godly. While many of these churches will proudly exhibit their use of computers and audio-visual aides in ministry in too many cases the most important tool is sorely deficient, the truth of God's word. Yes change, focusing on facts instead of frills, knowledge instead of numbers and staying in step with scripture instead of society. I am not advocating the church become something that the founders would not recognize that is where we are headed if not there already. We need to get back to the basics, back to the Bible. With advances in education among those in leadership our understanding of scripture should be increasing by leaps and bounds. Instead some of the very doctrines that define the Pentecostal church are stuck in the mud of tradition, politics and stubbornness. We worship in Spirit and truth, but when we focus too much on what we feel and excitement and signs and miracles and wonders and healing the balance shifts too far to the left and the "truth" gets neglected. Jesus said, "I am the way the truth and the life." The problem is in many cases as Jack Nicholson said, "You can't handle the truth."

About the Author

Growing up as the son of a preacher made life very interesting. Growing up the eldest of ten children made it more so. As such Eugene G. Akins found himself exposed to the burden of responsibility at a very early age. So some things he handled very well others not so much. You can imagine when an eight-year old is cast in a role almost as a parent mistakes are going to be made and he made some doozies. Ultimately, through the good and the bad he learned to trust that what he was being taught by his parents was right.

At age thirty-seven everything changed. He left a good job to go back to school. He left his wife taking care of an adolescent son and a handicapped daughter and he almost left the church. After a series of high profile sex related incidents locally and nationally in church circles, he began to question what he had been taught. Many of the biblical principles and doctrine he grew up on did not seem to be playing out in the lives of many church leaders and denominations. He began to question whether he had come to believe in a fairy tale or if he was a victim of a grand con game. He did not want to make another mistake. He had questions that people seemed to ignore and he wanted, needed answers. Again, he felt the burden of responsibility but now imposed upon himself. He also felt a responsibility once he realized he was finding answers to questions that many others were also asking. So, from a smoldering religious ember a burning desire was ignited to find out if this child had been "raised up" in the way he should go or look to another path and move on.